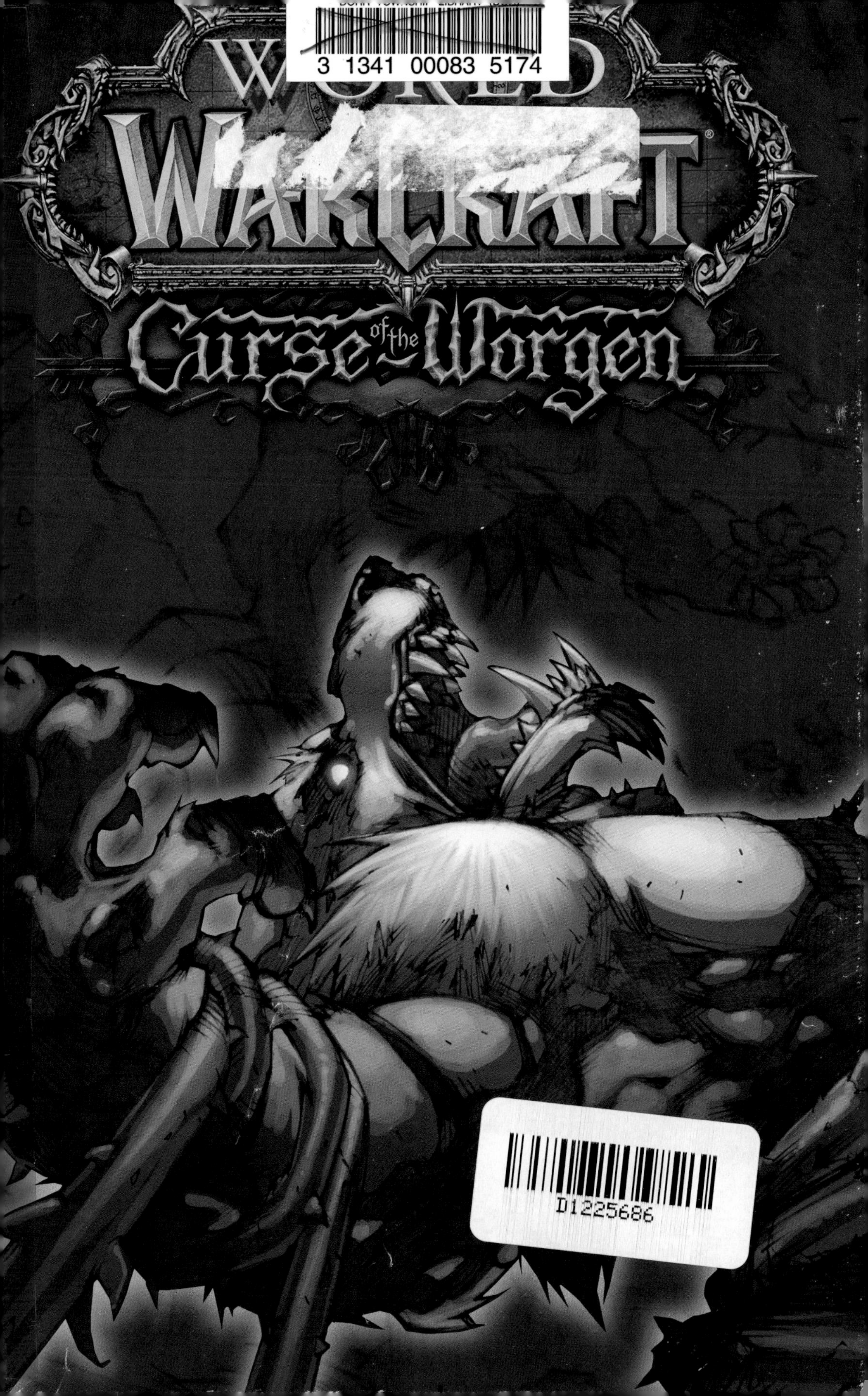
World of Warcraft
Curse of the Worgen

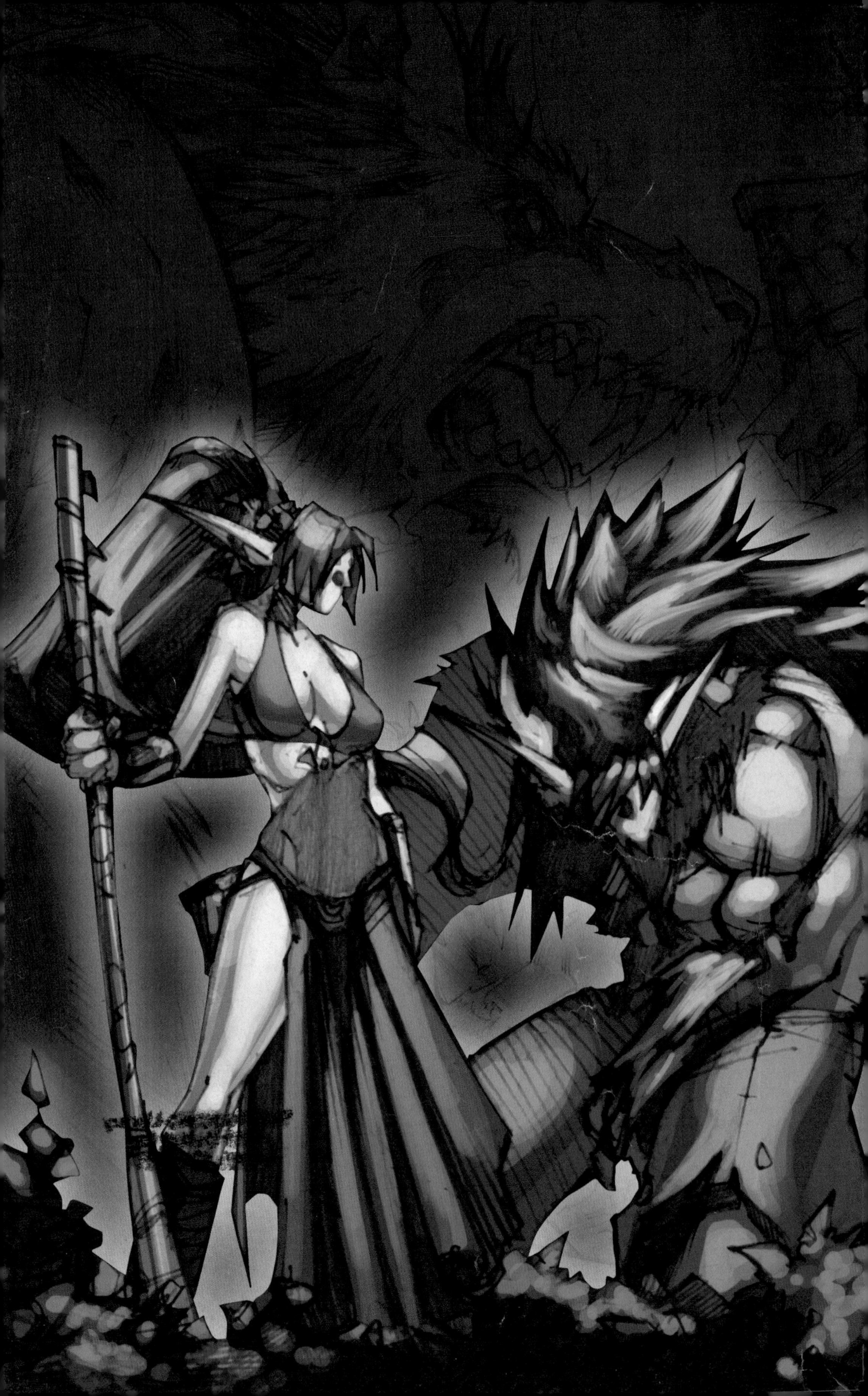

WORLD of WARCRAFT
Curse of the Worgen

WRITERS:
MICKY NEILSON & JAMES WAUGH

ARTISTS:
LUDO LULLABI & TONY WASHINGTON

LETTERER: WES ABBOTT

STORY CONSULTANTS
CHRIS METZEN, ALEX AFRASIABI & LUIS BARRIGA

COLLECTION COVER
BY WEI WANG

WORLD OF WARCRAFT: CURSE OF THE WORGEN

Published by DC Comics. Cover, compilation and epilogue Copyright © 2011 Blizzard Entertainment, Inc. All Rights Reserved.

Originally published in single magazine form in WORLD OF WARCRAFT: CURSE OF THE WORGEN 1-5 © 2011 Blizzard Entertainment, Inc. All Rights Reserved. Warcraft, World of Warcraft, and Blizzard Entertainment are registered trademarks of Blizzard Entertainment, Inc. The stories, characters and incidents featured in this publication are entirely fictional. DC Comics does not read or accept unsolicited submissions of ideas, stories or artwork.

DC Comics, 1700 Broadway, New York, NY 10019. A Warner Bros. Entertainment Company
Printed by RR Donnelley, Salem, VA, USA. 8/31/12. First Printing. ISBN: 978-1-4012-3445-4

Library of Congress Cataloging-in-Publication Data

Neilson, Micky.
World of warcraft : curse of the Worgen / Neilson, Waugh, Lullabi, Washington.
p. cm.
"Originally published in single magazine form in World Of Warcraft: Curse of the Worgen 1-5."
ISBN 978-1-4012-3445-4
1. World of Warcraft – Comic books, strips, etc. 2. Imaginary wars and battles – Comic books, strips, etc. 3. Graphic novels. I. Waugh, James (James M.) II. Lullabi, Ludo. III. Washington, Tony. IV. Title. V. Title: Curse of the Worgen.
PN6728.W69N46 2012
741.5'973 – dc23
2012026980

SUSTAINABLE FORESTRY INITIATIVE
Certified Chain of Custody
At Least 25% Certified Forest Content
www.sfiprogram.org
SFI-01042
APPLIES TO TEXT STOCK ONLY

LICENSED BLIZZARD ENTERTAINMENT PRODUCT

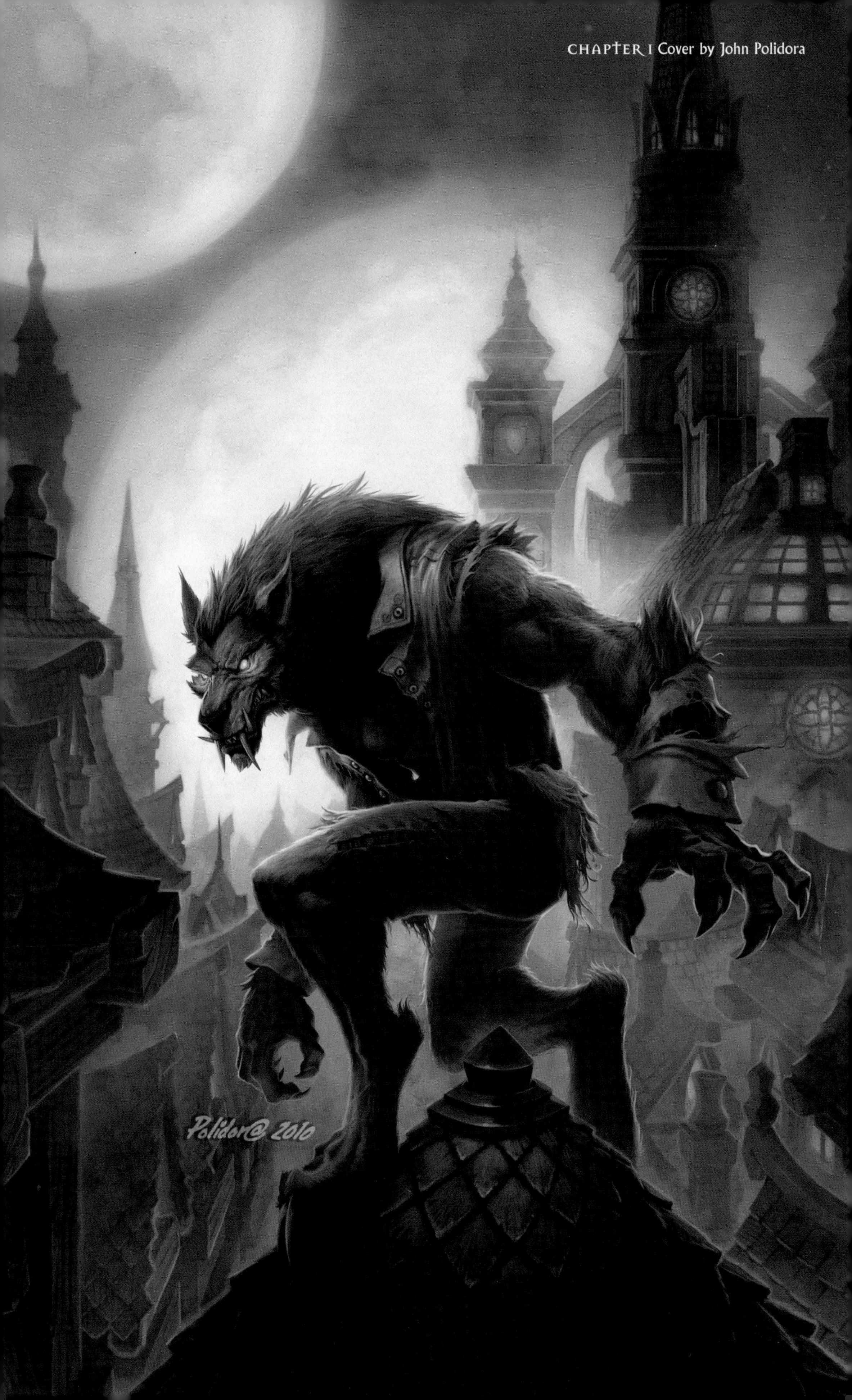
Polidor@ 2010

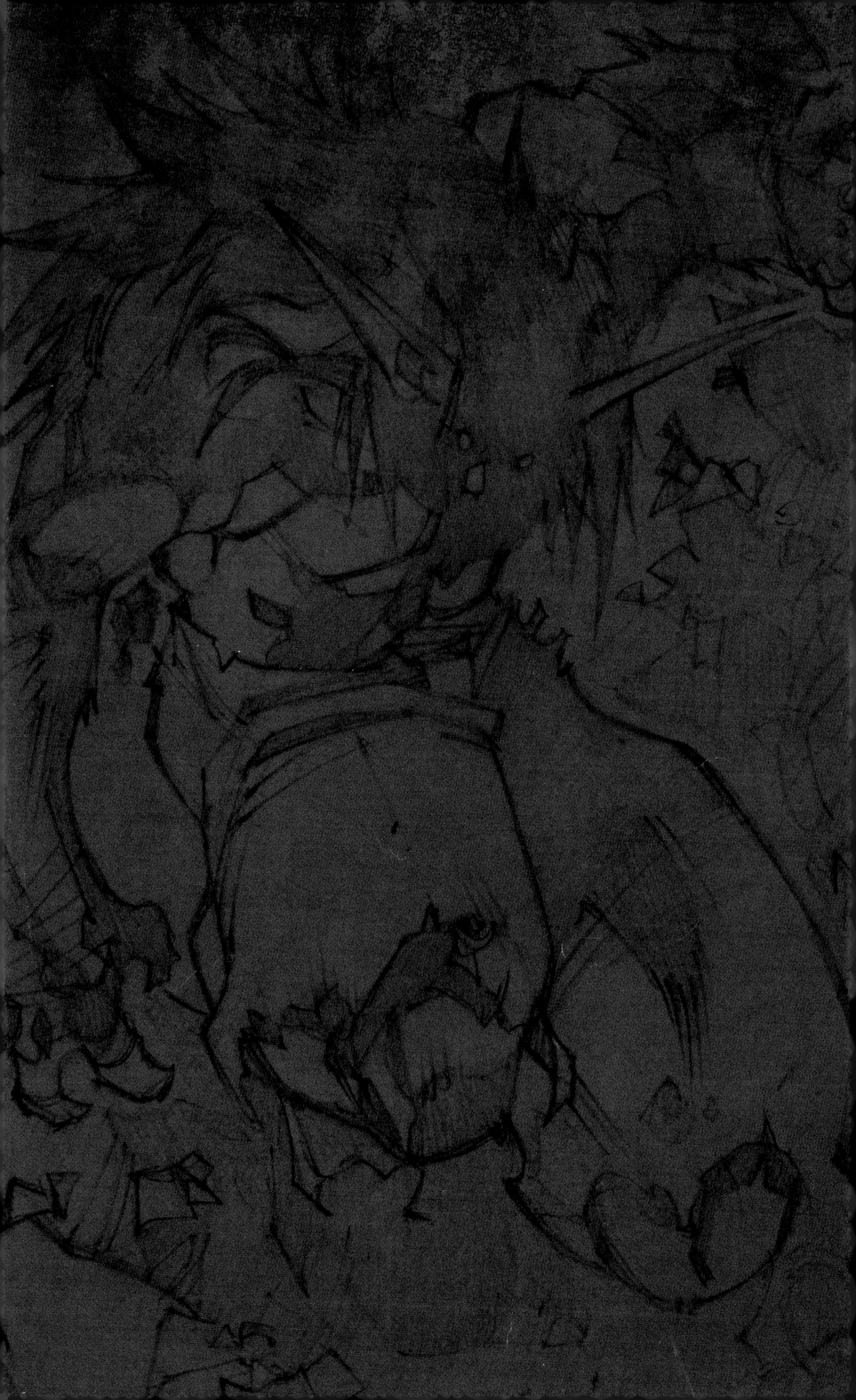

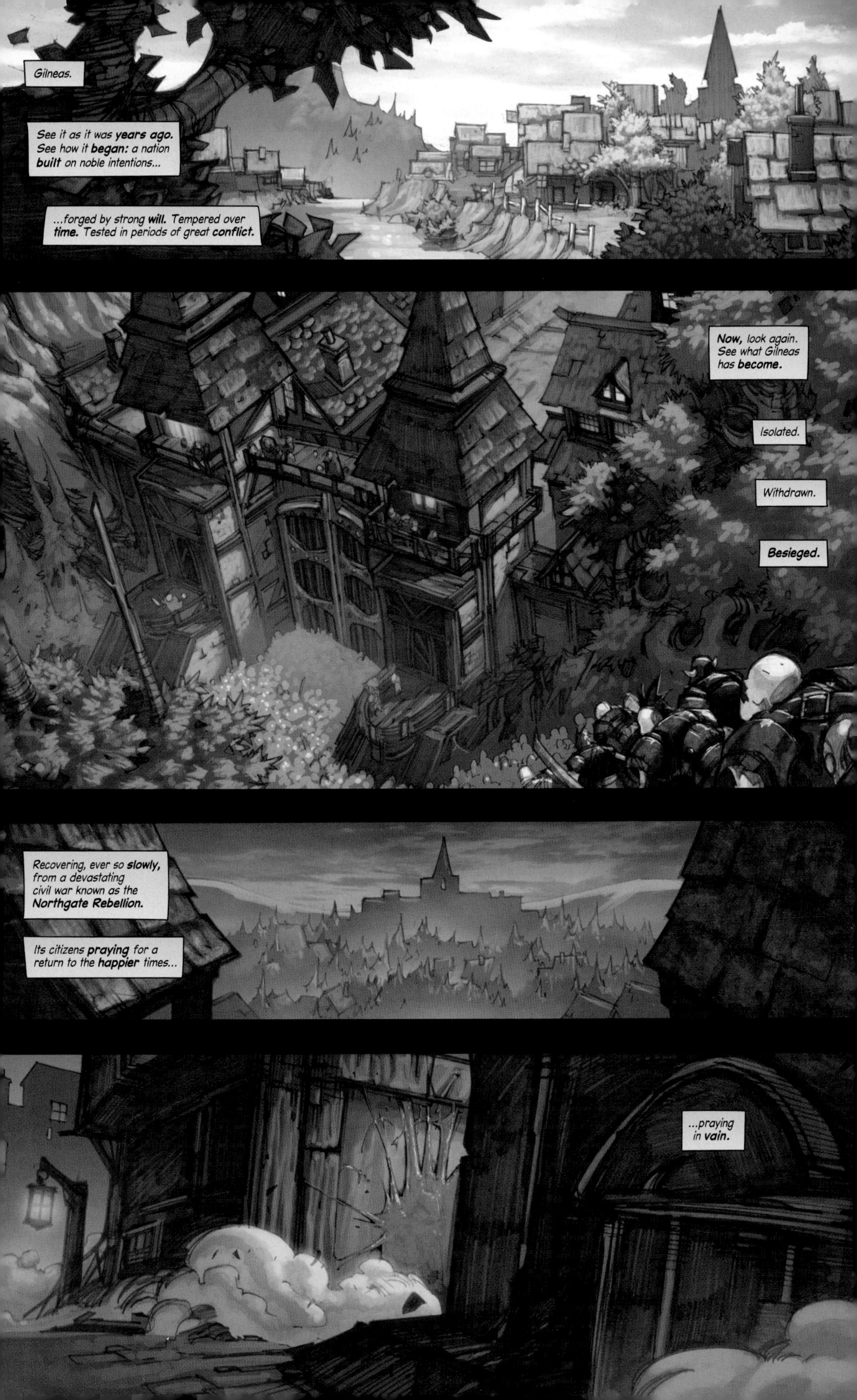
Gilneas.
See it as it was years ago. See how it began: a nation built on noble intentions...
...forged by strong will. Tempered over time. Tested in periods of great conflict.
Now, look again. See what Gilneas has become.
Isolated.
Withdrawn.
Besieged.
Recovering, ever so slowly, from a devastating civil war known as the Northgate Rebellion.
Its citizens praying for a return to the happier times...
...praying in vain.

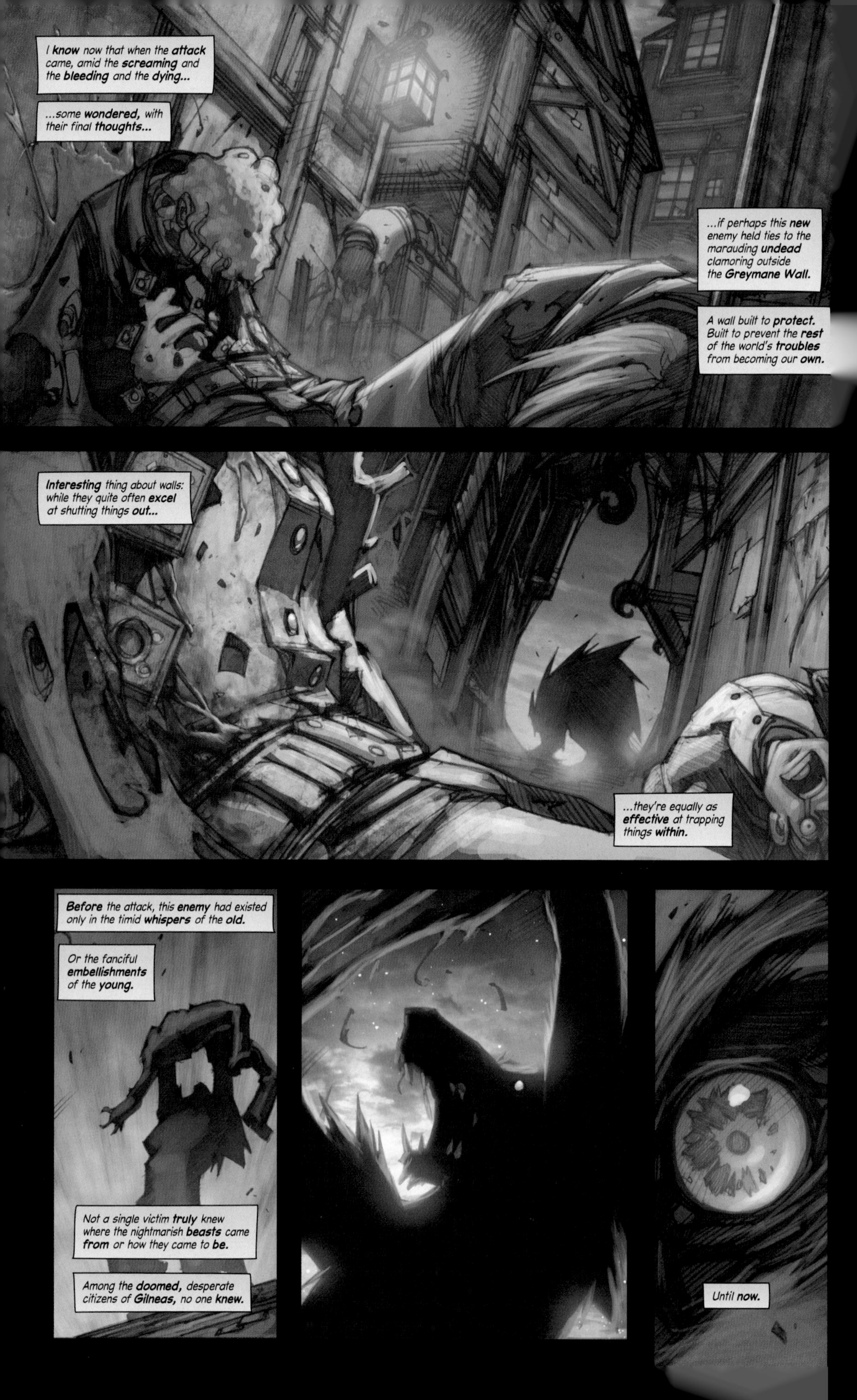
I know now that when the attack came, amid the screaming and the bleeding and the dying...
...some wondered, with their final thoughts...
...if perhaps this new enemy held ties to the marauding undead clamoring outside the Greymane Wall.
A wall built to protect. Built to prevent the rest of the world's troubles from becoming our own.
Interesting thing about walls: while they quite often excel at shutting things out...
...they're equally as effective at trapping things within.
Before the attack, this enemy had existed only in the timid whispers of the old.
Or the fanciful embellishments of the young.
Not a single victim truly knew where the nightmarish beasts came from or how they came to be.
Among the doomed, desperate citizens of Gilneas, no one knew.
Until now.

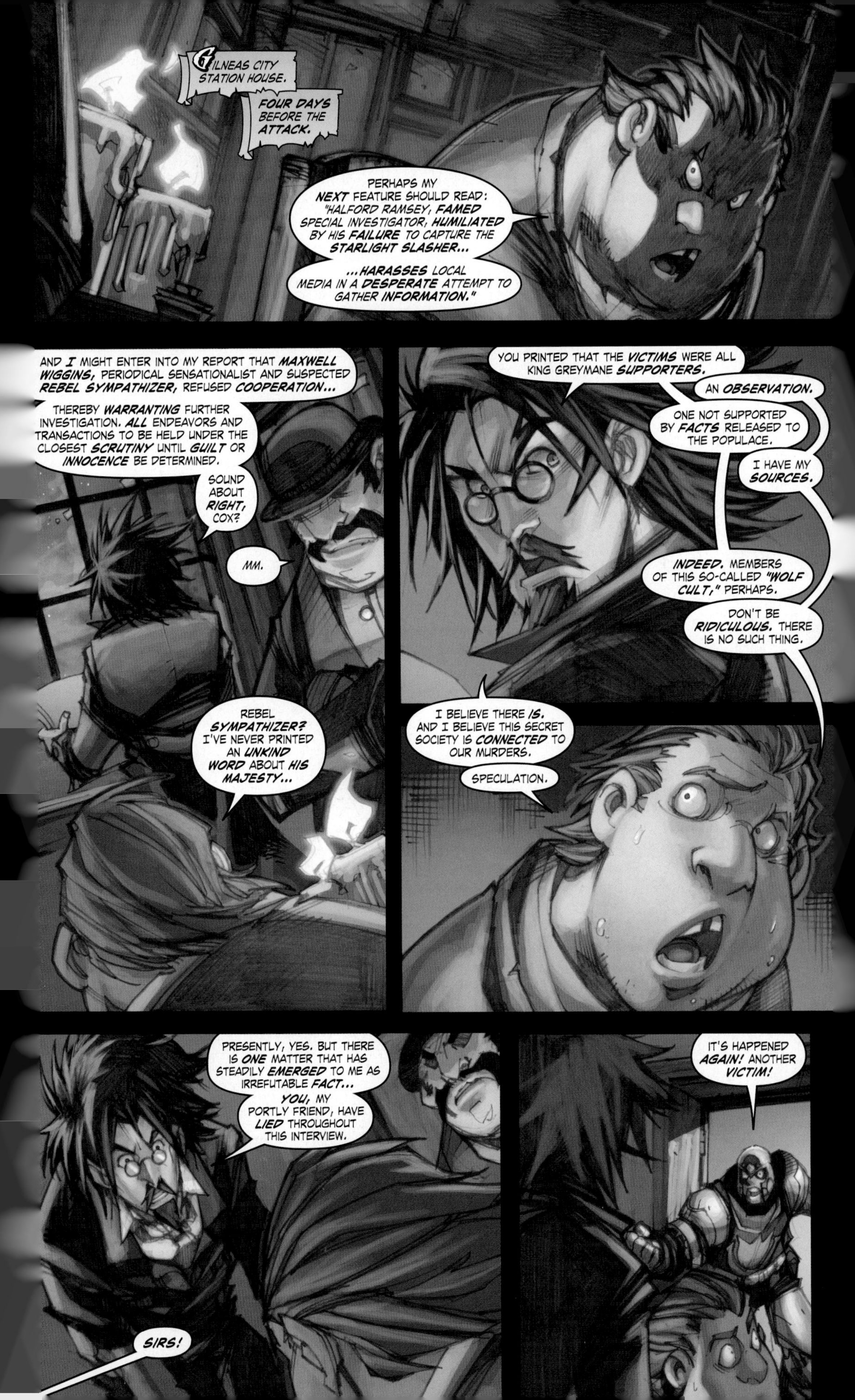
GILNEAS CITY STATION HOUSE.
FOUR DAYS BEFORE THE ATTACK.
PERHAPS MY NEXT FEATURE SHOULD READ: "HALFORD RAMSEY, FAMED SPECIAL INVESTIGATOR, HUMILIATED BY HIS FAILURE TO CAPTURE THE STARLIGHT SLASHER...
...HARASSES LOCAL MEDIA IN A DESPERATE ATTEMPT TO GATHER INFORMATION."
AND I MIGHT ENTER INTO MY REPORT THAT MAXWELL WIGGINS, PERIODICAL SENSATIONALIST AND SUSPECTED REBEL SYMPATHIZER, REFUSED COOPERATION...
THEREBY WARRANTING FURTHER INVESTIGATION. ALL ENDEAVORS AND TRANSACTIONS TO BE HELD UNDER THE CLOSEST SCRUTINY UNTIL GUILT OR INNOCENCE BE DETERMINED.
SOUND ABOUT RIGHT, COX?
MM.
REBEL SYMPATHIZER? I'VE NEVER PRINTED AN UNKIND WORD ABOUT HIS MAJESTY...
YOU PRINTED THAT THE VICTIMS WERE ALL KING GREYMANE SUPPORTERS.
AN OBSERVATION.
ONE NOT SUPPORTED BY FACTS RELEASED TO THE POPULACE.
I HAVE MY SOURCES.
INDEED. MEMBERS OF THIS SO-CALLED "WOLF CULT," PERHAPS.
DON'T BE RIDICULOUS. THERE IS NO SUCH THING.
I BELIEVE THERE IS. AND I BELIEVE THIS SECRET SOCIETY IS CONNECTED TO OUR MURDERS.
SPECULATION.
PRESENTLY, YES. BUT THERE IS ONE MATTER THAT HAS STEADILY EMERGED TO ME AS IRREFUTABLE FACT...
YOU, MY PORTLY FRIEND, HAVE LIED THROUGHOUT THIS INTERVIEW.
SIRS!
IT'S HAPPENED AGAIN! ANOTHER VICTIM!

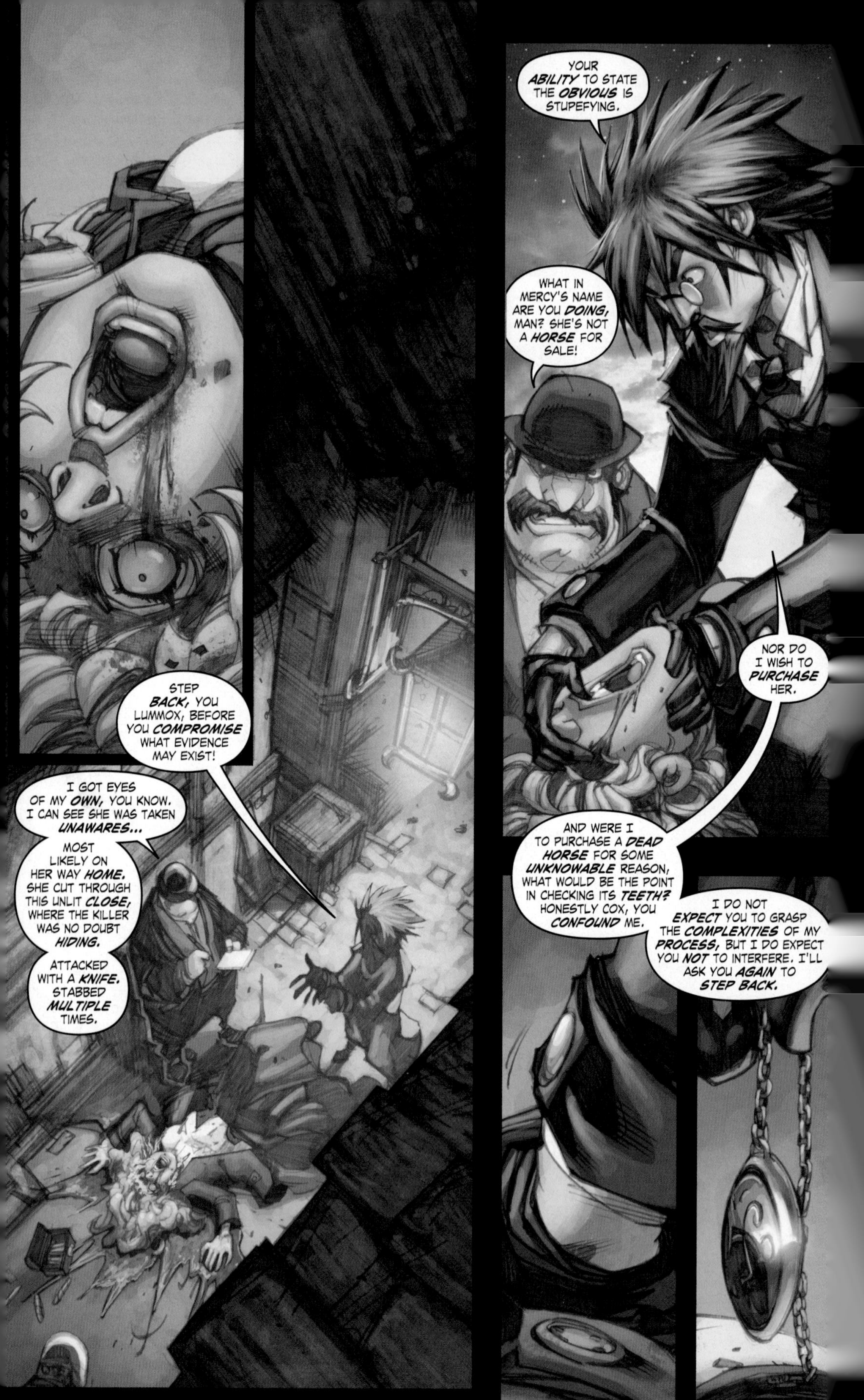
YOUR ABILITY TO STATE THE OBVIOUS IS STUPEFYING.
WHAT IN MERCY'S NAME ARE YOU DOING, MAN? SHE'S NOT A HORSE FOR SALE!
NOR DO I WISH TO PURCHASE HER.
STEP BACK, YOU LUMMOX, BEFORE YOU COMPROMISE WHAT EVIDENCE MAY EXIST!
I GOT EYES OF MY OWN, YOU KNOW. I CAN SEE SHE WAS TAKEN UNAWARES...
MOST LIKELY ON HER WAY HOME. SHE CUT THROUGH THIS UNLIT CLOSE, WHERE THE KILLER WAS NO DOUBT HIDING.
ATTACKED WITH A KNIFE. STABBED MULTIPLE TIMES.
AND WERE I TO PURCHASE A DEAD HORSE FOR SOME UNKNOWABLE REASON, WHAT WOULD BE THE POINT IN CHECKING ITS TEETH? HONESTLY COX, YOU CONFOUND ME.
I DO NOT EXPECT YOU TO GRASP THE COMPLEXITIES OF MY PROCESS, BUT I DO EXPECT YOU NOT TO INTERFERE. I'LL ASK YOU AGAIN TO STEP BACK.

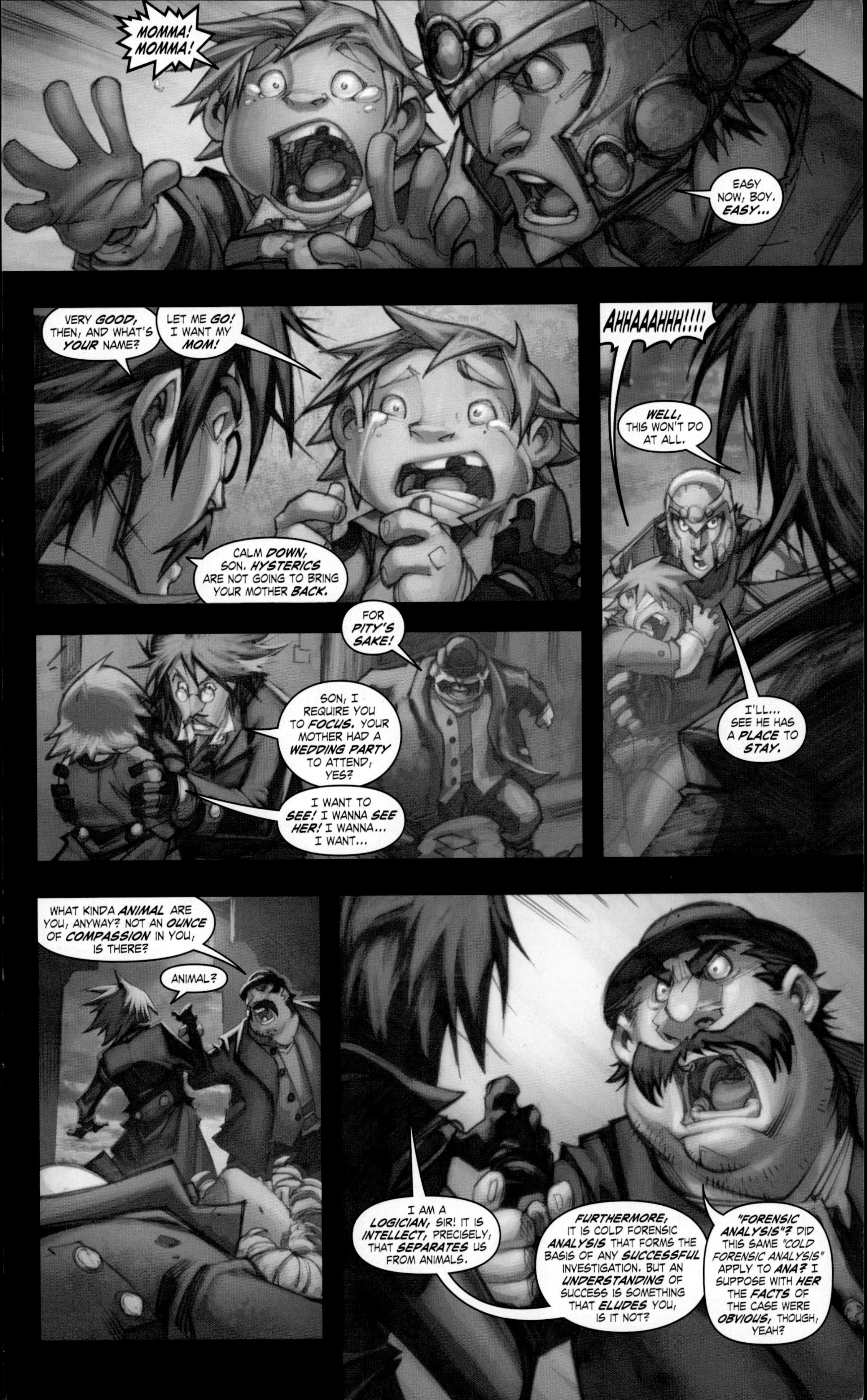
MOMMA! MOMMA!
EASY NOW, BOY. EASY...
VERY GOOD, THEN, AND WHAT'S YOUR NAME?
LET ME GO! I WANT MY MOM!
CALM DOWN, SON. HYSTERICS ARE NOT GOING TO BRING YOUR MOTHER BACK.
FOR PITY'S SAKE!
SON, I REQUIRE YOU TO FOCUS. YOUR MOTHER HAD A WEDDING PARTY TO ATTEND, YES?
I WANT TO SEE! I WANNA SEE HER! I WANNA... I WANT...
AHHAAAHHH!!!!
WELL, THIS WON'T DO AT ALL.
I'LL... SEE HE HAS A PLACE TO STAY.
WHAT KINDA ANIMAL ARE YOU, ANYWAY? NOT AN OUNCE OF COMPASSION IN YOU, IS THERE?
ANIMAL?
I AM A LOGICIAN, SIR! IT IS INTELLECT, PRECISELY, THAT SEPARATES US FROM ANIMALS.
FURTHERMORE, IT IS COLD FORENSIC ANALYSIS THAT FORMS THE BASIS OF ANY SUCCESSFUL INVESTIGATION. BUT AN UNDERSTANDING OF SUCCESS IS SOMETHING THAT ELUDES YOU, IS IT NOT?
"FORENSIC ANALYSIS"? DID THIS SAME "COLD FORENSIC ANALYSIS" APPLY TO ANA? I SUPPOSE WITH HER THE FACTS OF THE CASE WERE OBVIOUS, THOUGH, YEAH?

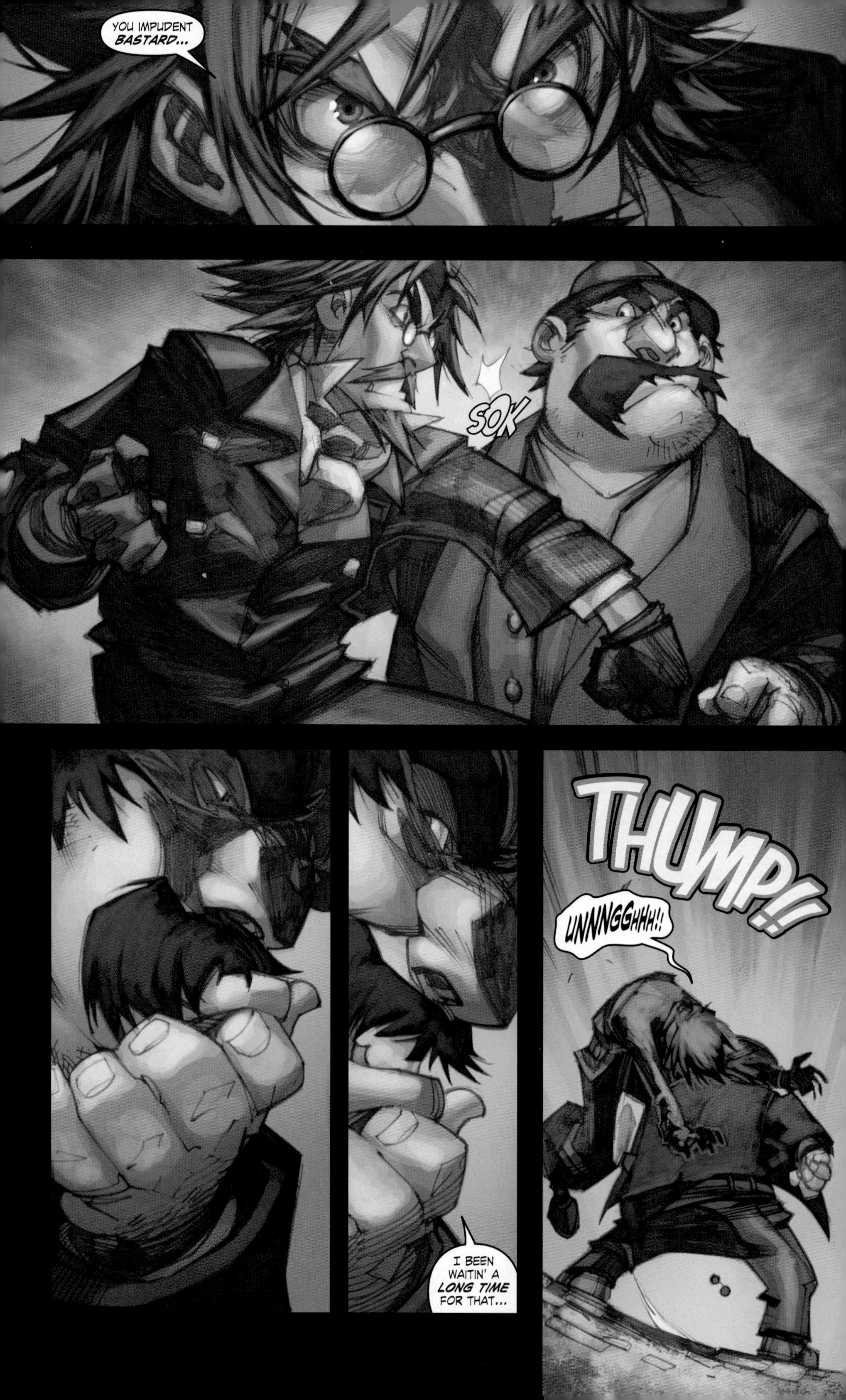
YOU IMPUDENT BASTARD...
SOK
I BEEN WAITIN' A LONG TIME FOR THAT...
THUMP!!
UNNNGGHHH!!

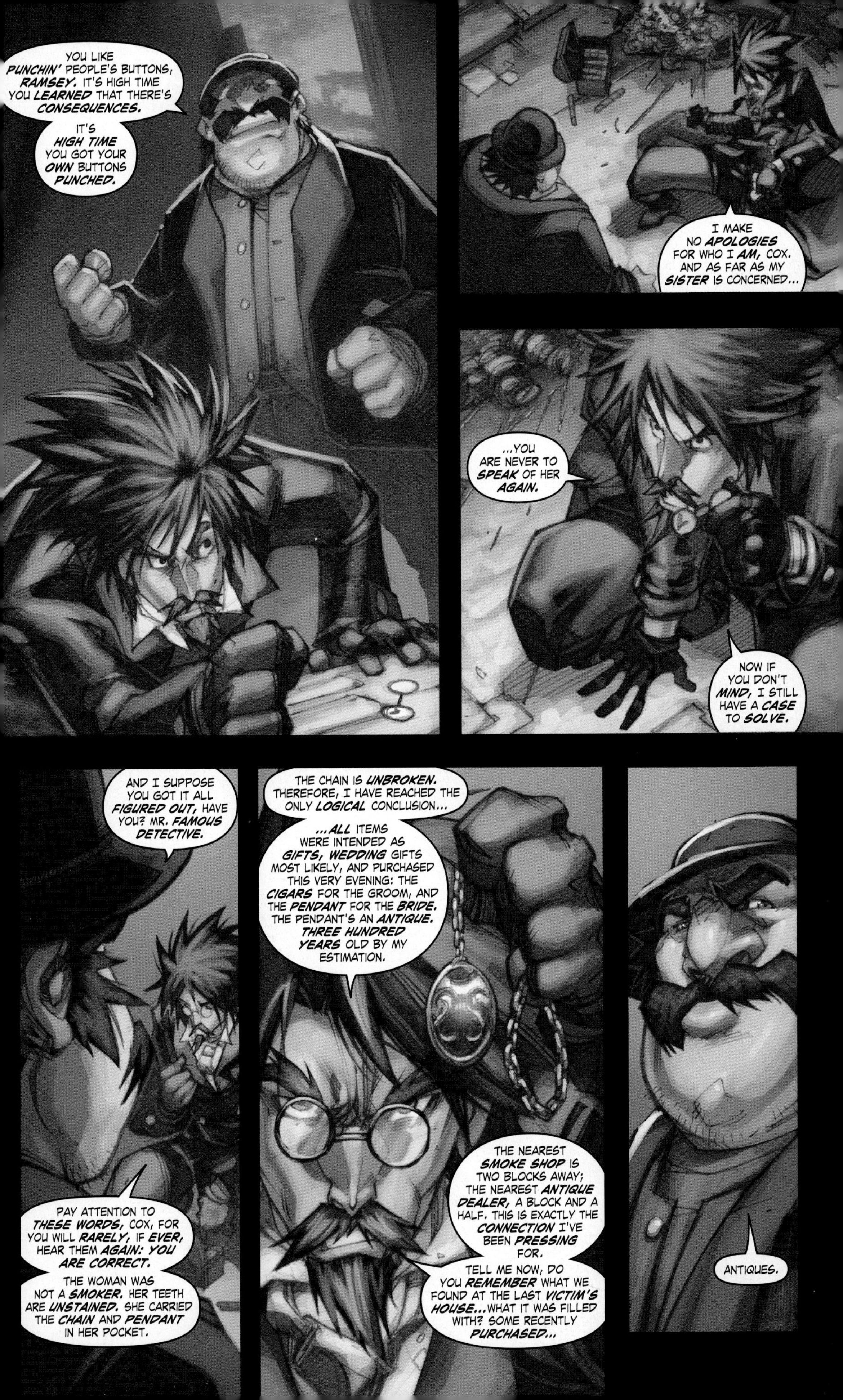
YOU LIKE PUNCHIN' PEOPLE'S BUTTONS, RAMSEY. IT'S HIGH TIME YOU LEARNED THAT THERE'S CONSEQUENCES.
IT'S HIGH TIME YOU GOT YOUR OWN BUTTONS PUNCHED.
I MAKE NO APOLOGIES FOR WHO I AM, COX. AND AS FAR AS MY SISTER IS CONCERNED...
...YOU ARE NEVER TO SPEAK OF HER AGAIN.
NOW IF YOU DON'T MIND, I STILL HAVE A CASE TO SOLVE.
AND I SUPPOSE YOU GOT IT ALL FIGURED OUT, HAVE YOU? MR. FAMOUS DETECTIVE.
PAY ATTENTION TO THESE WORDS, COX, FOR YOU WILL RARELY, IF EVER, HEAR THEM AGAIN: YOU ARE CORRECT.
THE WOMAN WAS NOT A SMOKER. HER TEETH ARE UNSTAINED. SHE CARRIED THE CHAIN AND PENDANT IN HER POCKET.
THE CHAIN IS UNBROKEN. THEREFORE, I HAVE REACHED THE ONLY LOGICAL CONCLUSION...
...ALL ITEMS WERE INTENDED AS GIFTS, WEDDING GIFTS MOST LIKELY, AND PURCHASED THIS VERY EVENING: THE CIGARS FOR THE GROOM, AND THE PENDANT FOR THE BRIDE. THE PENDANT'S AN ANTIQUE. THREE HUNDRED YEARS OLD BY MY ESTIMATION.
THE NEAREST SMOKE SHOP IS TWO BLOCKS AWAY; THE NEAREST ANTIQUE DEALER, A BLOCK AND A HALF. THIS IS EXACTLY THE CONNECTION I'VE BEEN PRESSING FOR.
TELL ME NOW, DO YOU REMEMBER WHAT WE FOUND AT THE LAST VICTIM'S HOUSE...WHAT IT WAS FILLED WITH? SOME RECENTLY PURCHASED...
ANTIQUES.

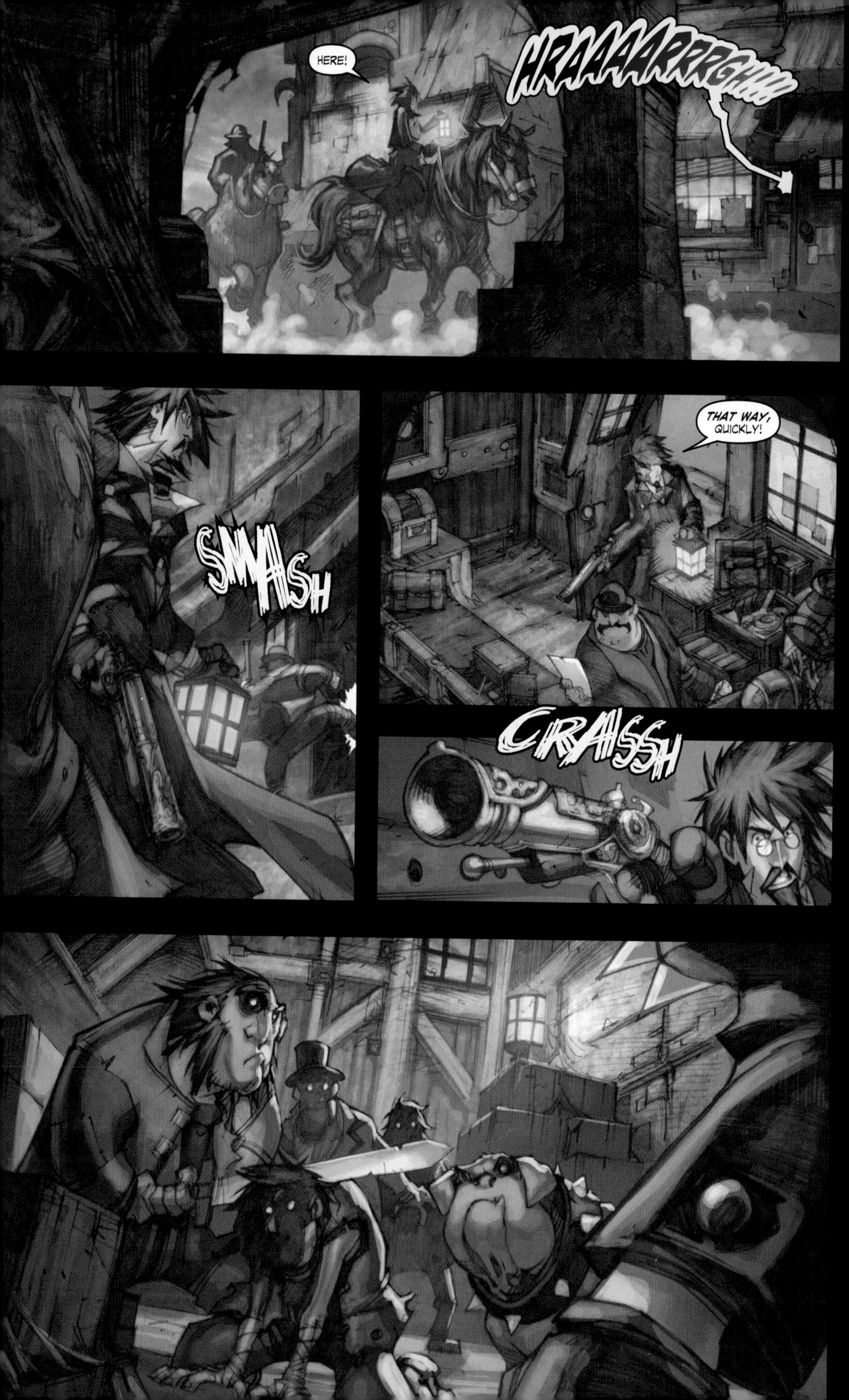
HERE!
HRAAAARRRGH!!!
SMASH
THAT WAY, QUICKLY!
CRASSH

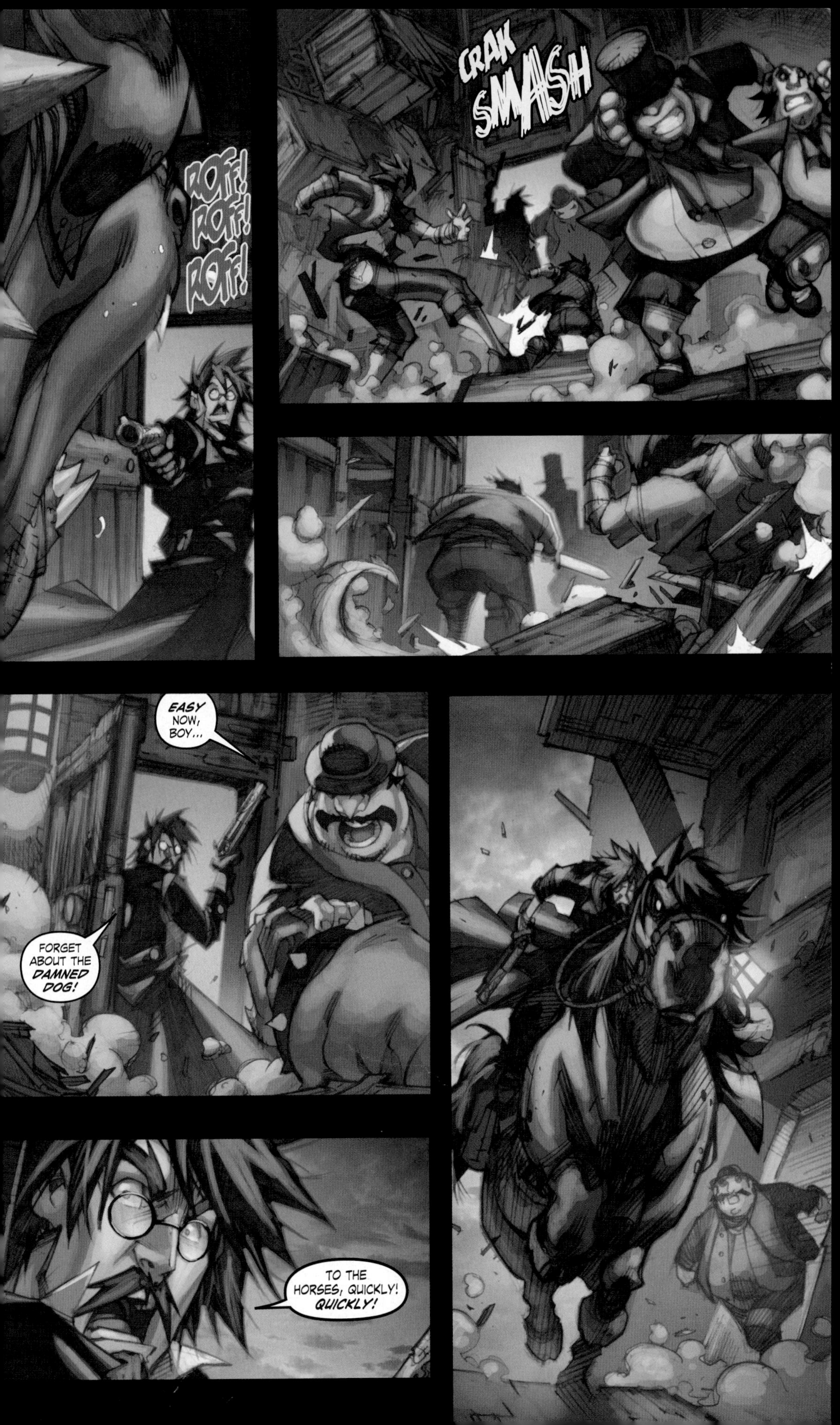
ROFF! ROFF! ROFF!
CRAK SMASH
EASY NOW, BOY...
FORGET ABOUT THE DAMNED DOG!
TO THE HORSES, QUICKLY! QUICKLY!

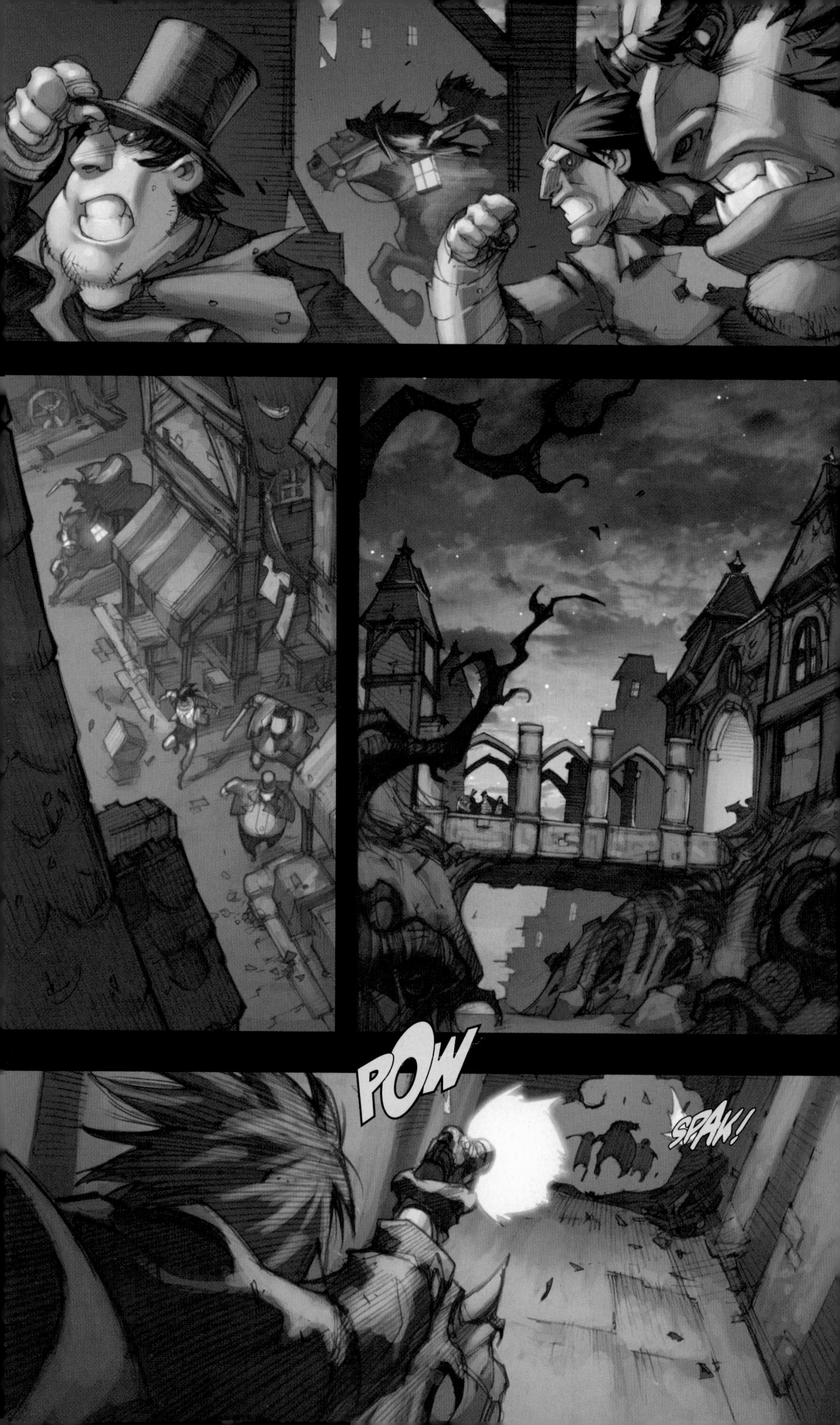
POW
SPAK!

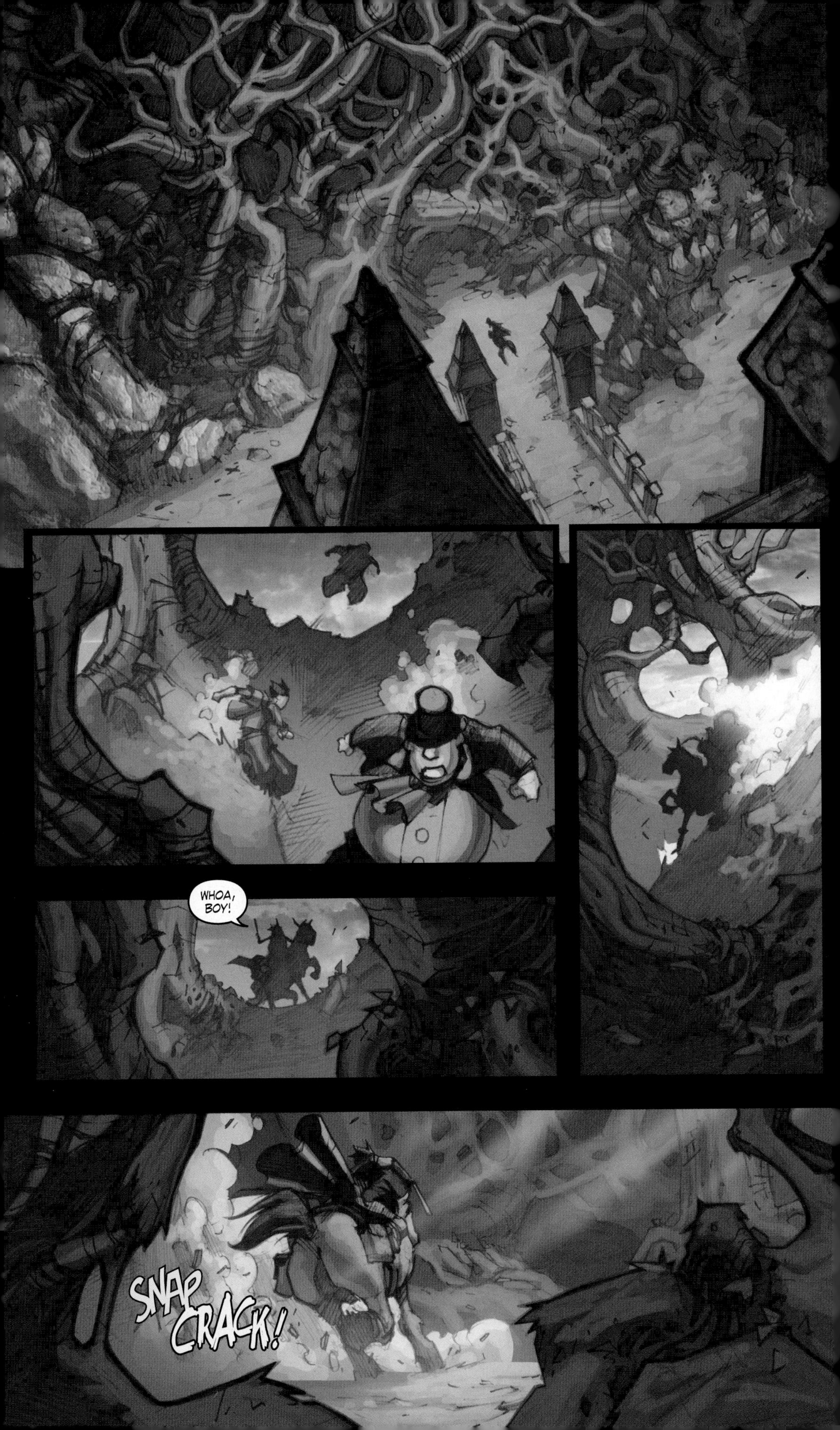
WHOA, BOY!
SNAP CRACK!

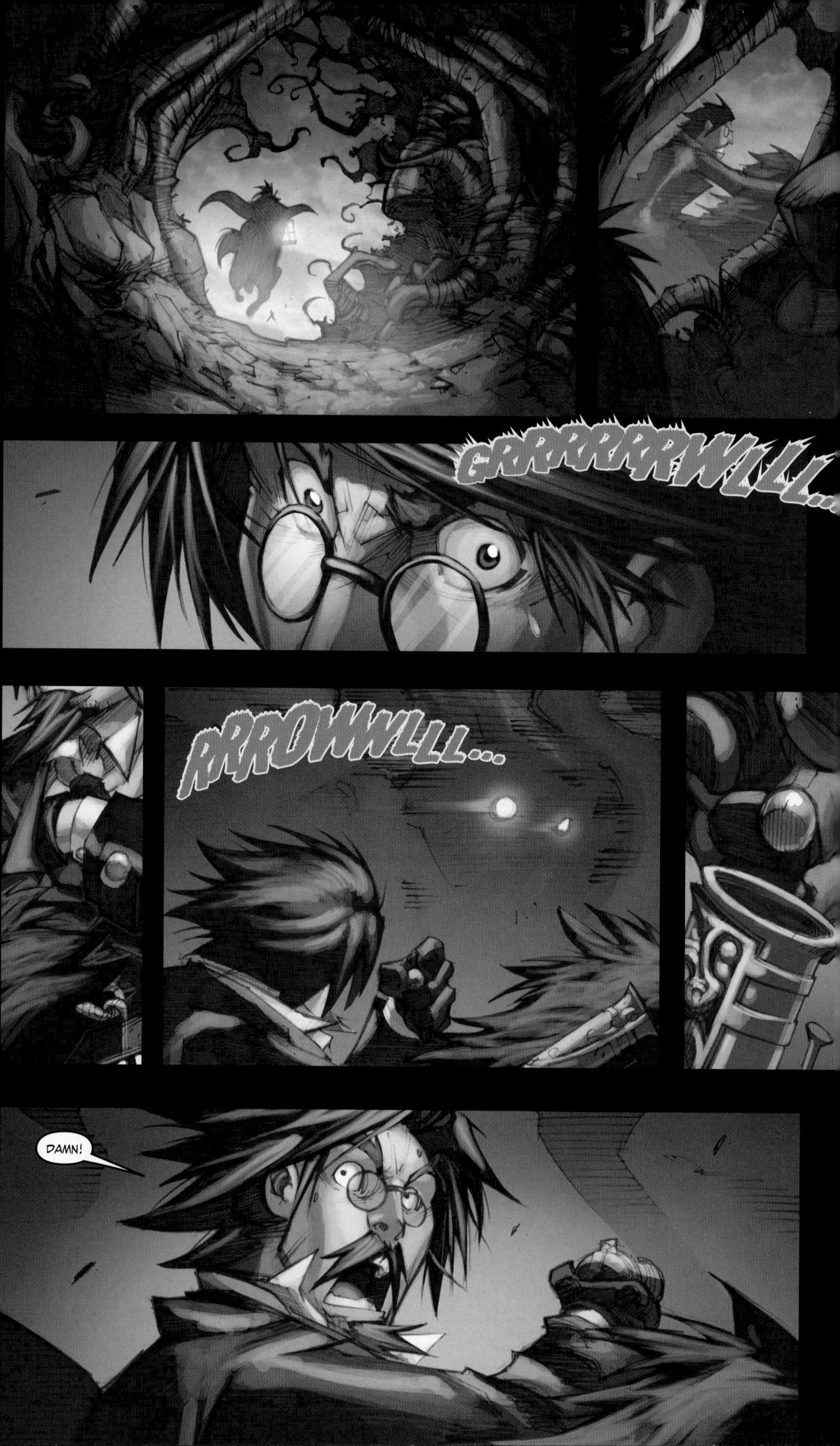
GRRRRRRRRWLLL...
RRRROWWLLL...
DAMN!

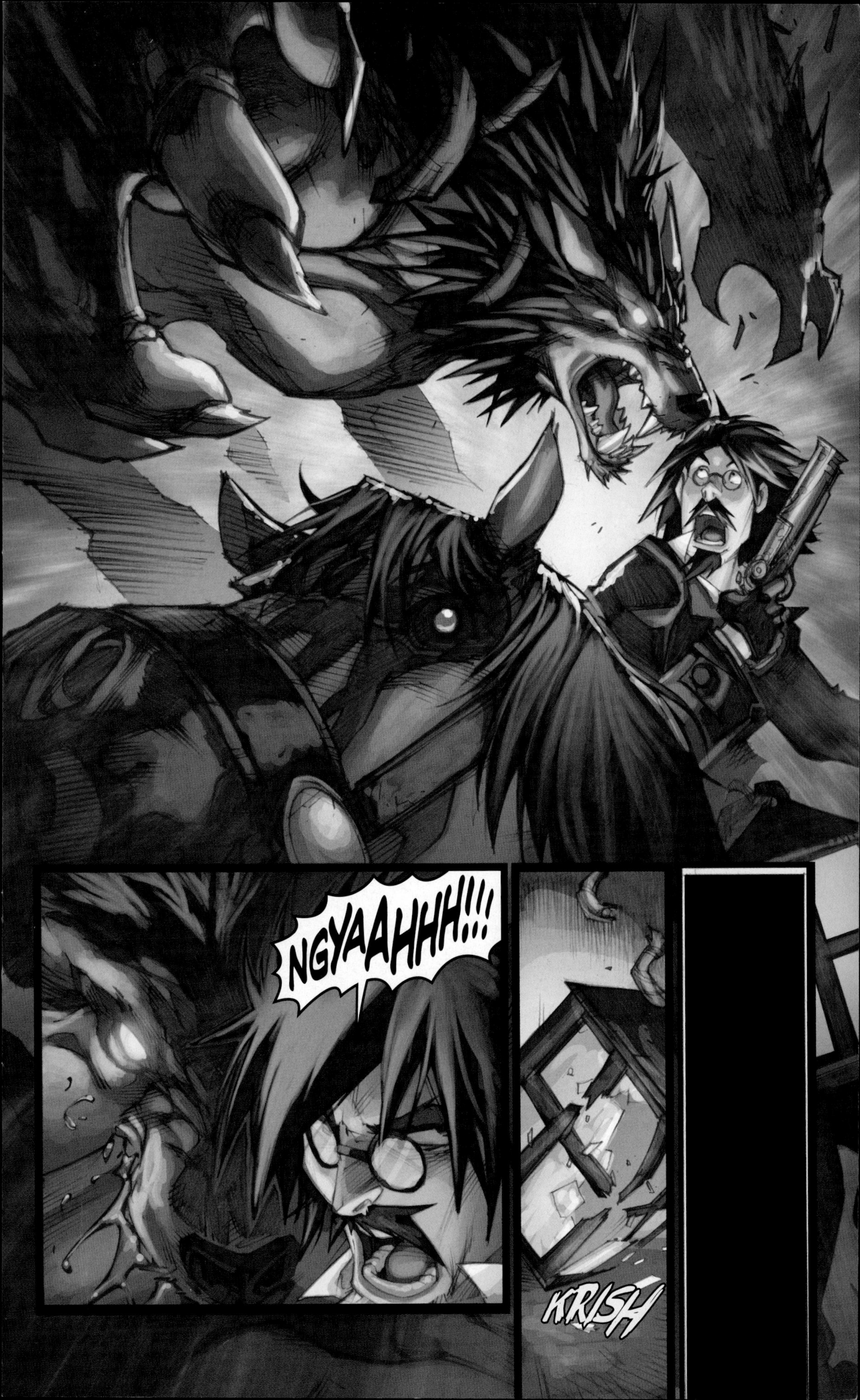
NGYAAHHH!!!
KRISH

The **pain** in my **shoulder** informed me that I was **alive.**

In a manor house... **abandoned** after the war. It was then that I caught the **scent...**

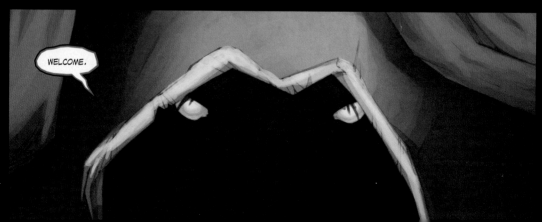

WELCOME.

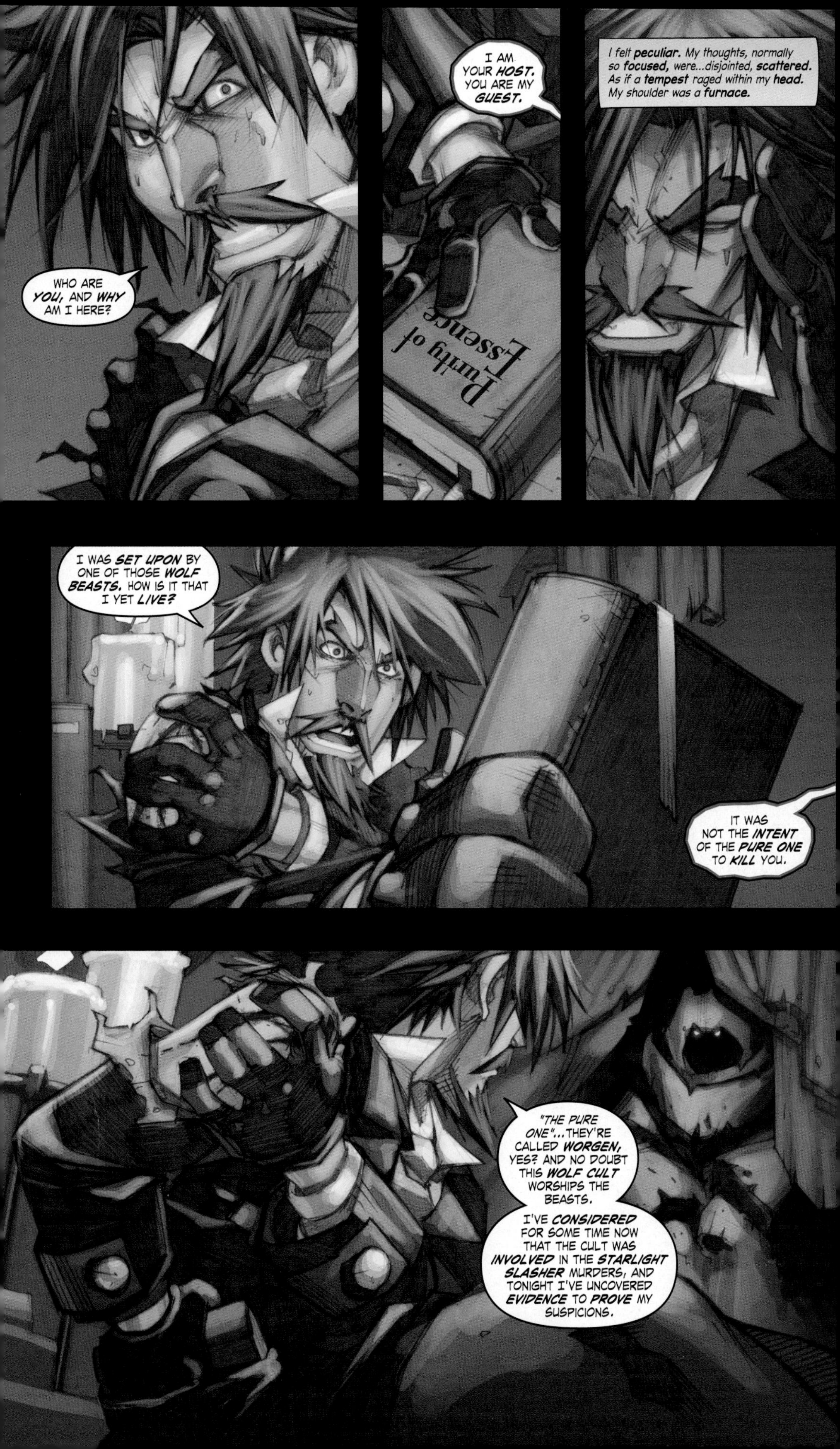
WHO ARE YOU, AND WHY AM I HERE?
I AM YOUR HOST. YOU ARE MY GUEST.
I felt peculiar. My thoughts, normally so focused, were...disjointed, scattered. As if a tempest raged within my head. My shoulder was a furnace.
Purity of Essence
I WAS SET UPON BY ONE OF THOSE WOLF BEASTS. HOW IS IT THAT I YET LIVE?
IT WAS NOT THE INTENT OF THE PURE ONE TO KILL YOU.
"THE PURE ONE"...THEY'RE CALLED WORGEN, YES? AND NO DOUBT THIS WOLF CULT WORSHIPS THE BEASTS.
I'VE CONSIDERED FOR SOME TIME NOW THAT THE CULT WAS INVOLVED IN THE STARLIGHT SLASHER MURDERS, AND TONIGHT I'VE UNCOVERED EVIDENCE TO PROVE MY SUSPICIONS.

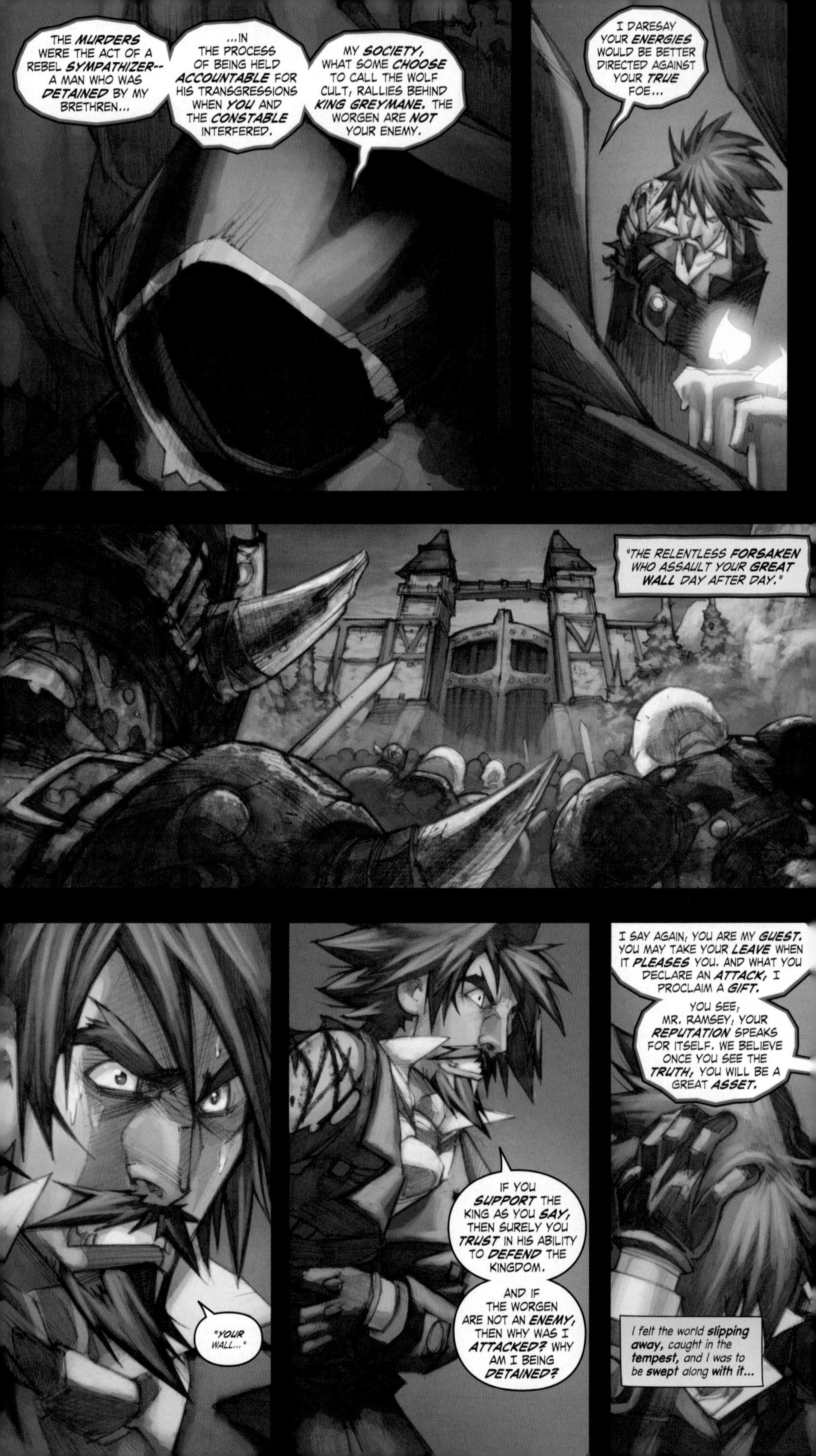
THE MURDERS WERE THE ACT OF A REBEL SYMPATHIZER-- A MAN WHO WAS DETAINED BY MY BRETHREN...
...IN THE PROCESS OF BEING HELD ACCOUNTABLE FOR HIS TRANSGRESSIONS WHEN YOU AND THE CONSTABLE INTERFERED.
MY SOCIETY, WHAT SOME CHOOSE TO CALL THE WOLF CULT, RALLIES BEHIND KING GREYMANE. THE WORGEN ARE NOT YOUR ENEMY.
I DARESAY YOUR ENERGIES WOULD BE BETTER DIRECTED AGAINST YOUR TRUE FOE...
"THE RELENTLESS FORSAKEN WHO ASSAULT YOUR GREAT WALL DAY AFTER DAY."
"YOUR WALL..."
IF YOU SUPPORT THE KING AS YOU SAY, THEN SURELY YOU TRUST IN HIS ABILITY TO DEFEND THE KINGDOM.
AND IF THE WORGEN ARE NOT AN ENEMY, THEN WHY WAS I ATTACKED? WHY AM I BEING DETAINED?
I SAY AGAIN, YOU ARE MY GUEST. YOU MAY TAKE YOUR LEAVE WHEN IT PLEASES YOU. AND WHAT YOU DECLARE AN ATTACK, I PROCLAIM A GIFT.
YOU SEE, MR. RAMSEY, YOUR REPUTATION SPEAKS FOR ITSELF. WE BELIEVE ONCE YOU SEE THE TRUTH, YOU WILL BE A GREAT ASSET.
I felt the world slipping away, caught in the tempest, and I was to be swept along with it...

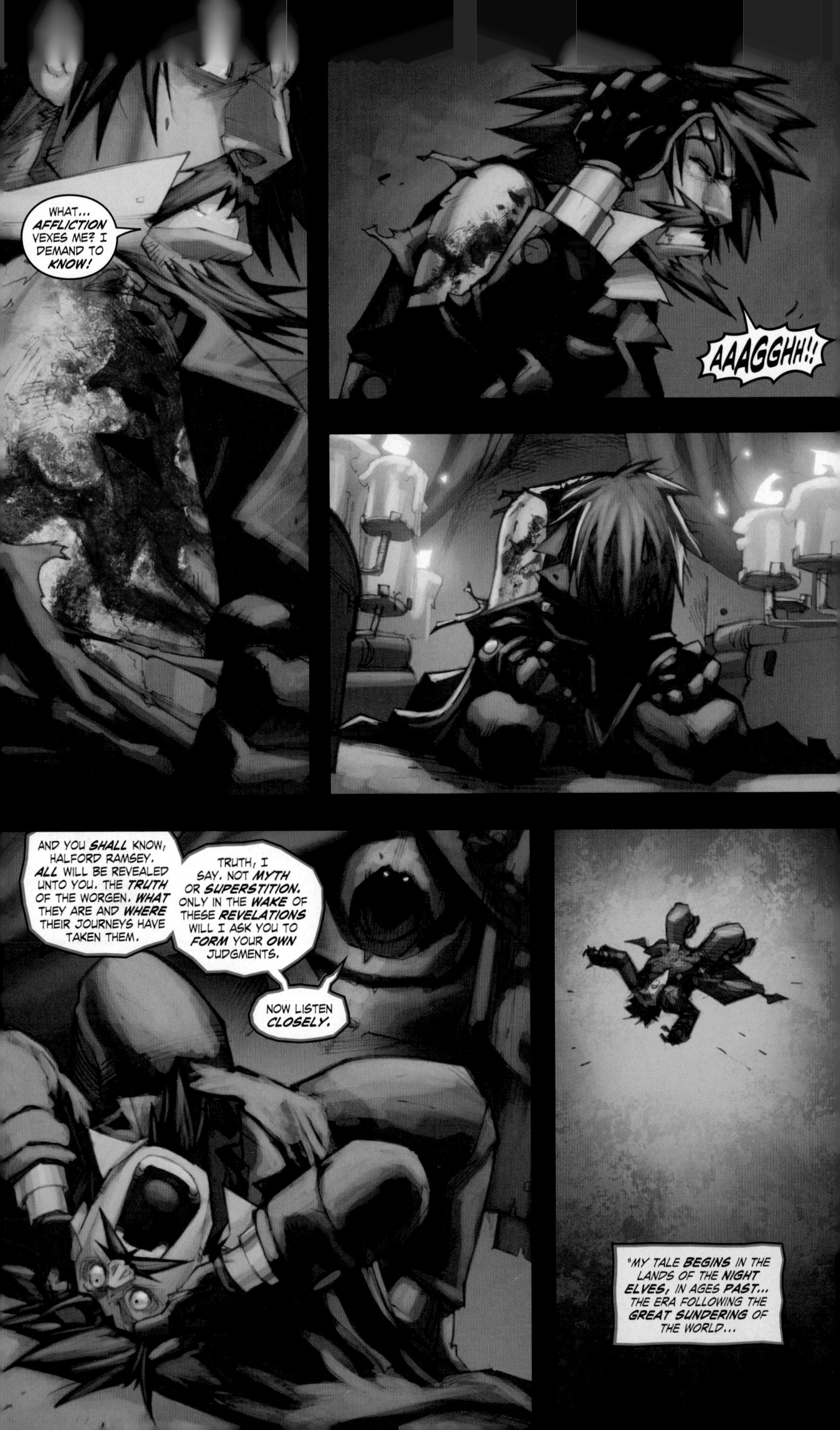
WHAT... AFFLICTION VEXES ME? I DEMAND TO KNOW!
AAAGGHH!!
AND YOU SHALL KNOW, HALFORD RAMSEY. ALL WILL BE REVEALED UNTO YOU. THE TRUTH OF THE WORGEN. WHAT THEY ARE AND WHERE THEIR JOURNEYS HAVE TAKEN THEM.
TRUTH, I SAY. NOT MYTH OR SUPERSTITION. ONLY IN THE WAKE OF THESE REVELATIONS WILL I ASK YOU TO FORM YOUR OWN JUDGMENTS.
NOW LISTEN CLOSELY.
"MY TALE BEGINS IN THE LANDS OF THE NIGHT ELVES, IN AGES PAST... THE ERA FOLLOWING THE GREAT SUNDERING OF THE WORLD...

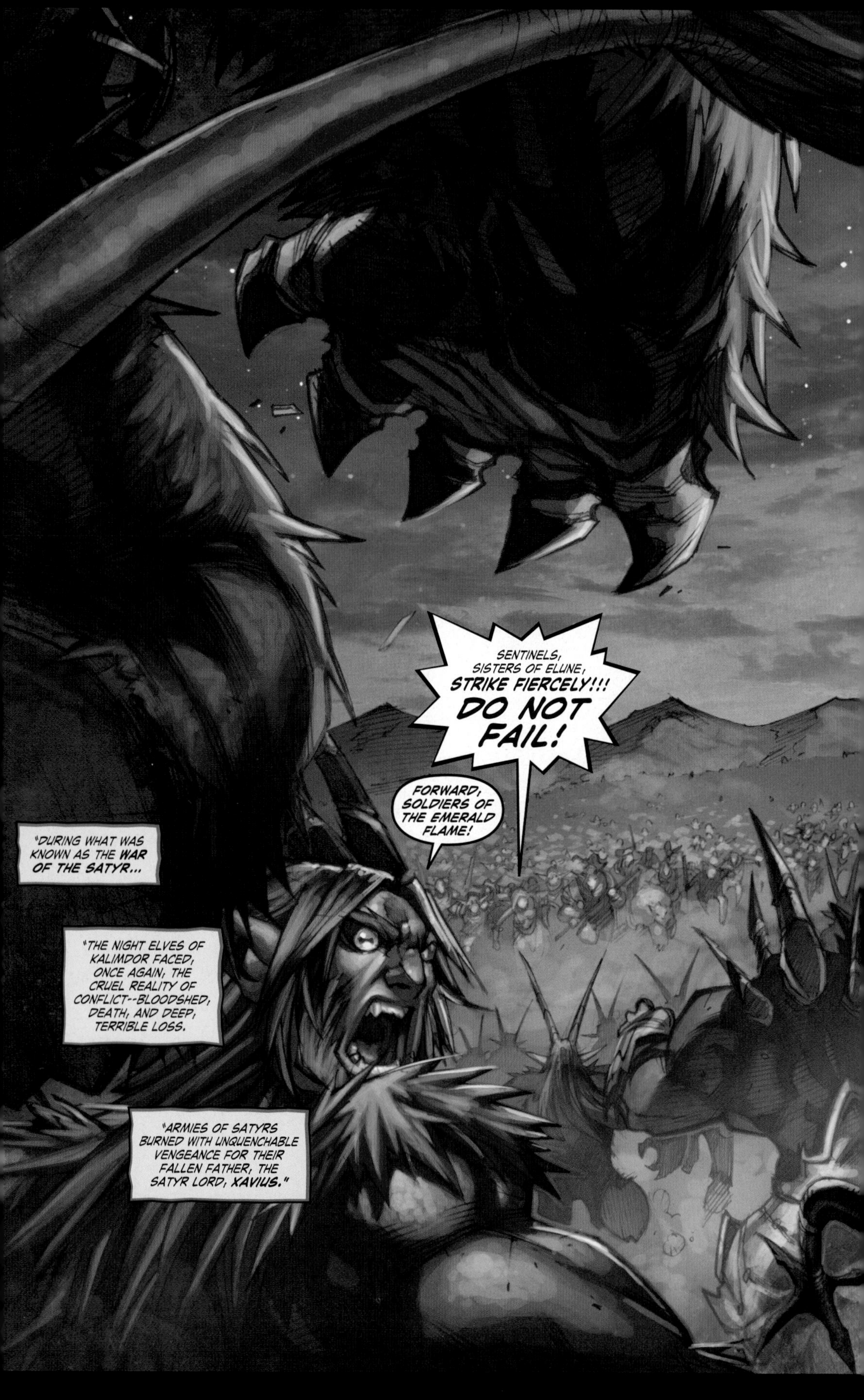
SENTINELS, SISTERS OF ELUNE, STRIKE FIERCELY!!! DO NOT FAIL!
FORWARD, SOLDIERS OF THE EMERALD FLAME!
"DURING WHAT WAS KNOWN AS THE WAR OF THE SATYR...
"THE NIGHT ELVES OF KALIMDOR FACED, ONCE AGAIN, THE CRUEL REALITY OF CONFLICT--BLOODSHED, DEATH, AND DEEP, TERRIBLE LOSS.
"ARMIES OF SATYRS BURNED WITH UNQUENCHABLE VENGEANCE FOR THEIR FALLEN FATHER, THE SATYR LORD, XAVIUS."

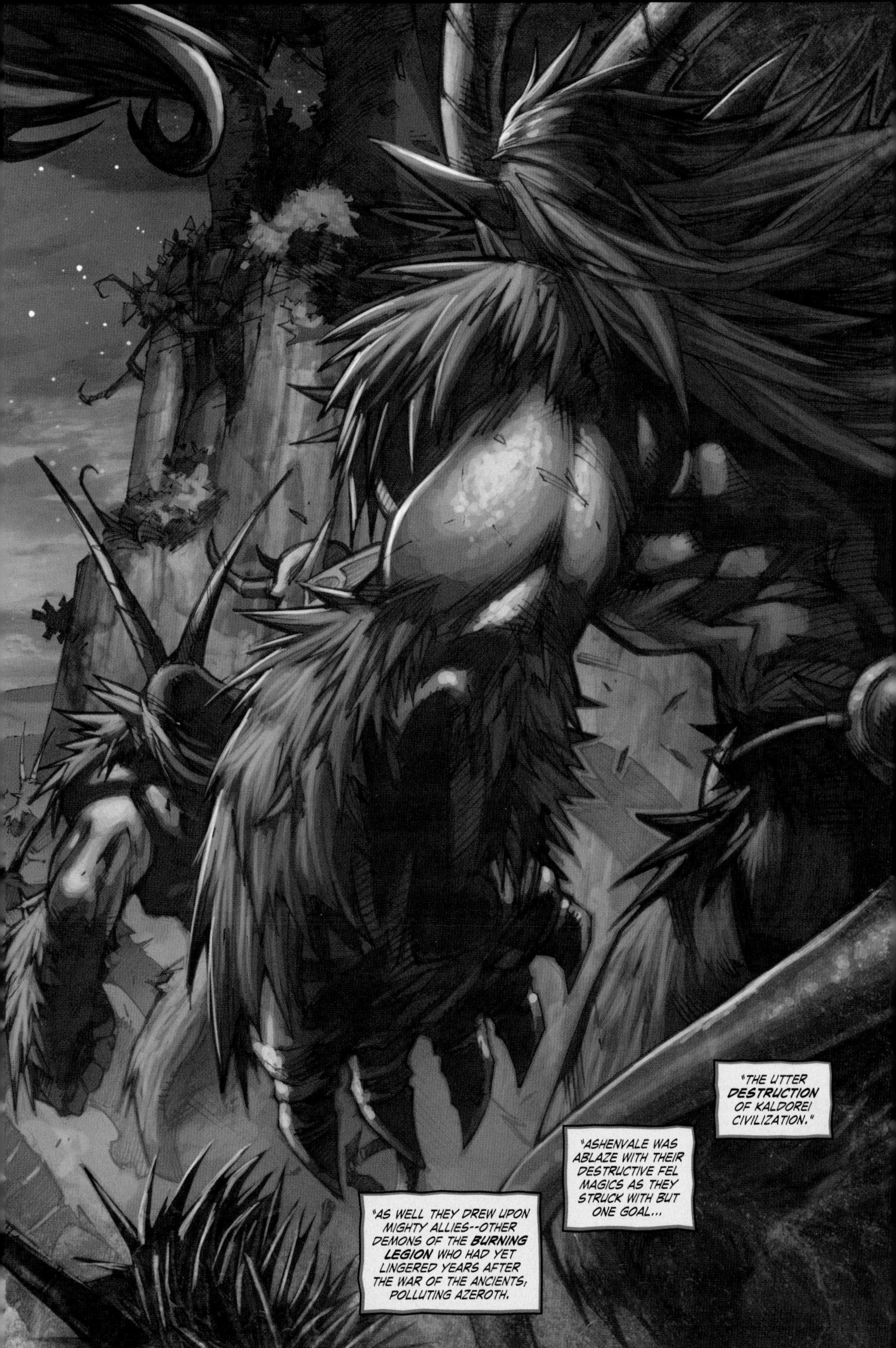
"AS WELL THEY DREW UPON MIGHTY ALLIES--OTHER DEMONS OF THE BURNING LEGION WHO HAD YET LINGERED YEARS AFTER THE WAR OF THE ANCIENTS, POLLUTING AZEROTH.
"ASHENVALE WAS ABLAZE WITH THEIR DESTRUCTIVE FEL MAGICS AS THEY STRUCK WITH BUT ONE GOAL...
"THE UTTER DESTRUCTION OF KALDOREI CIVILIZATION."

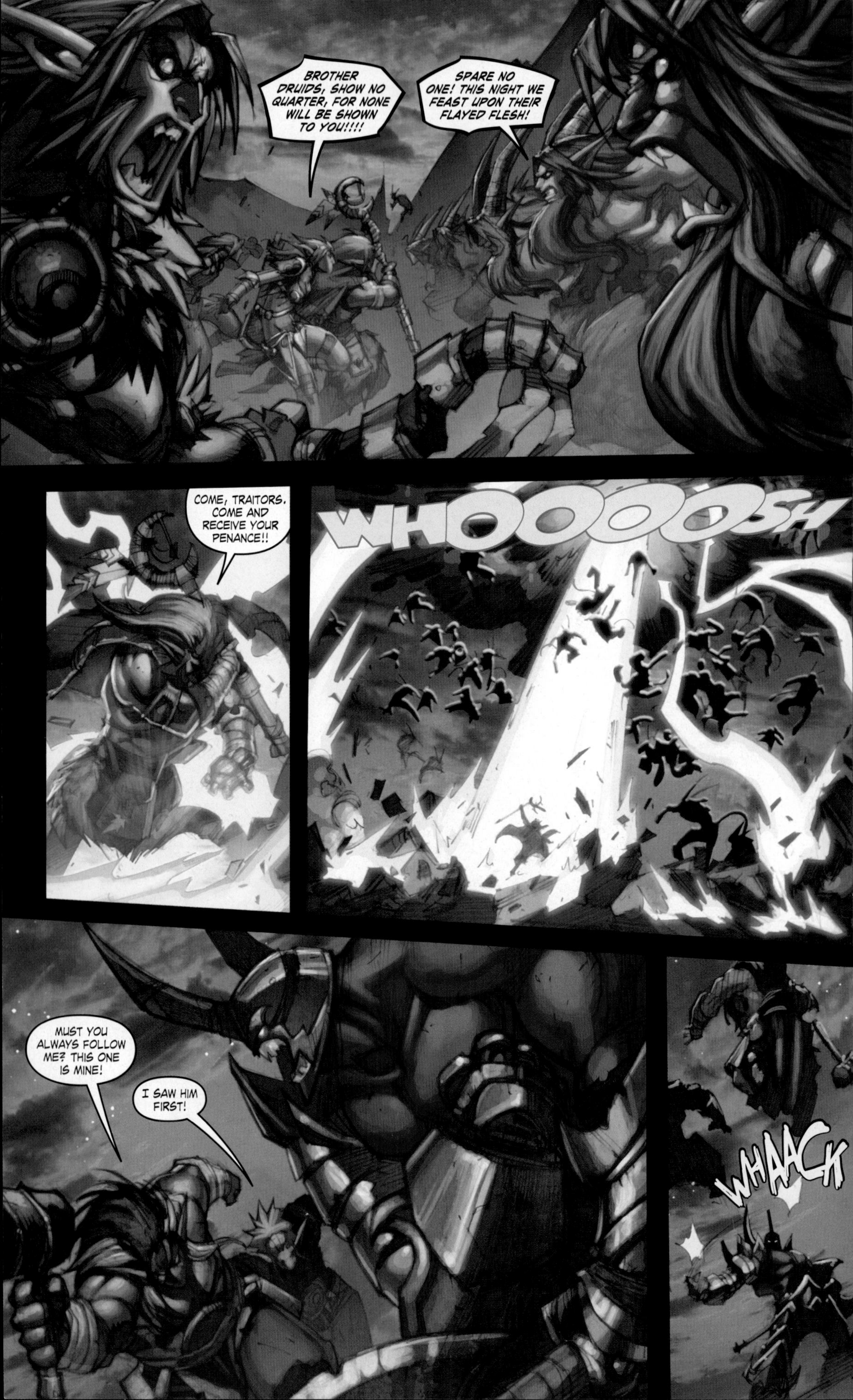

BROTHER DRUIDS, SHOW NO QUARTER, FOR NONE WILL BE SHOWN TO YOU!!!!
SPARE NO ONE! THIS NIGHT WE FEAST UPON THEIR FLAYED FLESH!
COME, TRAITORS. COME AND RECEIVE YOUR PENANCE!!
WHOOOOOSH
MUST YOU ALWAYS FOLLOW ME? THIS ONE IS MINE!
I SAW HIM FIRST!
WHAACK

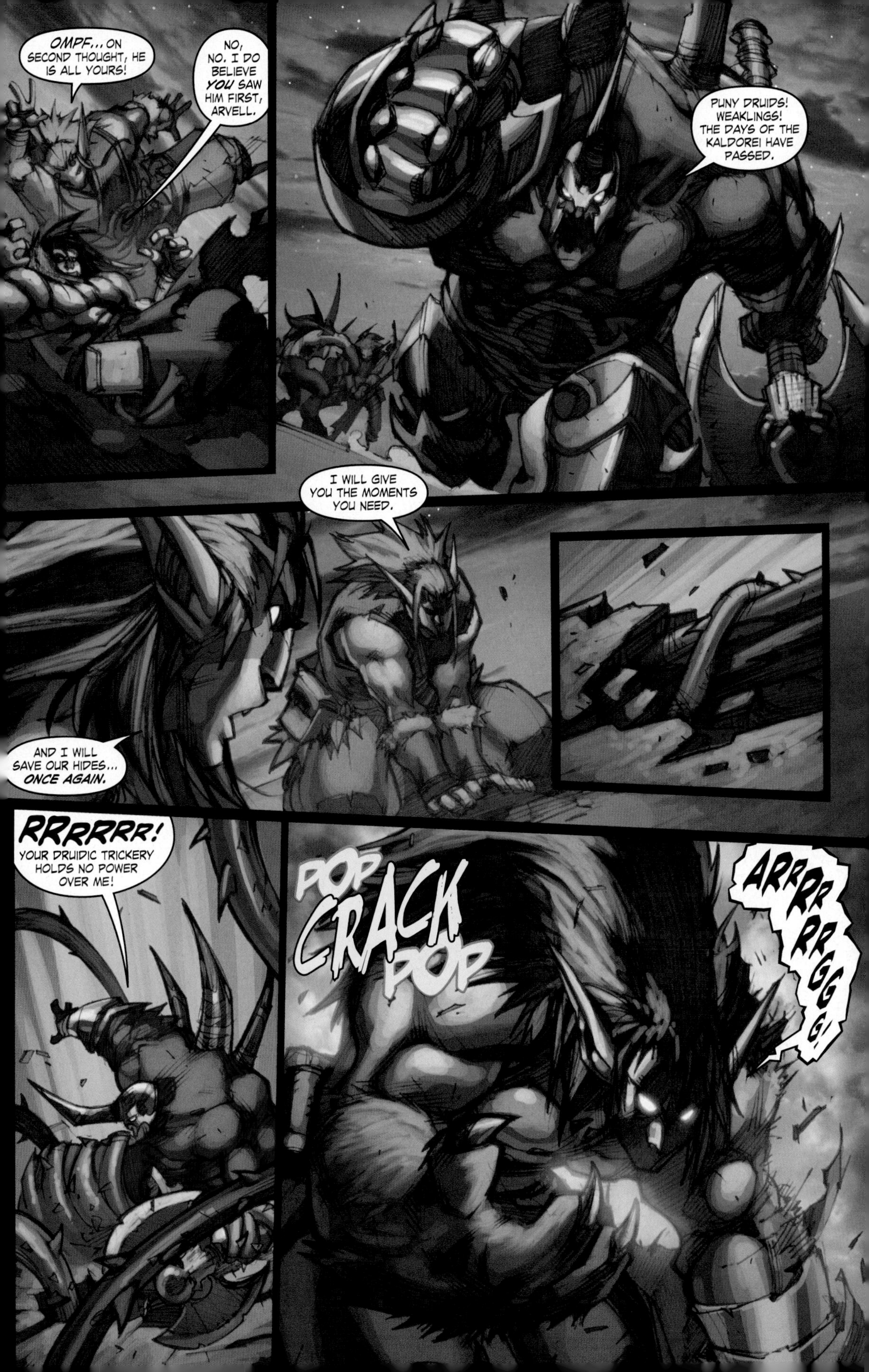
OMPF... ON SECOND THOUGHT, HE IS ALL YOURS!
NO, NO. I DO BELIEVE YOU SAW HIM FIRST, ARVELL.
PUNY DRUIDS! WEAKLINGS! THE DAYS OF THE KALDOREI HAVE PASSED.
I WILL GIVE YOU THE MOMENTS YOU NEED.
AND I WILL SAVE OUR HIDES... ONCE AGAIN.
RRRRRR! YOUR DRUIDIC TRICKERY HOLDS NO POWER OVER ME!
POP
CRACK
POP
ARRRRRRGGG!

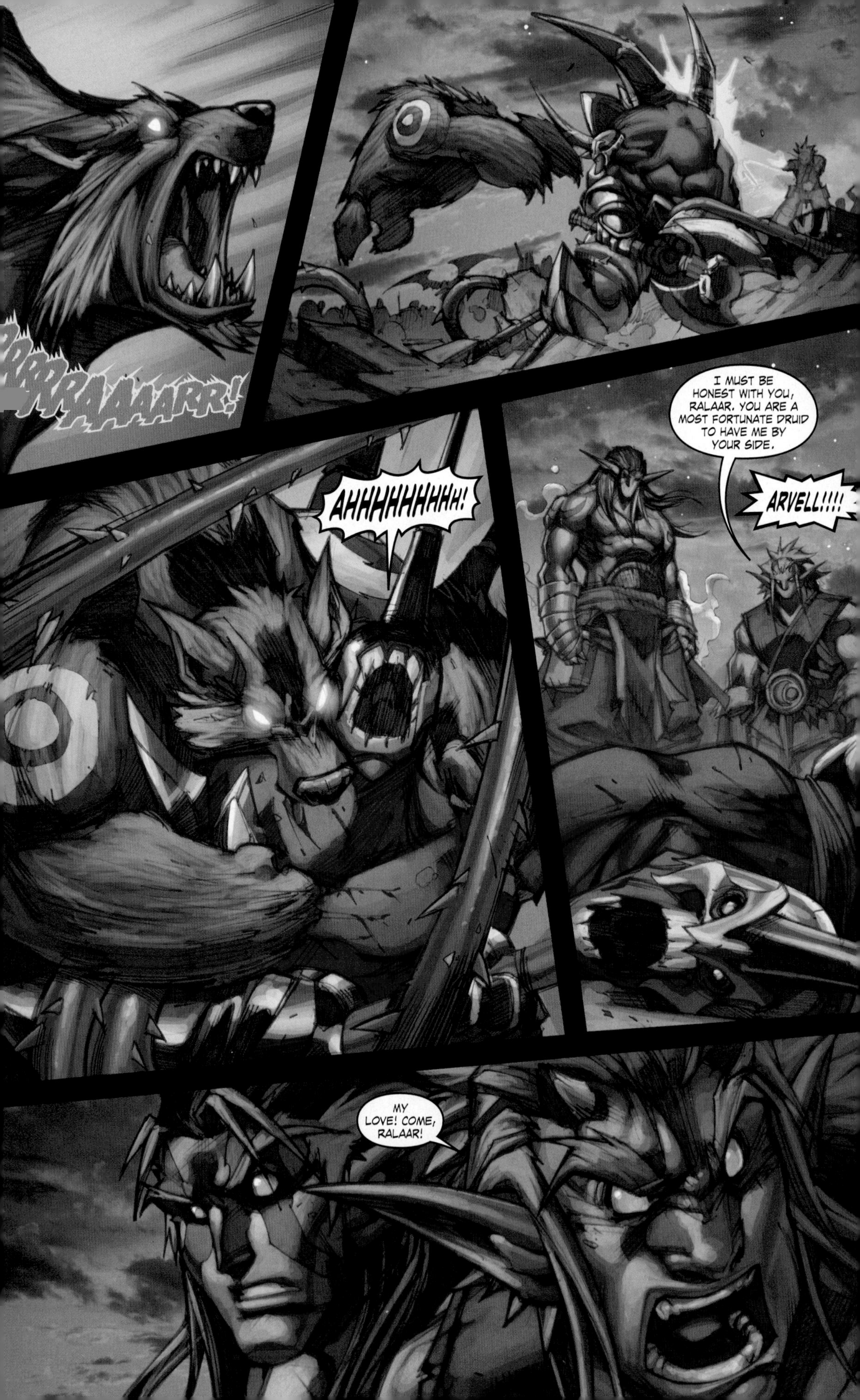
RRRRAAAAARR!
AHHHHHHHHH!
I MUST BE HONEST WITH YOU, RALAAR. YOU ARE A MOST FORTUNATE DRUID TO HAVE ME BY YOUR SIDE.
ARVELL!!!!
MY LOVE! COME, RALAAR!

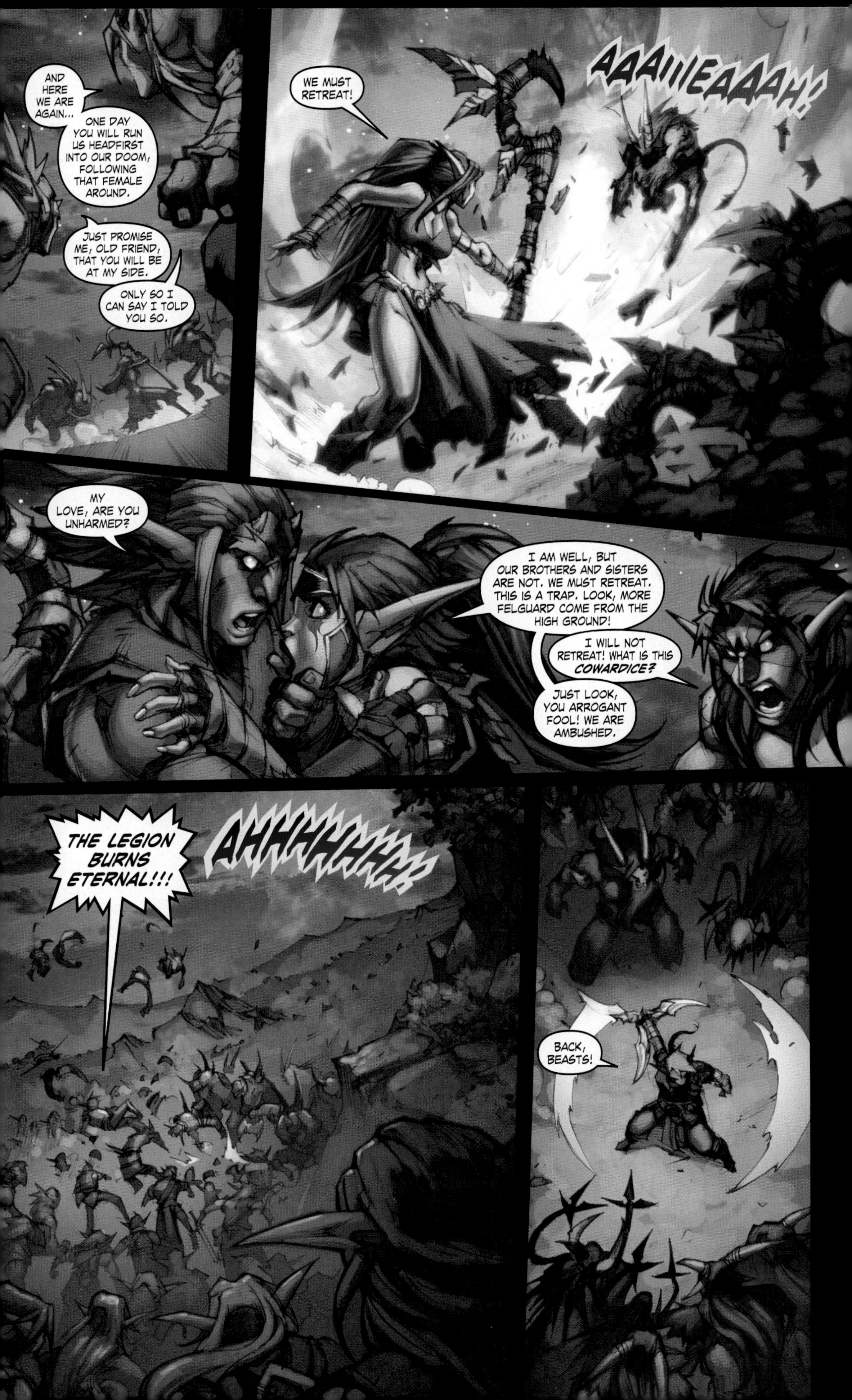
AND HERE WE ARE AGAIN...
ONE DAY YOU WILL RUN US HEADFIRST INTO OUR DOOM, FOLLOWING THAT FEMALE AROUND.
JUST PROMISE ME, OLD FRIEND, THAT YOU WILL BE AT MY SIDE.
ONLY SO I CAN SAY I TOLD YOU SO.
WE MUST RETREAT!
AAAIIIEAAAH!
MY LOVE, ARE YOU UNHARMED?
I AM WELL, BUT OUR BROTHERS AND SISTERS ARE NOT. WE MUST RETREAT. THIS IS A TRAP. LOOK, MORE FELGUARD COME FROM THE HIGH GROUND!
I WILL NOT RETREAT! WHAT IS THIS COWARDICE?
JUST LOOK, YOU ARROGANT FOOL! WE ARE AMBUSHED.
THE LEGION BURNS ETERNAL!!!
AHHHHHH!
BACK, BEASTS!

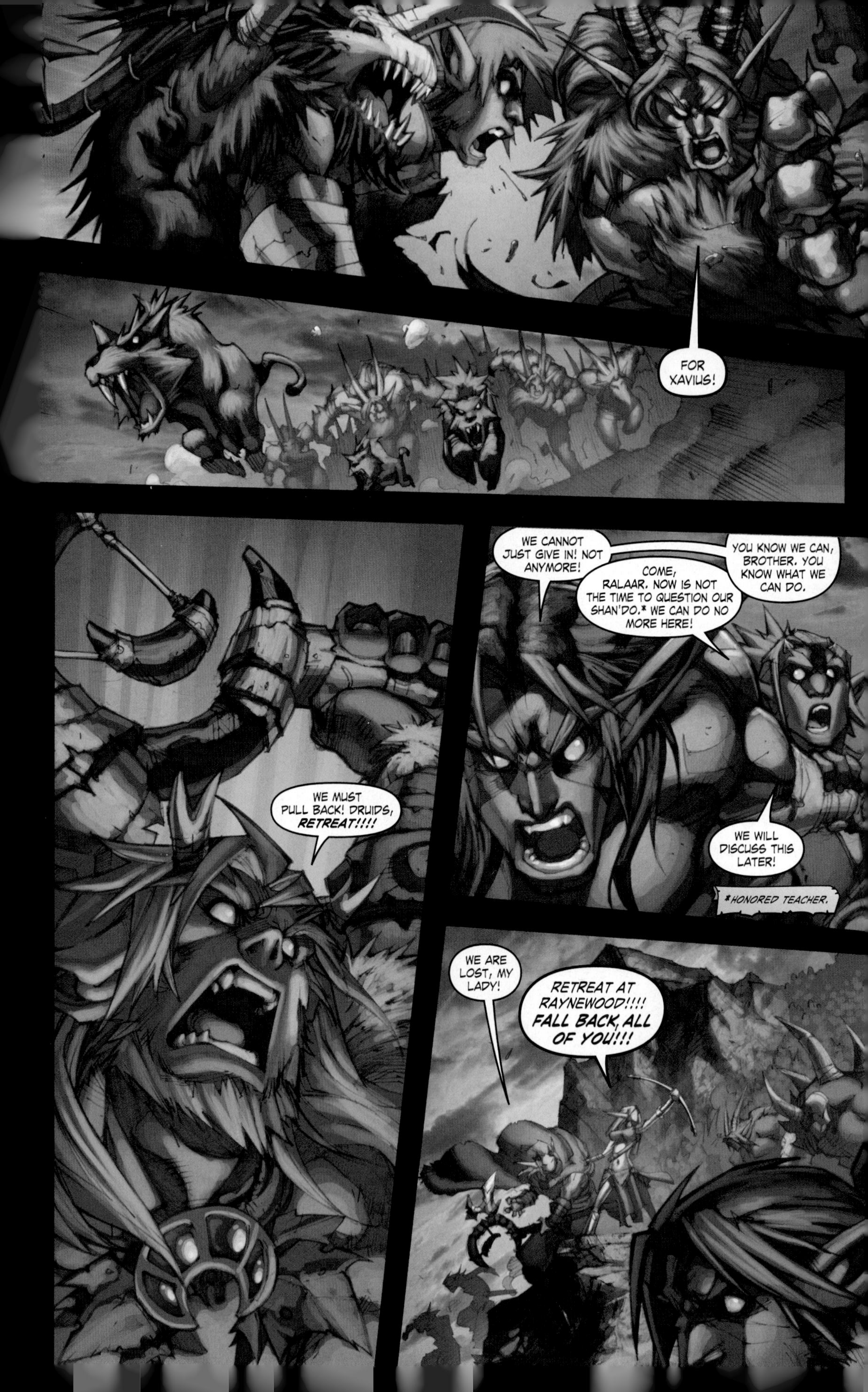
FOR XAVIUS!
WE MUST PULL BACK! DRUIDS, RETREAT!!!!
WE CANNOT JUST GIVE IN! NOT ANYMORE!
COME, RALAAR. NOW IS NOT THE TIME TO QUESTION OUR SHAN'DO.* WE CAN DO NO MORE HERE!
YOU KNOW WE CAN, BROTHER. YOU KNOW WHAT WE CAN DO.
WE WILL DISCUSS THIS LATER!
*HONORED TEACHER.
WE ARE LOST, MY LADY!
RETREAT AT RAYNEWOOD!!!! FALL BACK, ALL OF YOU!!!

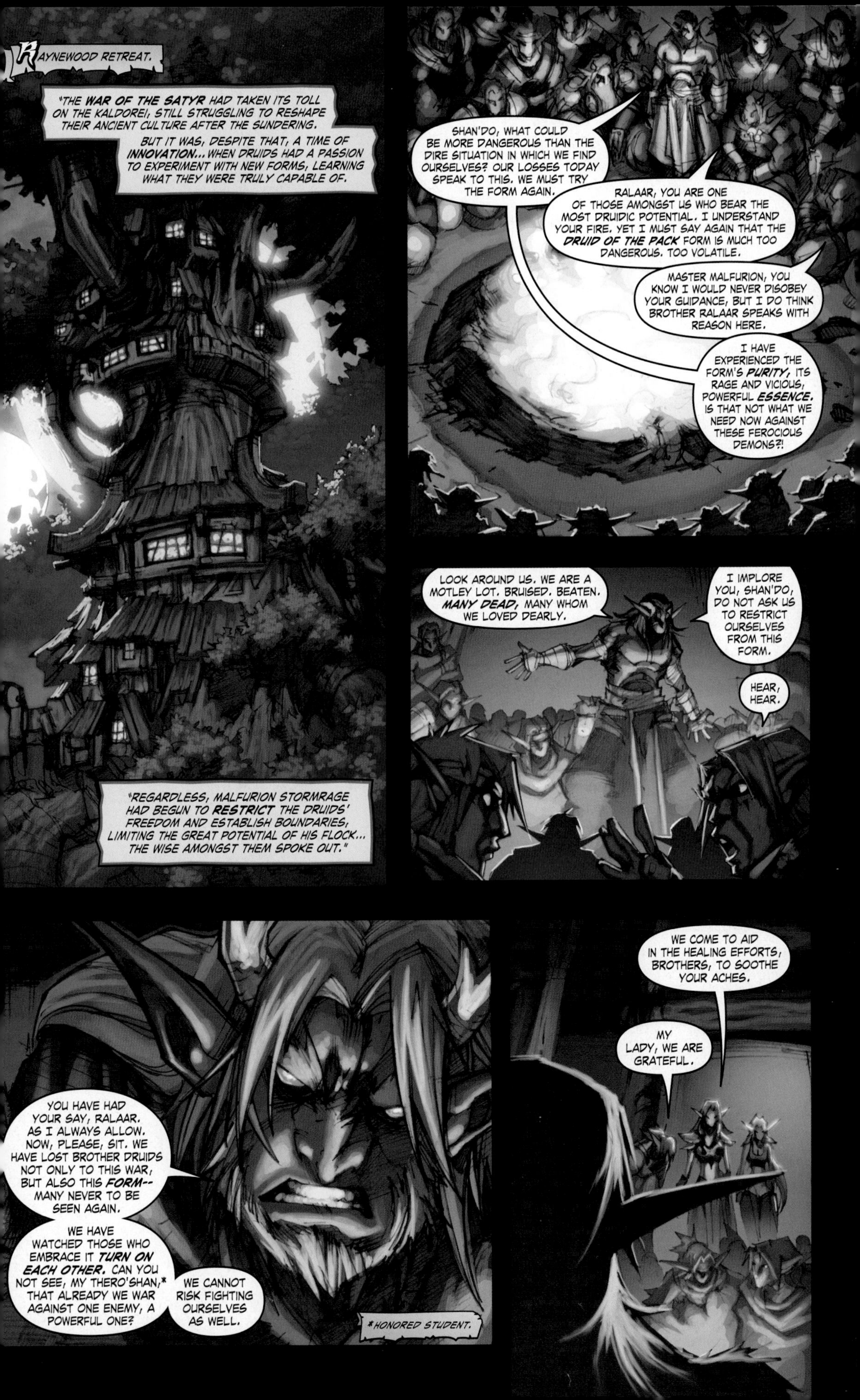
RAYNEWOOD RETREAT.
"THE WAR OF THE SATYR HAD TAKEN ITS TOLL ON THE KALDOREI, STILL STRUGGLING TO RESHAPE THEIR ANCIENT CULTURE AFTER THE SUNDERING.
BUT IT WAS, DESPITE THAT, A TIME OF INNOVATION... WHEN DRUIDS HAD A PASSION TO EXPERIMENT WITH NEW FORMS, LEARNING WHAT THEY WERE TRULY CAPABLE OF.
"REGARDLESS, MALFURION STORMRAGE HAD BEGUN TO RESTRICT THE DRUIDS' FREEDOM AND ESTABLISH BOUNDARIES, LIMITING THE GREAT POTENTIAL OF HIS FLOCK... THE WISE AMONGST THEM SPOKE OUT."
SHAN'DO, WHAT COULD BE MORE DANGEROUS THAN THE DIRE SITUATION IN WHICH WE FIND OURSELVES? OUR LOSSES TODAY SPEAK TO THIS. WE MUST TRY THE FORM AGAIN.
RALAAR, YOU ARE ONE OF THOSE AMONGST US WHO BEAR THE MOST DRUIDIC POTENTIAL. I UNDERSTAND YOUR FIRE. YET I MUST SAY AGAIN THAT THE DRUID OF THE PACK FORM IS MUCH TOO DANGEROUS. TOO VOLATILE.
MASTER MALFURION, YOU KNOW I WOULD NEVER DISOBEY YOUR GUIDANCE, BUT I DO THINK BROTHER RALAAR SPEAKS WITH REASON HERE.
I HAVE EXPERIENCED THE FORM'S PURITY, ITS RAGE AND VICIOUS, POWERFUL ESSENCE. IS THAT NOT WHAT WE NEED NOW AGAINST THESE FEROCIOUS DEMONS?!
LOOK AROUND US. WE ARE A MOTLEY LOT. BRUISED. BEATEN. MANY DEAD, MANY WHOM WE LOVED DEARLY.
I IMPLORE YOU, SHAN'DO, DO NOT ASK US TO RESTRICT OURSELVES FROM THIS FORM.
HEAR, HEAR.
YOU HAVE HAD YOUR SAY, RALAAR. AS I ALWAYS ALLOW. NOW, PLEASE, SIT. WE HAVE LOST BROTHER DRUIDS NOT ONLY TO THIS WAR, BUT ALSO THIS FORM-- MANY NEVER TO BE SEEN AGAIN.
WE HAVE WATCHED THOSE WHO EMBRACE IT TURN ON EACH OTHER. CAN YOU NOT SEE, MY THERO'SHAN,* THAT ALREADY WE WAR AGAINST ONE ENEMY, A POWERFUL ONE?
WE CANNOT RISK FIGHTING OURSELVES AS WELL.
*HONORED STUDENT.
WE COME TO AID IN THE HEALING EFFORTS, BROTHERS, TO SOOTHE YOUR ACHES.
MY LADY, WE ARE GRATEFUL.

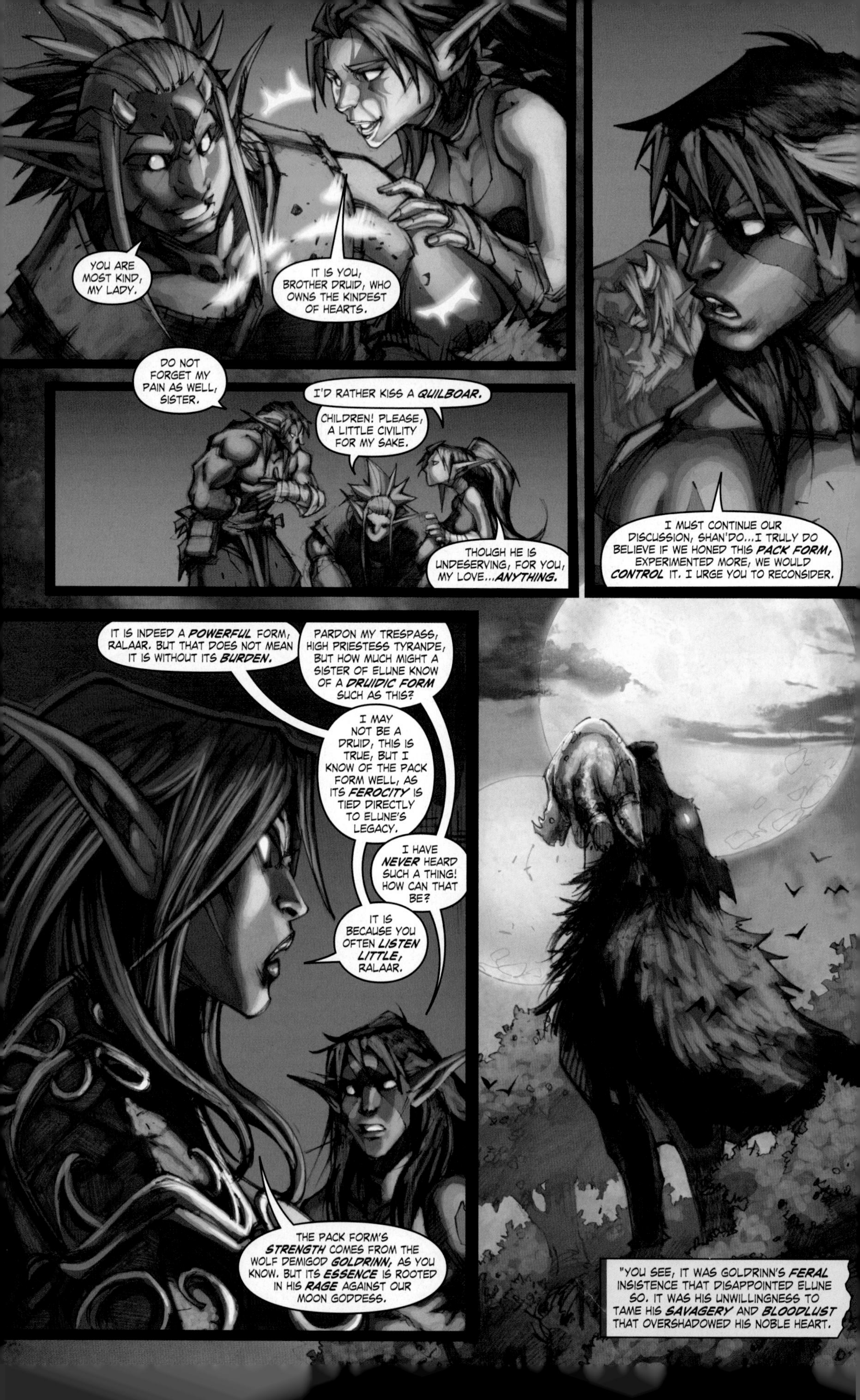
YOU ARE MOST KIND, MY LADY.
IT IS YOU, BROTHER DRUID, WHO OWNS THE KINDEST OF HEARTS.
DO NOT FORGET MY PAIN AS WELL, SISTER.
I'D RATHER KISS A QUILBOAR.
CHILDREN! PLEASE, A LITTLE CIVILITY FOR MY SAKE.
THOUGH HE IS UNDESERVING, FOR YOU, MY LOVE...ANYTHING.
I MUST CONTINUE OUR DISCUSSION, SHAN'DO...I TRULY DO BELIEVE IF WE HONED THIS PACK FORM, EXPERIMENTED MORE, WE WOULD CONTROL IT. I URGE YOU TO RECONSIDER.
IT IS INDEED A POWERFUL FORM, RALAAR. BUT THAT DOES NOT MEAN IT IS WITHOUT ITS BURDEN.
PARDON MY TRESPASS, HIGH PRIESTESS TYRANDE, BUT HOW MUCH MIGHT A SISTER OF ELUNE KNOW OF A DRUIDIC FORM SUCH AS THIS?
I MAY NOT BE A DRUID, THIS IS TRUE, BUT I KNOW OF THE PACK FORM WELL, AS ITS FEROCITY IS TIED DIRECTLY TO ELUNE'S LEGACY.
I HAVE NEVER HEARD SUCH A THING! HOW CAN THAT BE?
IT IS BECAUSE YOU OFTEN LISTEN LITTLE, RALAAR.
THE PACK FORM'S STRENGTH COMES FROM THE WOLF DEMIGOD GOLDRINN, AS YOU KNOW. BUT ITS ESSENCE IS ROOTED IN HIS RAGE AGAINST OUR MOON GODDESS.
"YOU SEE, IT WAS GOLDRINN'S FERAL INSISTENCE THAT DISAPPOINTED ELUNE SO. IT WAS HIS UNWILLINGNESS TO TAME HIS SAVAGERY AND BLOODLUST THAT OVERSHADOWED HIS NOBLE HEART.

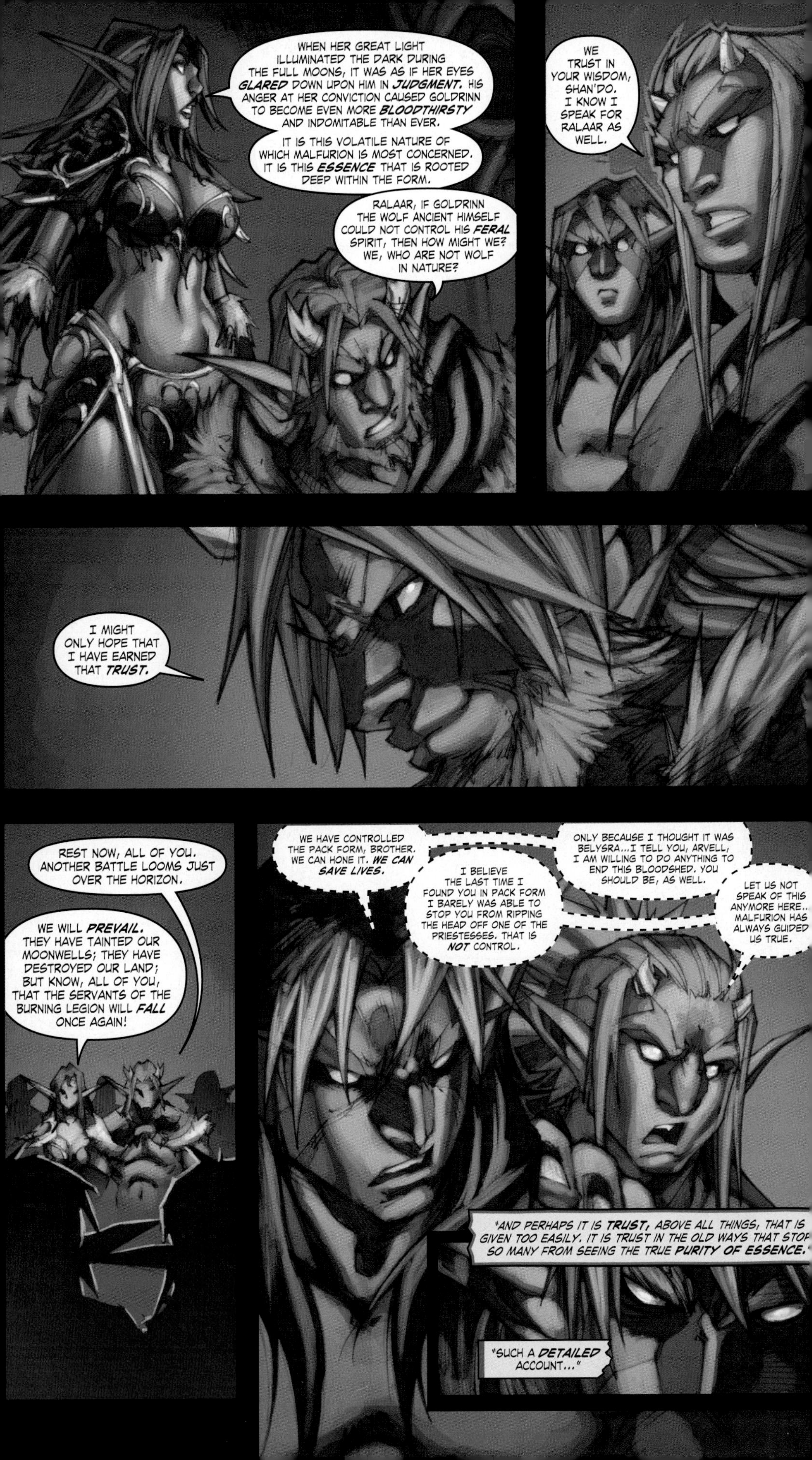
WHEN HER GREAT LIGHT ILLUMINATED THE DARK DURING THE FULL MOONS, IT WAS AS IF HER EYES *GLARED* DOWN UPON HIM IN *JUDGMENT.* HIS ANGER AT HER CONVICTION CAUSED GOLDRINN TO BECOME EVEN MORE *BLOODTHIRSTY* AND INDOMITABLE THAN EVER.
IT IS THIS VOLATILE NATURE OF WHICH MALFURION IS MOST CONCERNED. IT IS THIS *ESSENCE* THAT IS ROOTED DEEP WITHIN THE FORM.
RALAAR, IF GOLDRINN THE WOLF ANCIENT HIMSELF COULD NOT CONTROL HIS *FERAL* SPIRIT, THEN HOW MIGHT WE? WE, WHO ARE NOT WOLF IN NATURE?
WE TRUST IN YOUR WISDOM, SHAN'DO. I KNOW I SPEAK FOR RALAAR AS WELL.
I MIGHT ONLY HOPE THAT I HAVE EARNED THAT *TRUST.*
REST NOW, ALL OF YOU. ANOTHER BATTLE LOOMS JUST OVER THE HORIZON.
WE WILL *PREVAIL.* THEY HAVE TAINTED OUR MOONWELLS; THEY HAVE DESTROYED OUR LAND; BUT KNOW, ALL OF YOU, THAT THE SERVANTS OF THE BURNING LEGION WILL *FALL* ONCE AGAIN!
WE HAVE CONTROLLED THE PACK FORM, BROTHER. WE CAN HONE IT. *WE CAN SAVE LIVES.*
I BELIEVE THE LAST TIME I FOUND YOU IN PACK FORM I BARELY WAS ABLE TO STOP YOU FROM RIPPING THE HEAD OFF ONE OF THE PRIESTESSES. THAT IS *NOT* CONTROL.
ONLY BECAUSE I THOUGHT IT WAS BELYSRA...I TELL YOU, ARVELL, I AM WILLING TO DO ANYTHING TO END THIS BLOODSHED. YOU SHOULD BE, AS WELL.
LET US NOT SPEAK OF THIS ANYMORE HERE... MALFURION HAS ALWAYS GUIDED US TRUE.
"AND PERHAPS IT IS *TRUST,* ABOVE ALL THINGS, THAT IS GIVEN TOO EASILY. IT IS TRUST IN THE OLD WAYS THAT STOP SO MANY FROM SEEING THE TRUE *PURITY OF ESSENCE.*"
"SUCH A *DETAILED* ACCOUNT..."

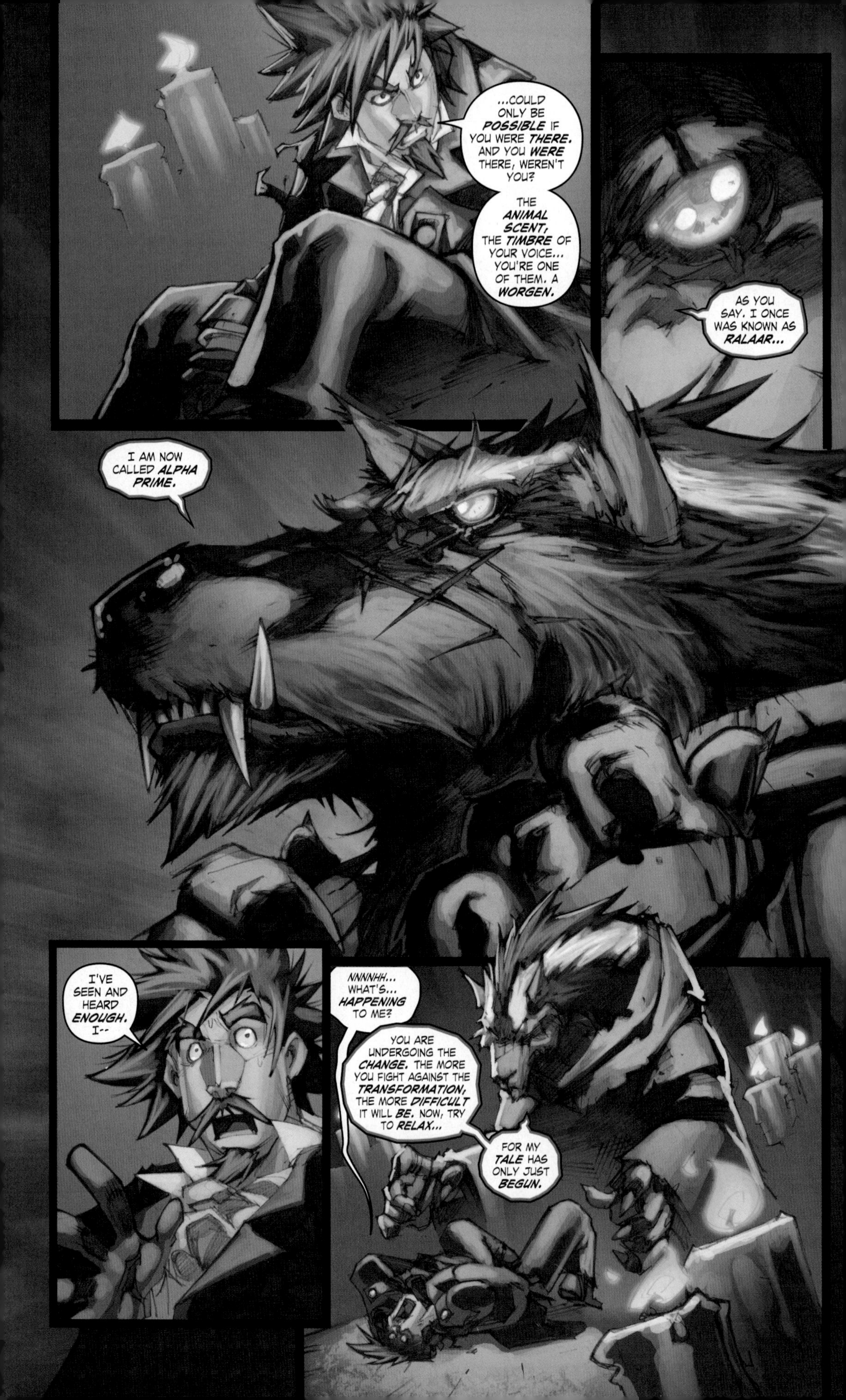

...COULD ONLY BE POSSIBLE IF YOU WERE THERE. AND YOU WERE THERE, WEREN'T YOU?
THE ANIMAL SCENT, THE TIMBRE OF YOUR VOICE... YOU'RE ONE OF THEM. A WORGEN.
AS YOU SAY. I ONCE WAS KNOWN AS RALAAR...
I AM NOW CALLED ALPHA PRIME.
I'VE SEEN AND HEARD ENOUGH. I--
NNNNHH... WHAT'S... HAPPENING TO ME?
YOU ARE UNDERGOING THE CHANGE. THE MORE YOU FIGHT AGAINST THE TRANSFORMATION, THE MORE DIFFICULT IT WILL BE. NOW, TRY TO RELAX...
FOR MY TALE HAS ONLY JUST BEGUN.

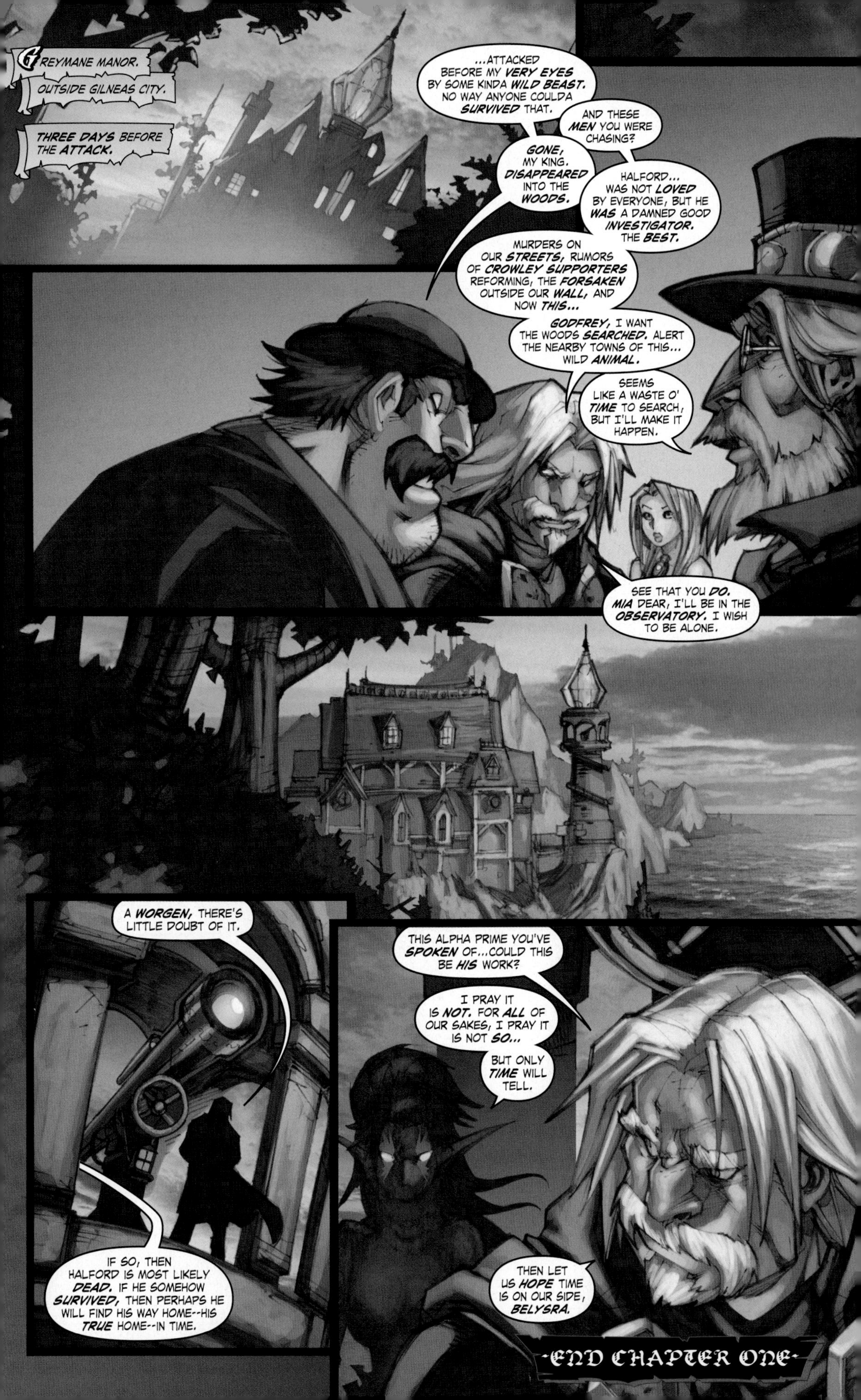
GREYMANE MANOR.
OUTSIDE GILNEAS CITY.
THREE DAYS BEFORE THE ATTACK.
...ATTACKED BEFORE MY VERY EYES BY SOME KINDA WILD BEAST. NO WAY ANYONE COULDA SURVIVED THAT.
AND THESE MEN YOU WERE CHASING?
GONE, MY KING. DISAPPEARED INTO THE WOODS.
HALFORD... WAS NOT LOVED BY EVERYONE, BUT HE WAS A DAMNED GOOD INVESTIGATOR. THE BEST.
MURDERS ON OUR STREETS, RUMORS OF CROWLEY SUPPORTERS REFORMING, THE FORSAKEN OUTSIDE OUR WALL, AND NOW THIS...
GODFREY, I WANT THE WOODS SEARCHED. ALERT THE NEARBY TOWNS OF THIS... WILD ANIMAL.
SEEMS LIKE A WASTE O' TIME TO SEARCH, BUT I'LL MAKE IT HAPPEN.
SEE THAT YOU DO. MIA DEAR, I'LL BE IN THE OBSERVATORY. I WISH TO BE ALONE.
A WORGEN, THERE'S LITTLE DOUBT OF IT.
IF SO, THEN HALFORD IS MOST LIKELY DEAD. IF HE SOMEHOW SURVIVED, THEN PERHAPS HE WILL FIND HIS WAY HOME--HIS TRUE HOME--IN TIME.
THIS ALPHA PRIME YOU'VE SPOKEN OF...COULD THIS BE HIS WORK?
I PRAY IT IS NOT. FOR ALL OF OUR SAKES, I PRAY IT IS NOT SO...
BUT ONLY TIME WILL TELL.
THEN LET US HOPE TIME IS ON OUR SIDE, BELYSRA.
-END CHAPTER ONE-

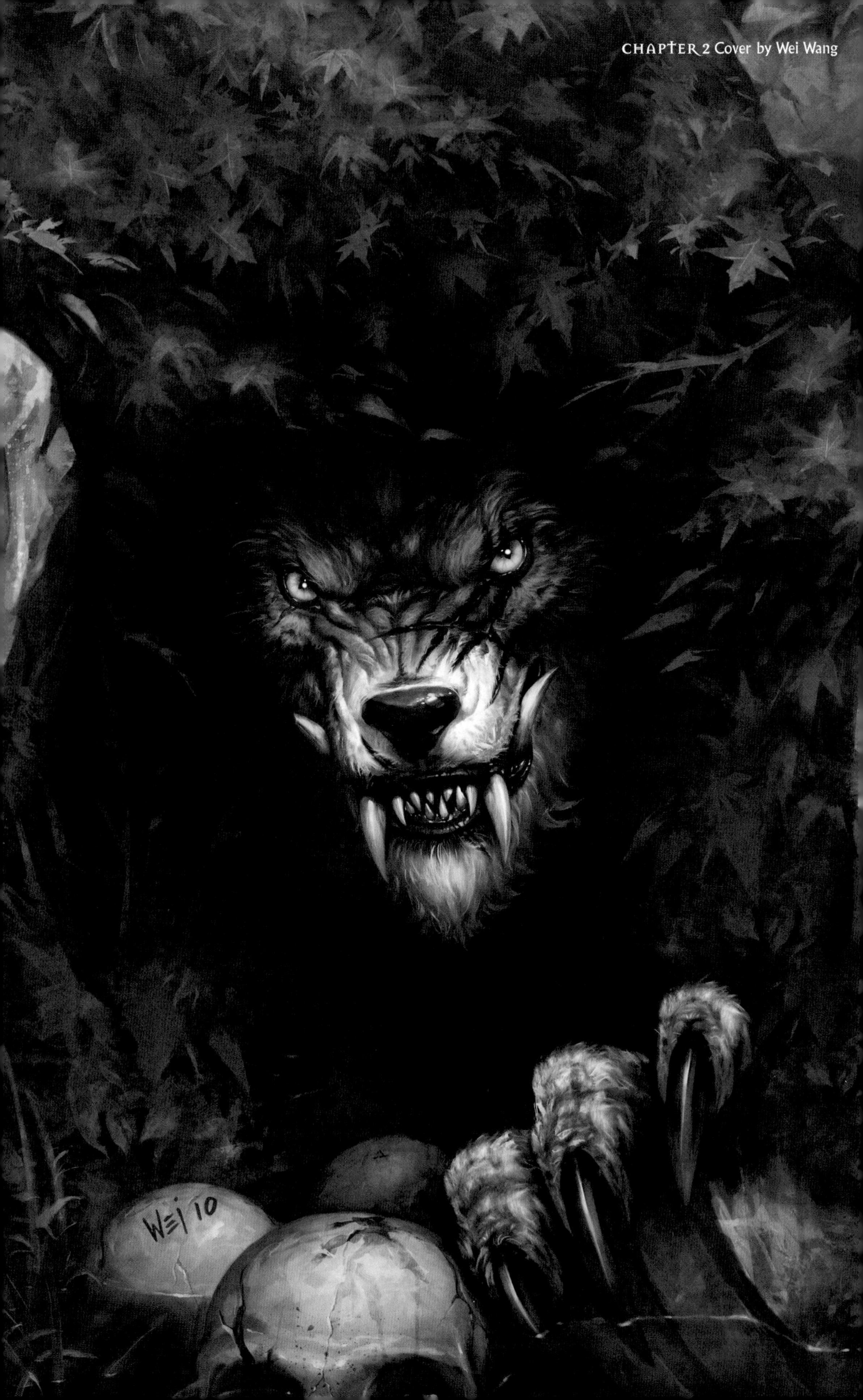
WEI 10

CHAPTER 2 Cover by Wei Wang

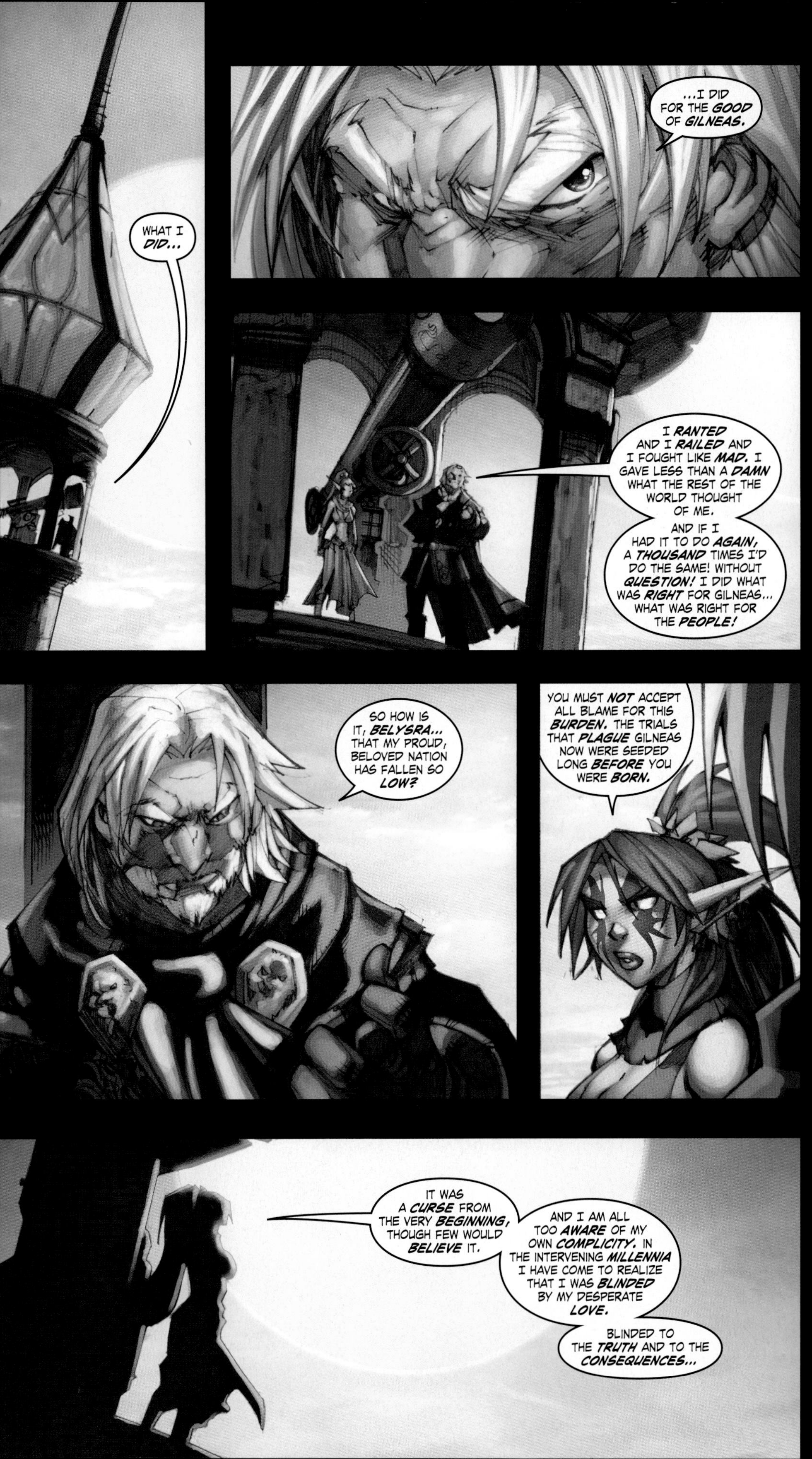

WHAT I DID...
...I DID FOR THE GOOD OF GILNEAS.
I RANTED AND I RAILED AND I FOUGHT LIKE MAD. I GAVE LESS THAN A DAMN WHAT THE REST OF THE WORLD THOUGHT OF ME.
AND IF I HAD IT TO DO AGAIN, A THOUSAND TIMES I'D DO THE SAME! WITHOUT QUESTION! I DID WHAT WAS RIGHT FOR GILNEAS... WHAT WAS RIGHT FOR THE PEOPLE!
SO HOW IS IT, BELYSRA... THAT MY PROUD, BELOVED NATION HAS FALLEN SO LOW?
YOU MUST NOT ACCEPT ALL BLAME FOR THIS BURDEN. THE TRIALS THAT PLAGUE GILNEAS NOW WERE SEEDED LONG BEFORE YOU WERE BORN.
IT WAS A CURSE FROM THE VERY BEGINNING, THOUGH FEW WOULD BELIEVE IT.
AND I AM ALL TOO AWARE OF MY OWN COMPLICITY. IN THE INTERVENING MILLENNIA I HAVE COME TO REALIZE THAT I WAS BLINDED BY MY DESPERATE LOVE.
BLINDED TO THE TRUTH AND TO THE CONSEQUENCES...

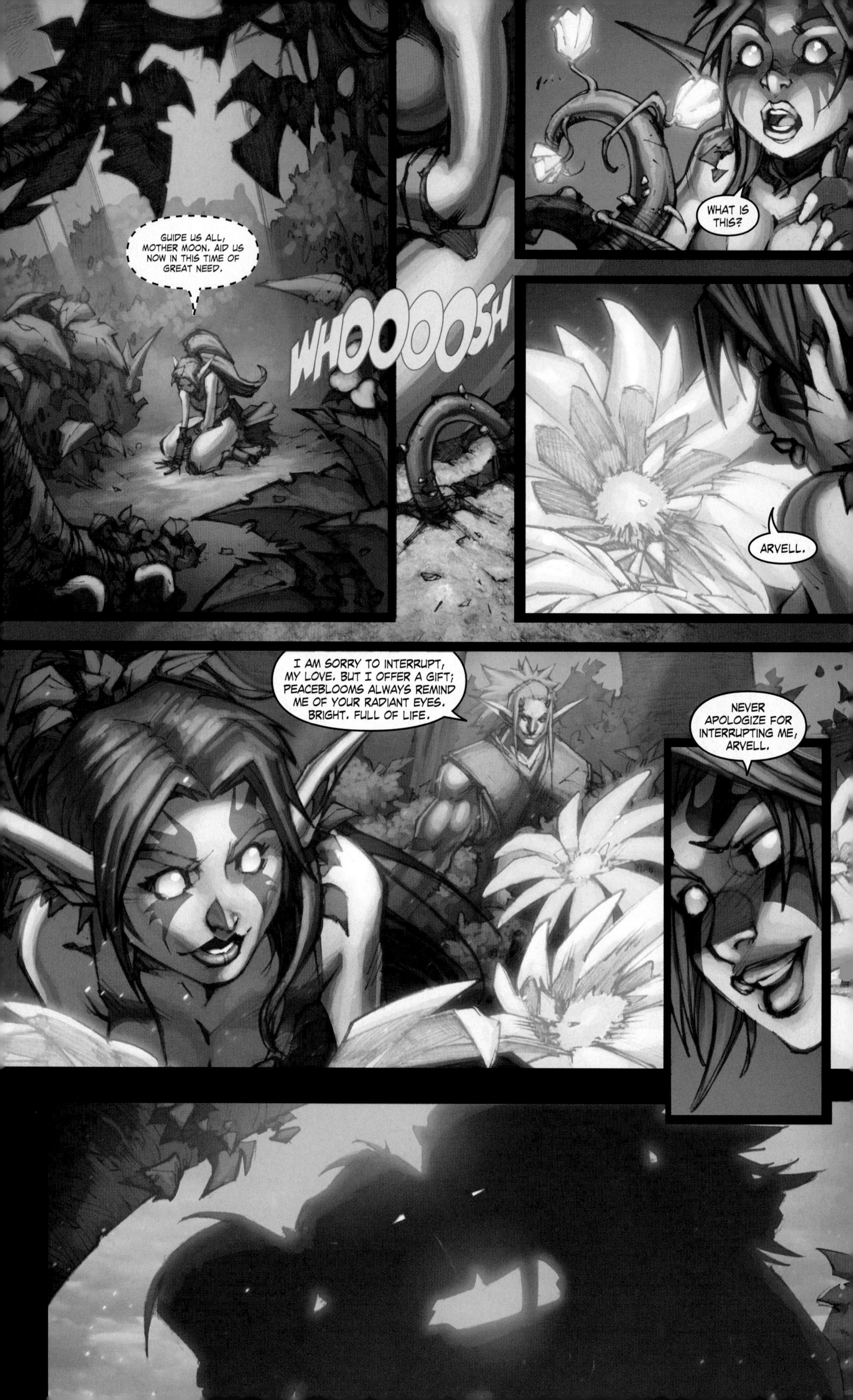
GUIDE US ALL, MOTHER MOON. AID US NOW IN THIS TIME OF GREAT NEED.
WHOOOOOSH
WHAT IS THIS?
ARVELL.
I AM SORRY TO INTERRUPT, MY LOVE. BUT I OFFER A GIFT; PEACEBLOOMS ALWAYS REMIND ME OF YOUR RADIANT EYES. BRIGHT. FULL OF LIFE.
NEVER APOLOGIZE FOR INTERRUPTING ME, ARVELL.

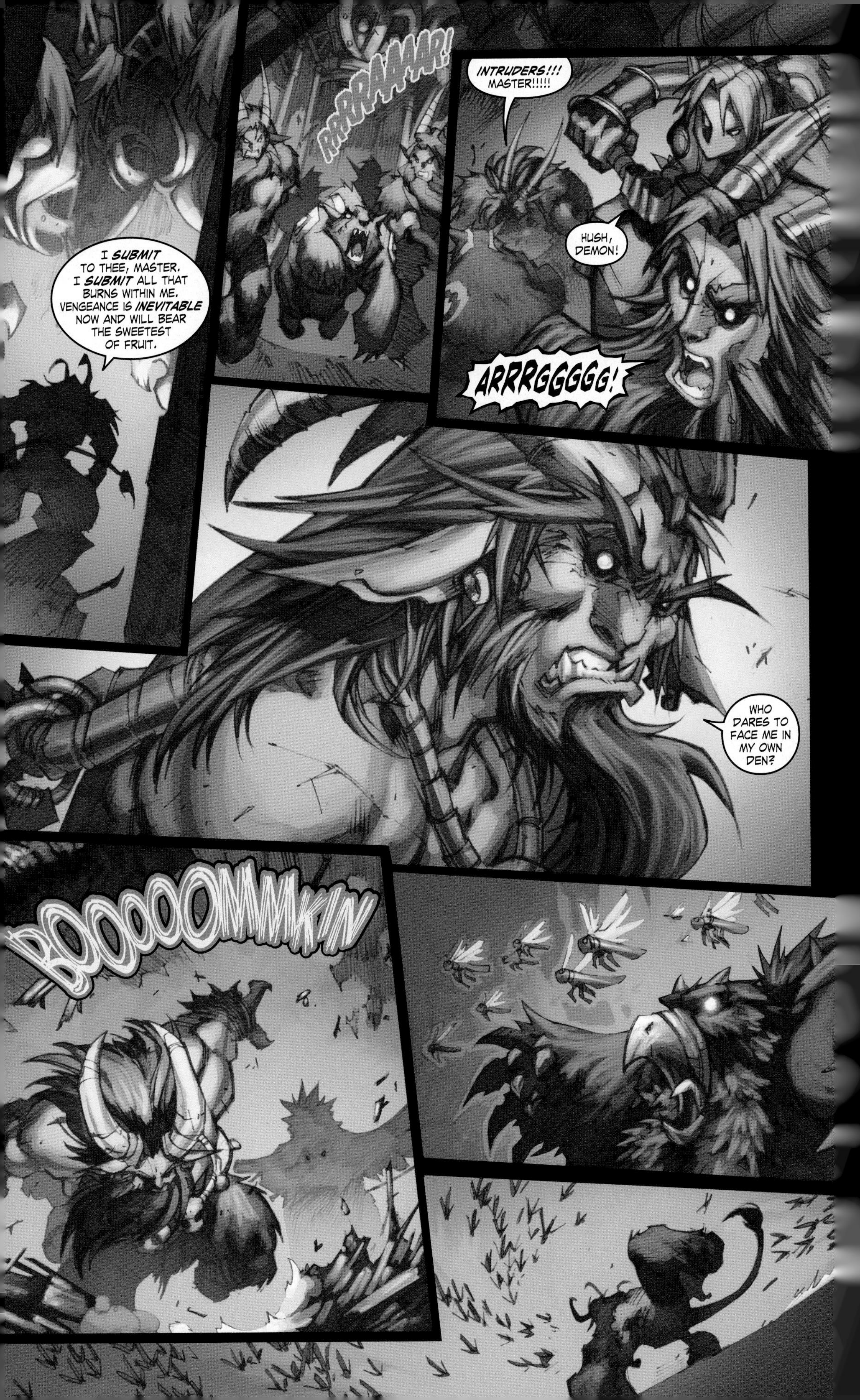
I SUBMIT TO THEE, MASTER. I SUBMIT ALL THAT BURNS WITHIN ME. VENGEANCE IS INEVITABLE NOW AND WILL BEAR THE SWEETEST OF FRUIT.
RRRRAAAAR!
INTRUDERS!!! MASTER!!!!!
HUSH, DEMON!
ARRRGGGGG!
WHO DARES TO FACE ME IN MY OWN DEN?
BOOOOOMMKIN

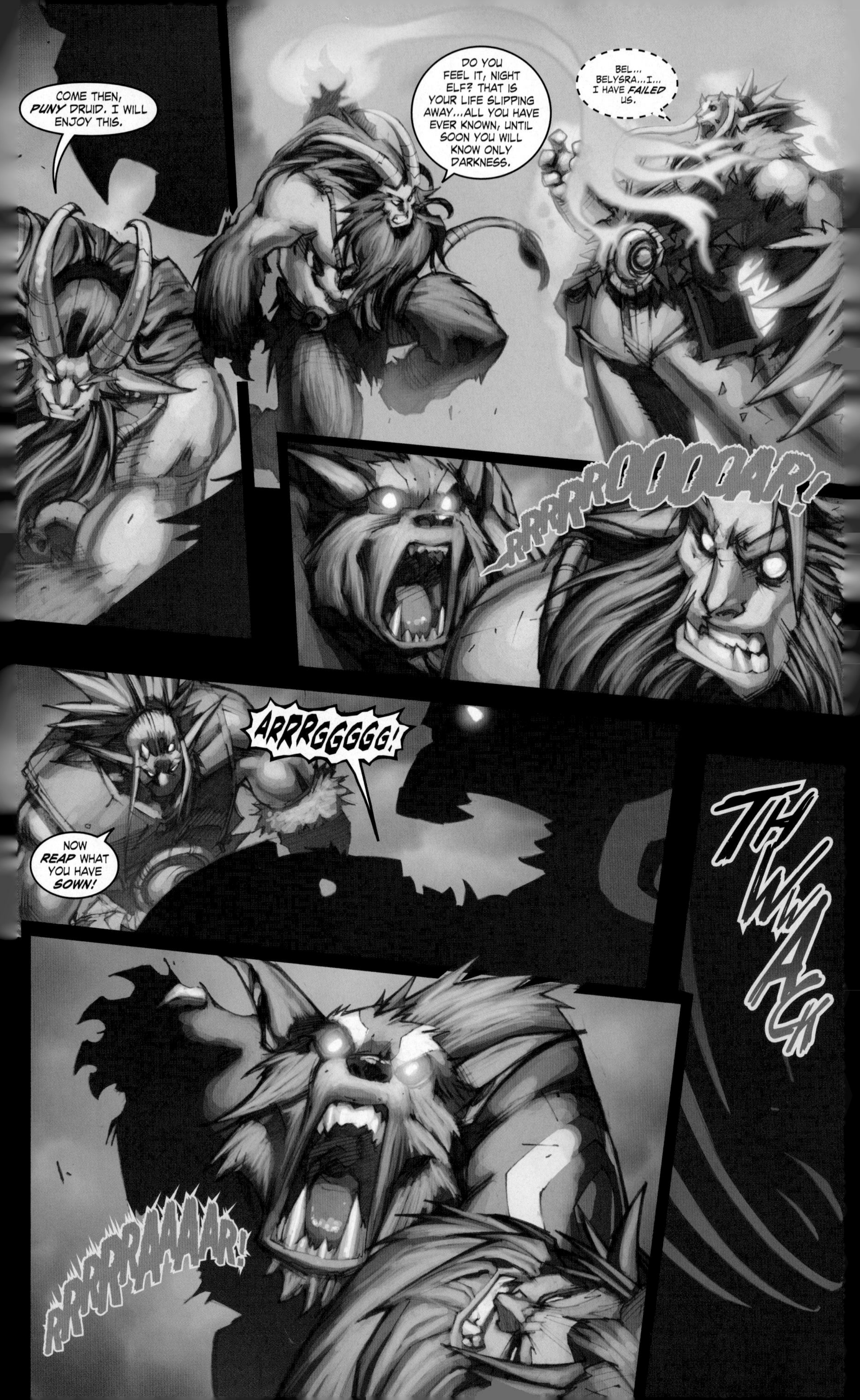
COME THEN, PUNY DRUID. I WILL ENJOY THIS.
DO YOU FEEL IT, NIGHT ELF? THAT IS YOUR LIFE SLIPPING AWAY...ALL YOU HAVE EVER KNOWN, UNTIL SOON YOU WILL KNOW ONLY DARKNESS.
BEL... BELYSRA...I... I HAVE FAILED US.
RRRRRROOOOOAR!
ARRRGGGGG!
NOW REAP WHAT YOU HAVE SOWN!
THWACK
RRRRRRAAAAR!

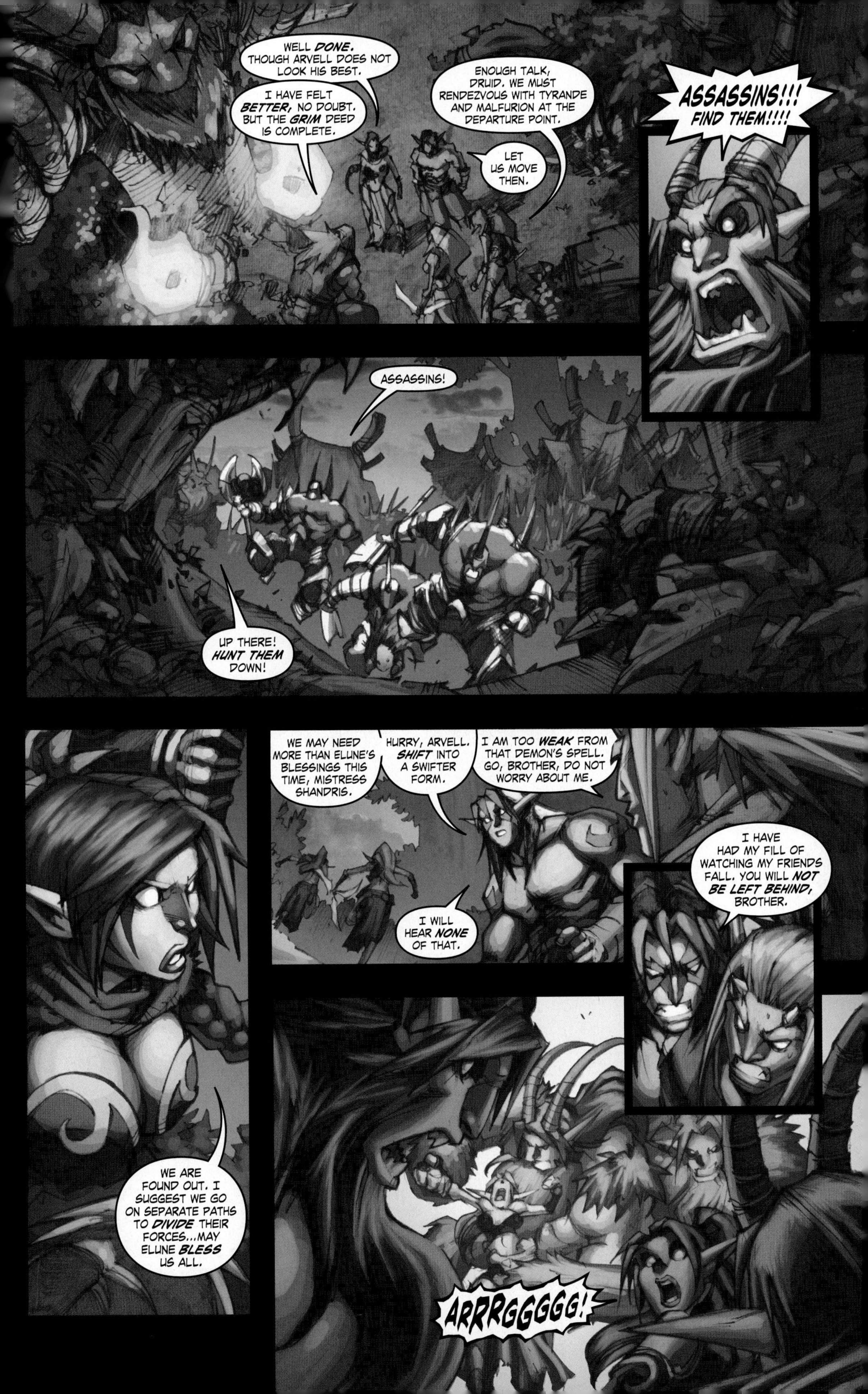

WELL DONE. THOUGH ARVELL DOES NOT LOOK HIS BEST.
I HAVE FELT BETTER, NO DOUBT. BUT THE GRIM DEED IS COMPLETE.
ENOUGH TALK, DRUID. WE MUST RENDEZVOUS WITH TYRANDE AND MALFURION AT THE DEPARTURE POINT.
LET US MOVE THEN.
ASSASSINS!!! FIND THEM!!!!
ASSASSINS!
UP THERE! HUNT THEM DOWN!
WE ARE FOUND OUT. I SUGGEST WE GO ON SEPARATE PATHS TO DIVIDE THEIR FORCES...MAY ELUNE BLESS US ALL.
WE MAY NEED MORE THAN ELUNE'S BLESSINGS THIS TIME, MISTRESS SHANDRIS.
HURRY, ARVELL. SHIFT INTO A SWIFTER FORM.
I AM TOO WEAK FROM THAT DEMON'S SPELL. GO, BROTHER, DO NOT WORRY ABOUT ME.
I WILL HEAR NONE OF THAT.
I HAVE HAD MY FILL OF WATCHING MY FRIENDS FALL. YOU WILL NOT BE LEFT BEHIND, BROTHER.
ARRRGGGGG!

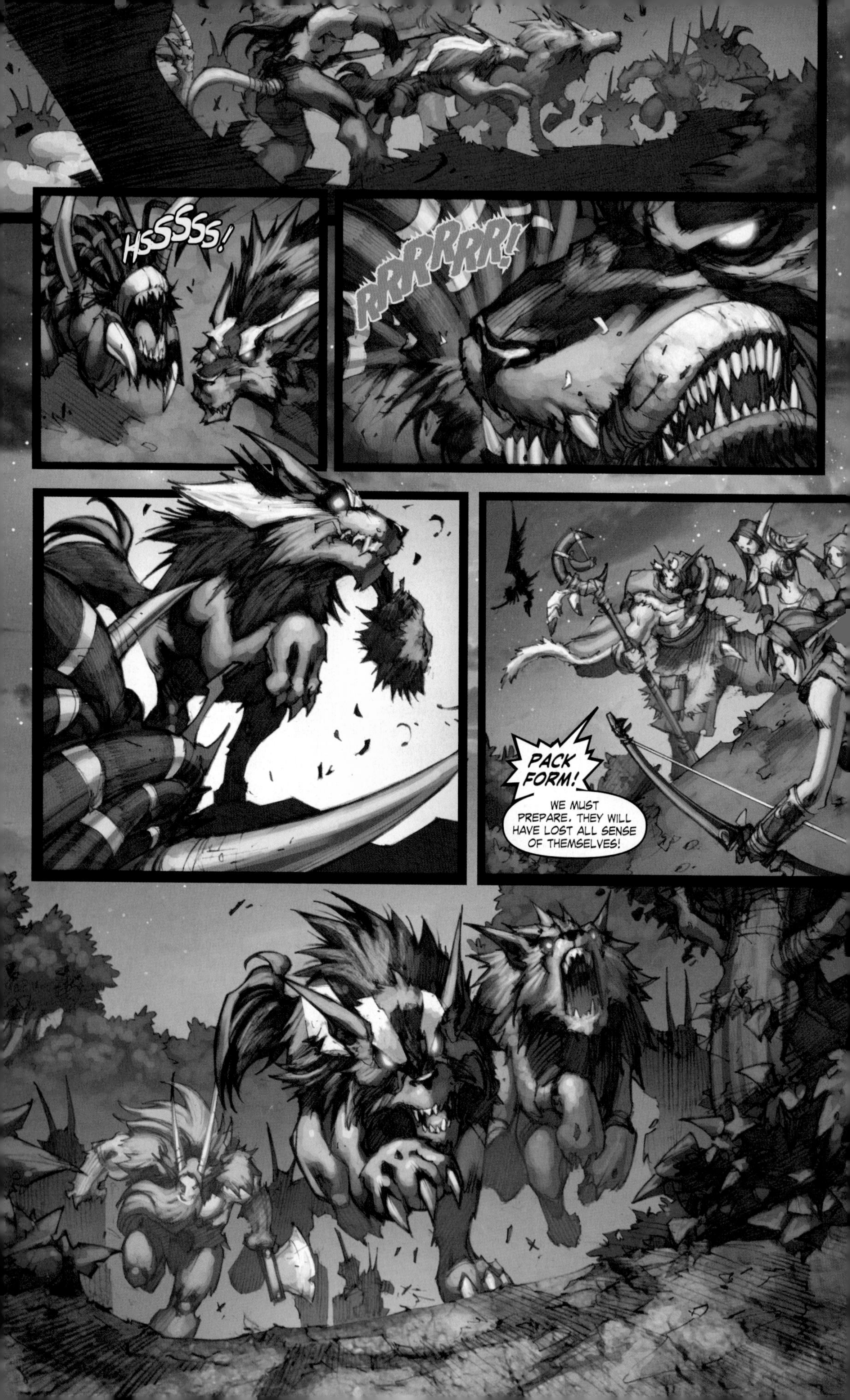
HSSSSS!
RRRRRR!
PACK FORM!
WE MUST PREPARE. THEY WILL HAVE LOST ALL SENSE OF THEMSELVES!

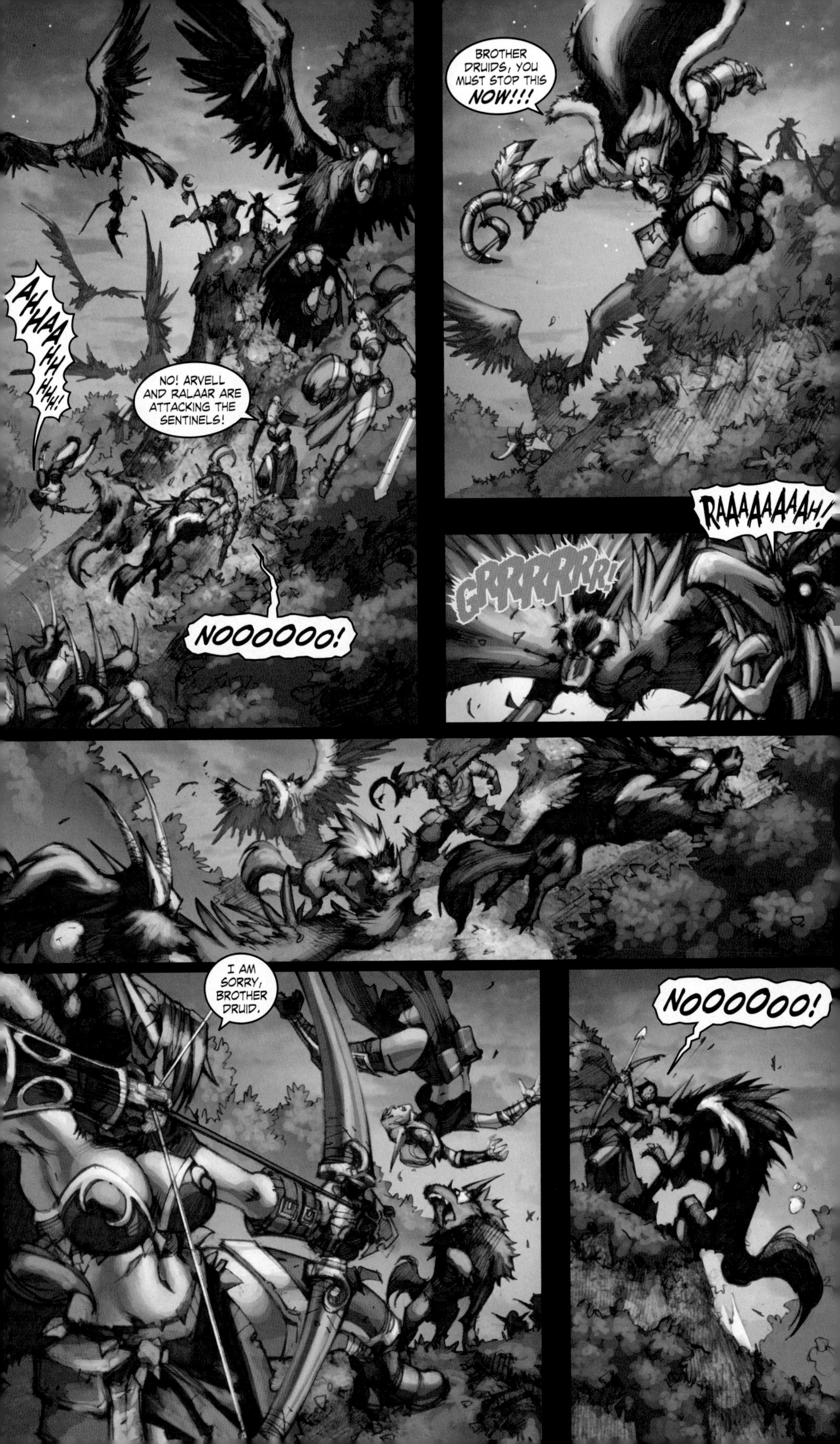
AHHAAHHHHH!
NO! ARVELL AND RALAAR ARE ATTACKING THE SENTINELS!
NOOOOOO!
BROTHER DRUIDS, YOU MUST STOP THIS NOW!!!
RAAAAAAAAH!
GRRRRRRR!
I AM SORRY, BROTHER DRUID.
NOOOOOO!

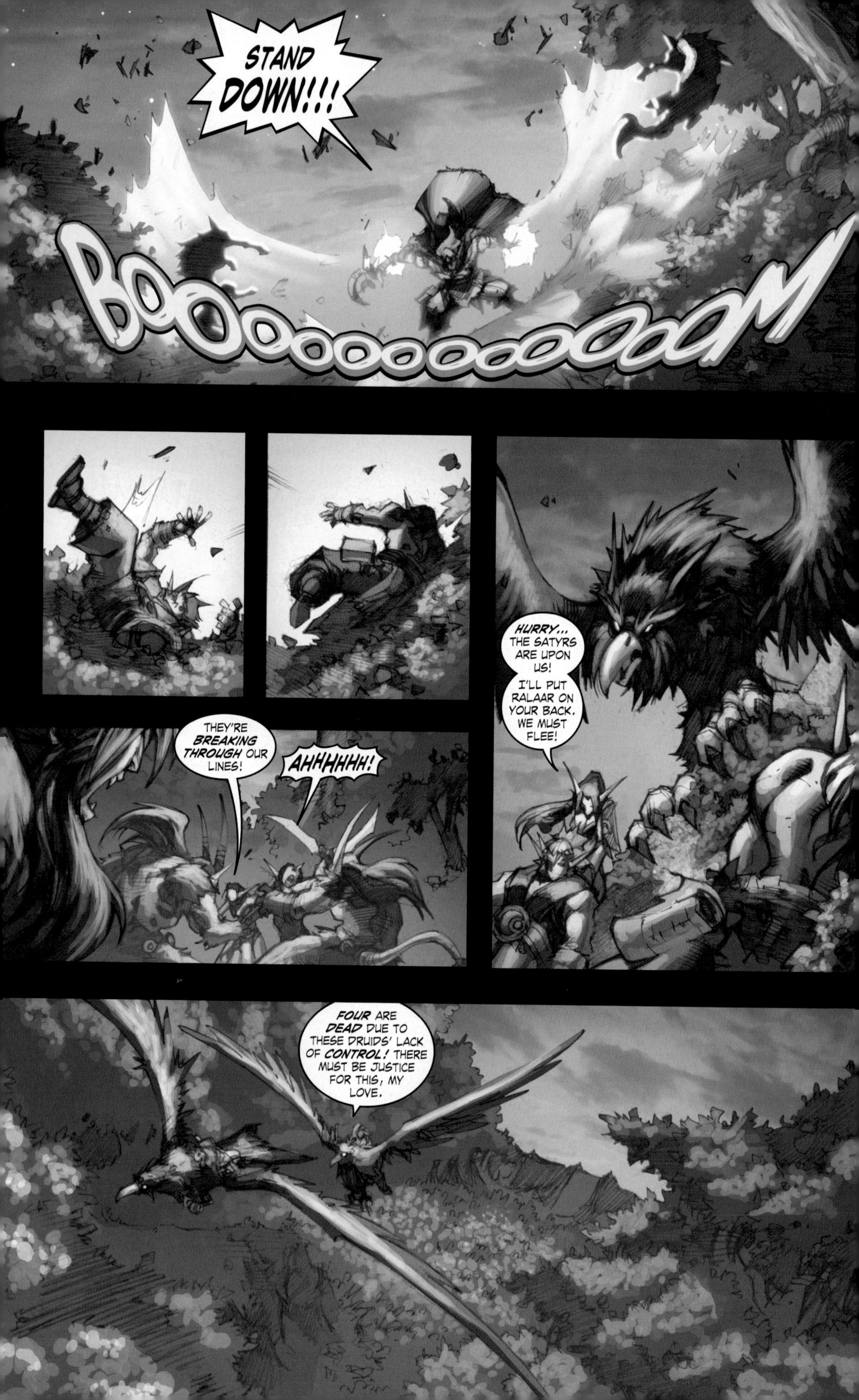
STAND DOWN!!!
BOOOOOOOOOOOOOOM
THEY'RE BREAKING THROUGH OUR LINES!
AHHHHHH!
HURRY... THE SATYRS ARE UPON US!
I'LL PUT RALAAR ON YOUR BACK. WE MUST FLEE!
FOUR ARE DEAD DUE TO THESE DRUIDS' LACK OF CONTROL! THERE MUST BE JUSTICE FOR THIS, MY LOVE.

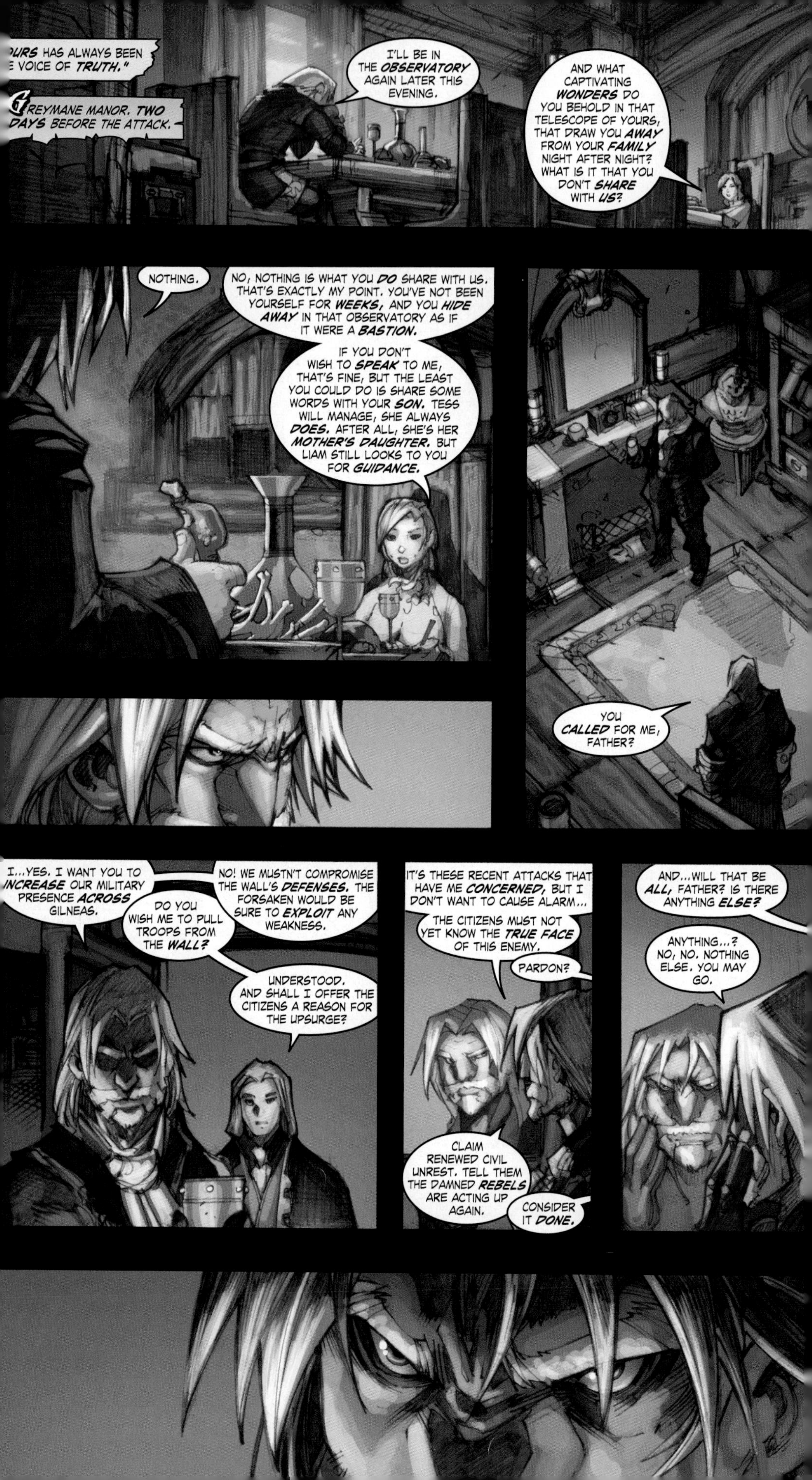

...OURS HAS ALWAYS BEEN ...E VOICE OF TRUTH."
GREYMANE MANOR. TWO DAYS BEFORE THE ATTACK.
I'LL BE IN THE OBSERVATORY AGAIN LATER THIS EVENING.
AND WHAT CAPTIVATING WONDERS DO YOU BEHOLD IN THAT TELESCOPE OF YOURS, THAT DRAW YOU AWAY FROM YOUR FAMILY NIGHT AFTER NIGHT? WHAT IS IT THAT YOU DON'T SHARE WITH US?
NOTHING.
NO, NOTHING IS WHAT YOU DO SHARE WITH US. THAT'S EXACTLY MY POINT. YOU'VE NOT BEEN YOURSELF FOR WEEKS, AND YOU HIDE AWAY IN THAT OBSERVATORY AS IF IT WERE A BASTION.
IF YOU DON'T WISH TO SPEAK TO ME, THAT'S FINE, BUT THE LEAST YOU COULD DO IS SHARE SOME WORDS WITH YOUR SON. TESS WILL MANAGE, SHE ALWAYS DOES. AFTER ALL, SHE'S HER MOTHER'S DAUGHTER. BUT LIAM STILL LOOKS TO YOU FOR GUIDANCE.
YOU CALLED FOR ME, FATHER?
I...YES. I WANT YOU TO INCREASE OUR MILITARY PRESENCE ACROSS GILNEAS.
DO YOU WISH ME TO PULL TROOPS FROM THE WALL?
NO! WE MUSTN'T COMPROMISE THE WALL'S DEFENSES. THE FORSAKEN WOULD BE SURE TO EXPLOIT ANY WEAKNESS.
UNDERSTOOD. AND SHALL I OFFER THE CITIZENS A REASON FOR THE UPSURGE?
IT'S THESE RECENT ATTACKS THAT HAVE ME CONCERNED, BUT I DON'T WANT TO CAUSE ALARM...
THE CITIZENS MUST NOT YET KNOW THE TRUE FACE OF THIS ENEMY.
PARDON?
CLAIM RENEWED CIVIL UNREST. TELL THEM THE DAMNED REBELS ARE ACTING UP AGAIN.
CONSIDER IT DONE.
AND...WILL THAT BE ALL, FATHER? IS THERE ANYTHING ELSE?
ANYTHING...? NO, NO. NOTHING ELSE. YOU MAY GO.

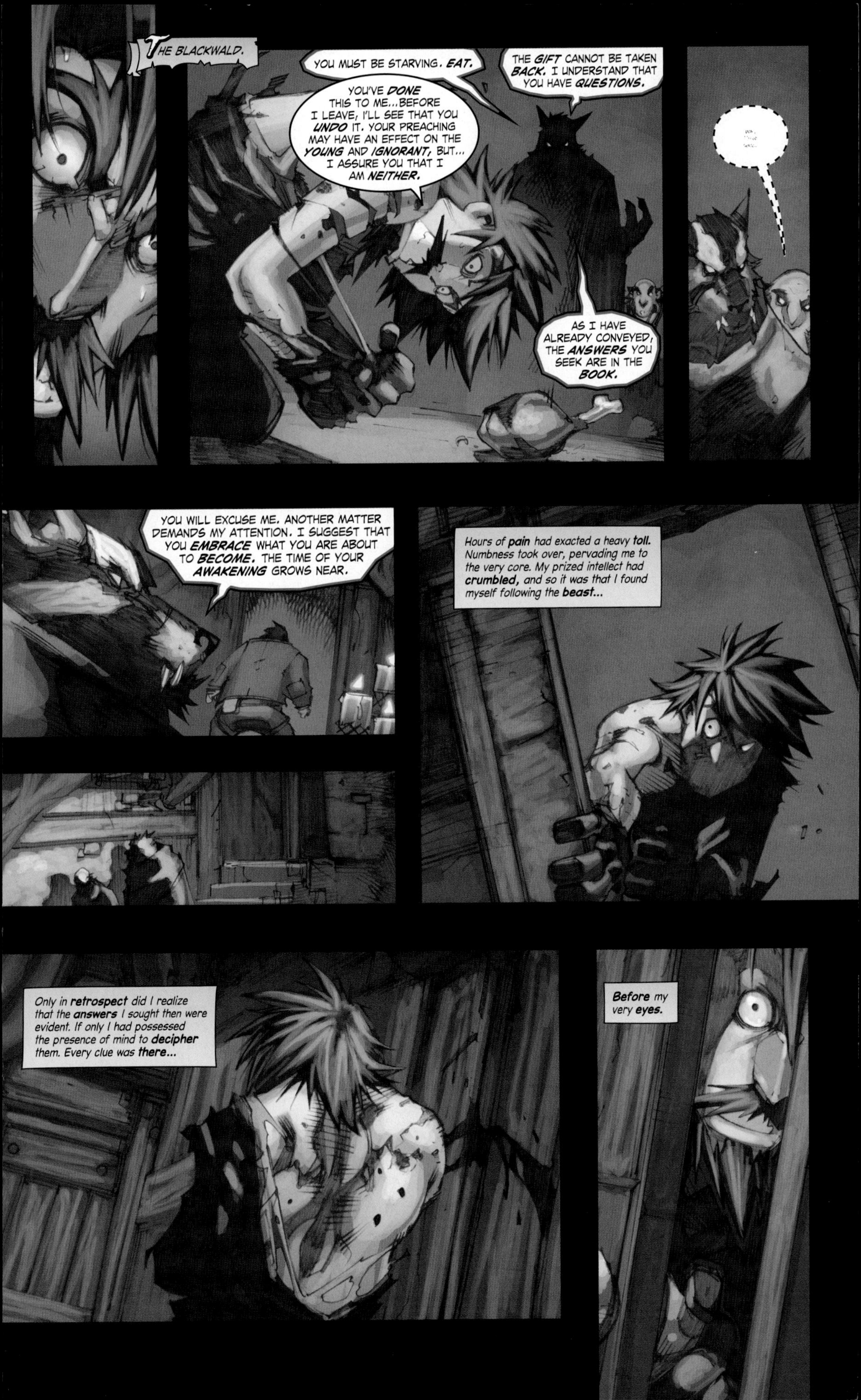
THE BLACKWALD.
YOU MUST BE STARVING. EAT.
YOU'VE DONE THIS TO ME...BEFORE I LEAVE, I'LL SEE THAT YOU UNDO IT. YOUR PREACHING MAY HAVE AN EFFECT ON THE YOUNG AND IGNORANT, BUT... I ASSURE YOU THAT I AM NEITHER.
THE GIFT CANNOT BE TAKEN BACK. I UNDERSTAND THAT YOU HAVE QUESTIONS.
AS I HAVE ALREADY CONVEYED, THE ANSWERS YOU SEEK ARE IN THE BOOK.
YOU WILL EXCUSE ME. ANOTHER MATTER DEMANDS MY ATTENTION. I SUGGEST THAT YOU EMBRACE WHAT YOU ARE ABOUT TO BECOME. THE TIME OF YOUR AWAKENING GROWS NEAR.
Hours of pain had exacted a heavy toll. Numbness took over, pervading me to the very core. My prized intellect had crumbled, and so it was that I found myself following the beast...
Only in retrospect did I realize that the answers I sought then were evident. If only I had possessed the presence of mind to decipher them. Every clue was there...
Before my very eyes.

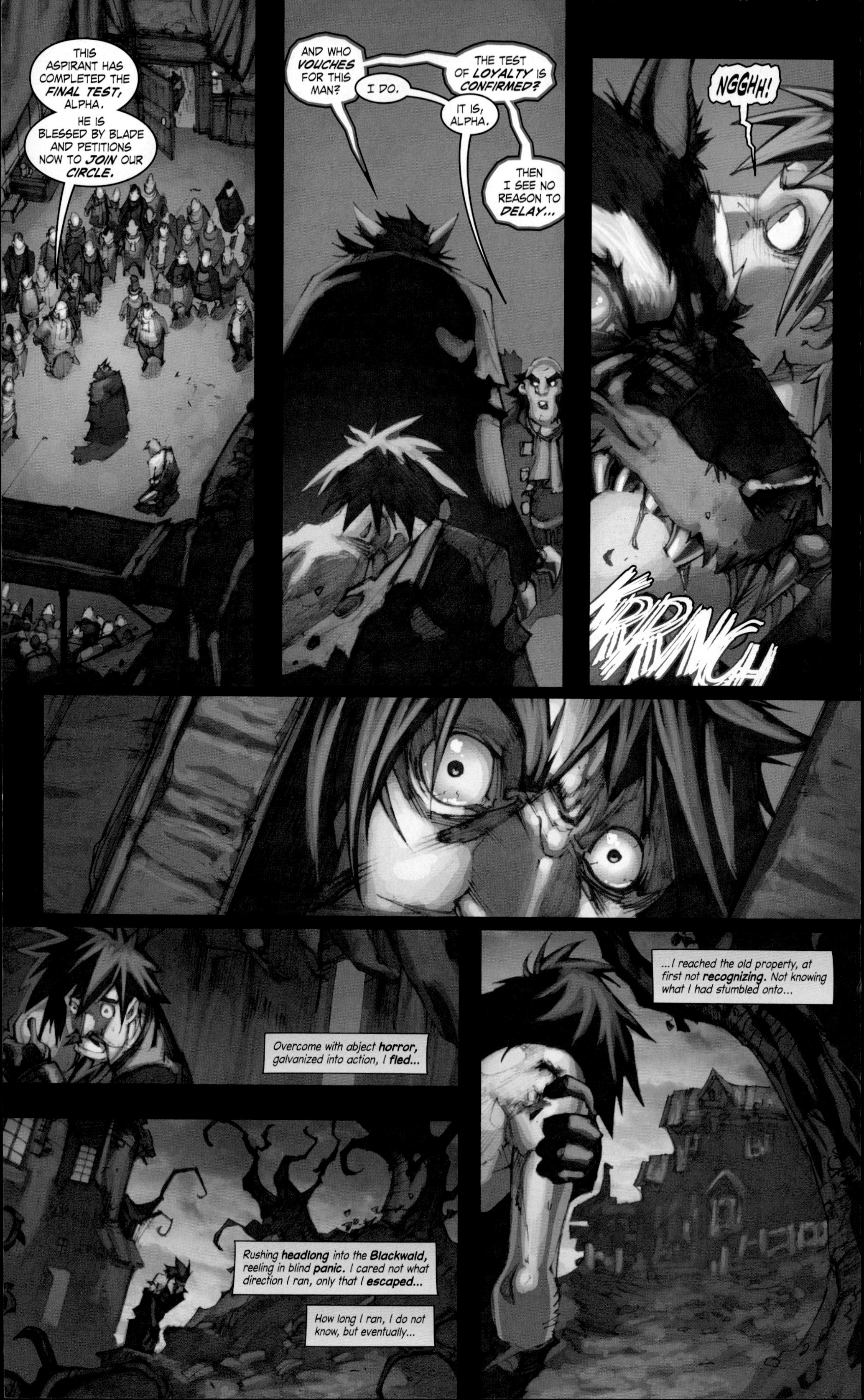
THIS ASPIRANT HAS COMPLETED THE FINAL TEST, ALPHA.
HE IS BLESSED BY BLADE AND PETITIONS NOW TO JOIN OUR CIRCLE.
AND WHO VOUCHES FOR THIS MAN?
I DO.
THE TEST OF LOYALTY IS CONFIRMED?
IT IS, ALPHA.
THEN I SEE NO REASON TO DELAY...
NGGHH!
KRRRNCH
Overcome with abject horror, galvanized into action, I fled...
Rushing headlong into the Blackwald, reeling in blind panic. I cared not what direction I ran, only that I escaped...
How long I ran, I do not know, but eventually...
...I reached the old property, at first not recognizing. Not knowing what I had stumbled onto...

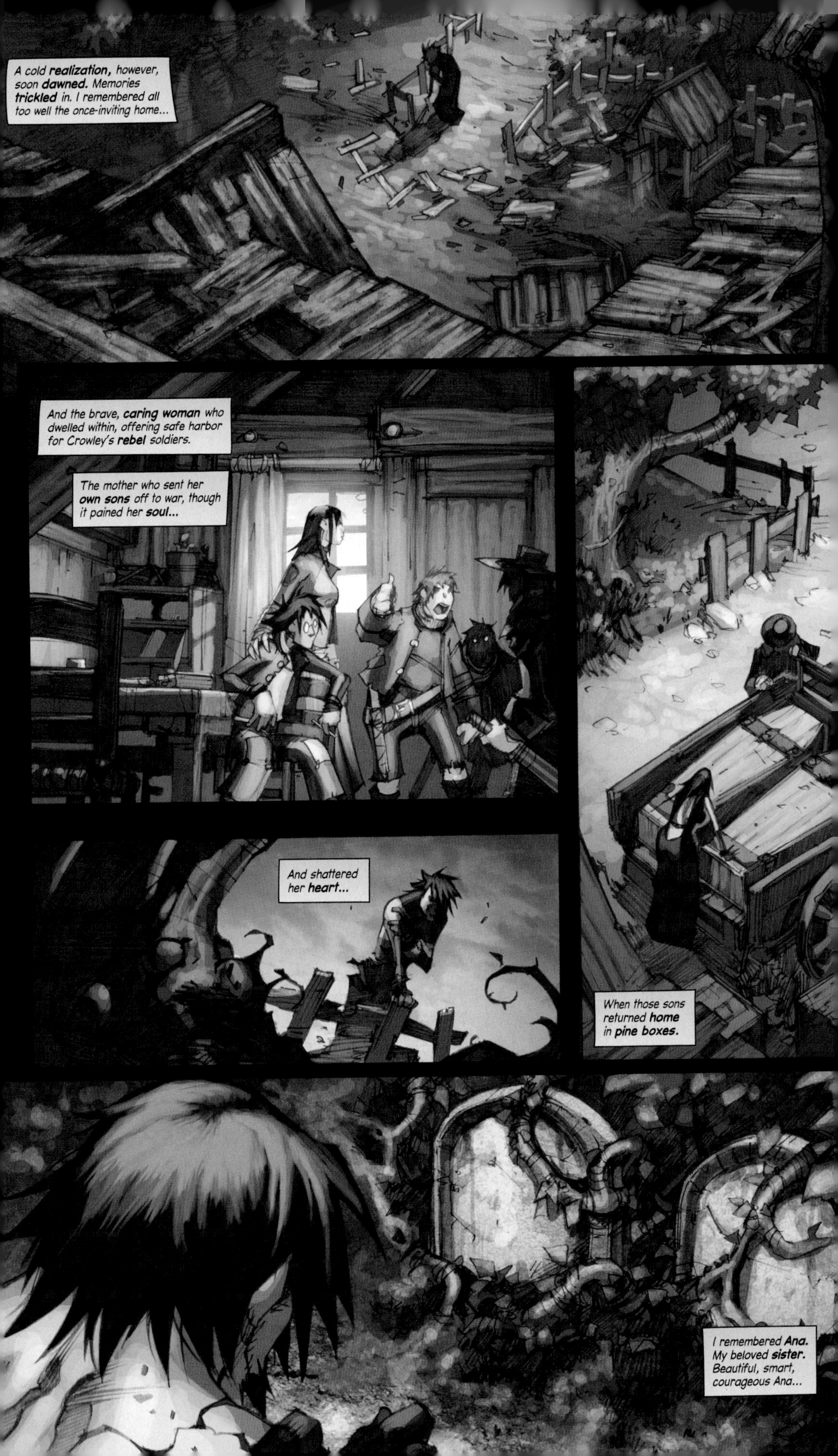
A cold realization, however, soon dawned. Memories trickled in. I remembered all too well the once-inviting home...
And the brave, caring woman who dwelled within, offering safe harbor for Crowley's rebel soldiers.
The mother who sent her own sons off to war, though it pained her soul...
When those sons returned home in pine boxes.
And shattered her heart...
I remembered Ana. My beloved sister. Beautiful, smart, courageous Ana...

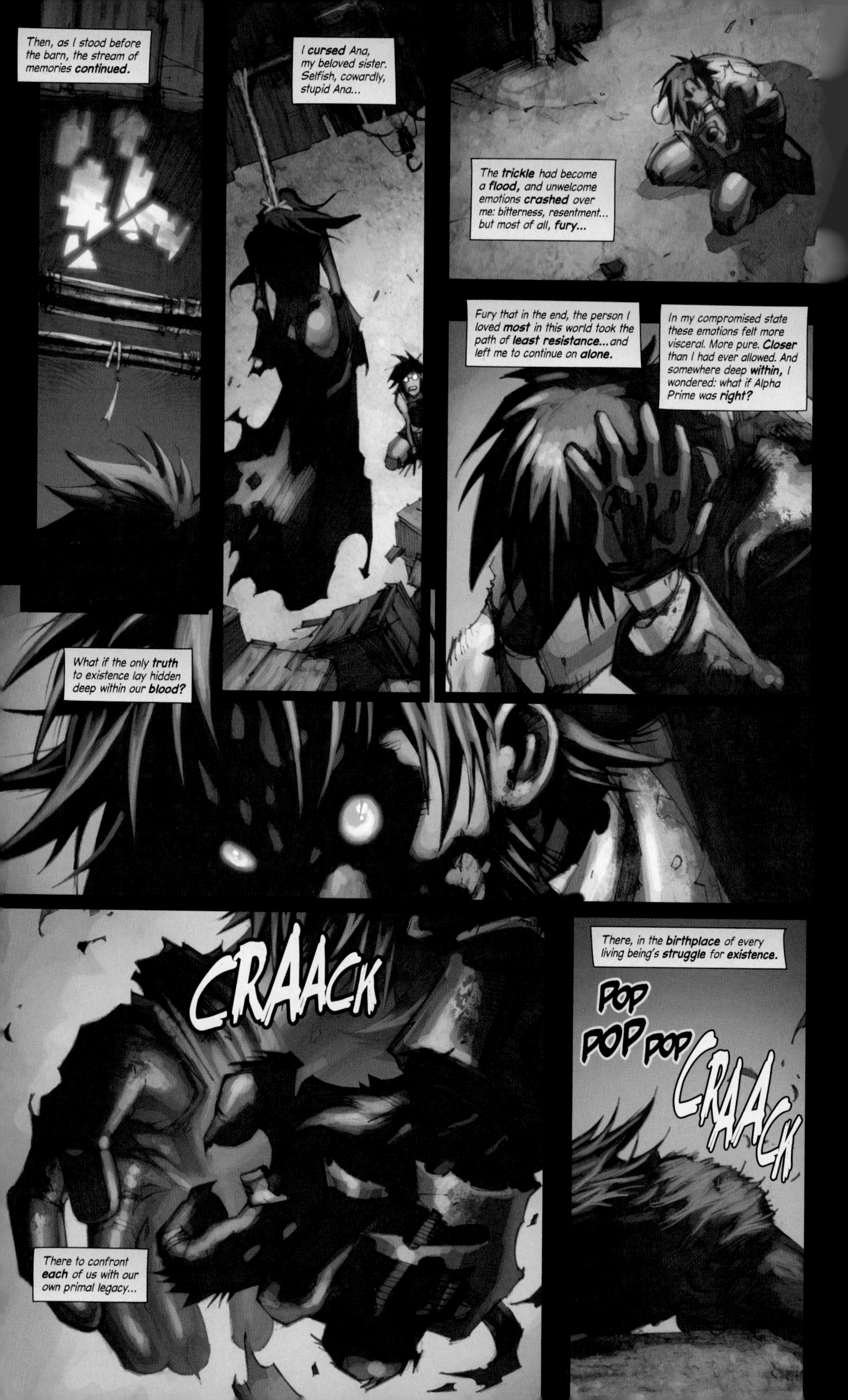
Then, as I stood before the barn, the stream of memories **continued.**
I **cursed** Ana, my beloved sister. Selfish, cowardly, stupid Ana...
The **trickle** had become a **flood,** and unwelcome emotions **crashed** over me: bitterness, resentment... but most of all, **fury...**
Fury that in the end, the person I loved **most** in this world took the path of **least resistance...** and left me to continue on **alone.**
In my compromised state these emotions felt more visceral. More pure. **Closer** than I had ever allowed. And somewhere deep **within,** I wondered: what if Alpha Prime was **right?**
What if the only **truth** to existence lay hidden deep within our **blood?**
CRAACK
There to confront **each** of us with our own primal legacy...
There, in the **birthplace** of every living being's **struggle** for **existence.**
POP
POP POP CRAACK

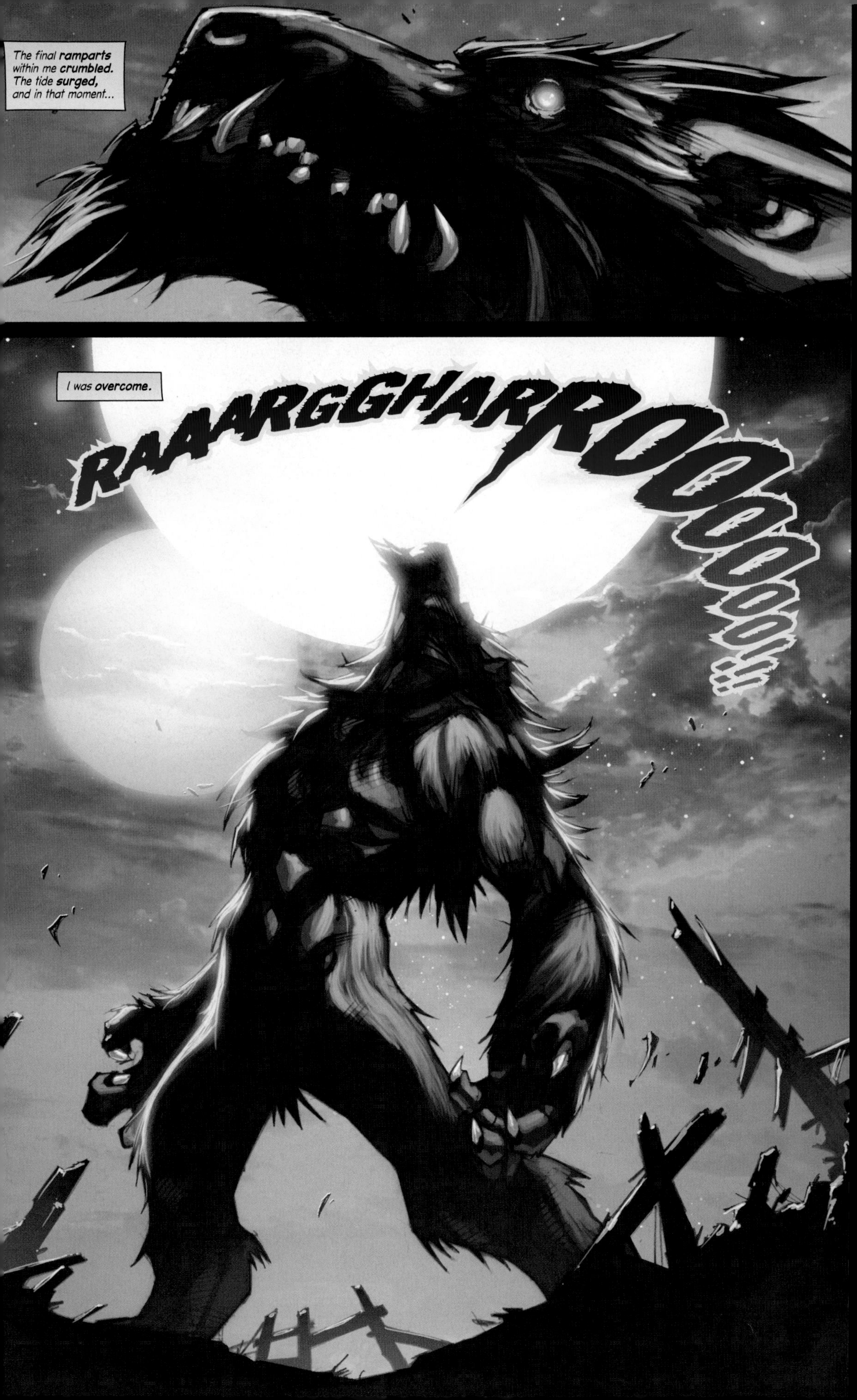
The final ramparts within me crumbled. The tide surged, and in that moment...
I was overcome.
RAAARGGHARROOOOOOOO!!!

LOVE...IT'S A *TRICKY THING*, IS IT NOT? NEVER EXACTLY BEEN MY AREA OF *STRENGTH*. ESPECIALLY NOW, WITH ALL MY TIME SPENT *HERE*, I'M SURE MY WIFE THINKS I'M PURSUING SOME *OTHER* ROMANTIC INTEREST.

WHY, YOUR *MAJESTY*, THERE *IS* QUITE AN AGE DIFFERENCE. I AM OLD ENOUGH TO BE YOUR GRANDMOTHER A *THOUSAND TIMES* OVER.

APOLOGIES. A MISGUIDED ATTEMPT AT BRINGING SOME LEVITY. IT *HELPS*, SOMETIMES.

YOU ARE *INDEED* MUCH OLDER AND WISER THAN I. SO WHAT *LESSON* DO YOU WISH TO CONVEY WITH THIS PART OF THE TALE? YOU SPEAK TO ME OF *FEAR* AND *LOSS*...

HOURS AGO I LEARNED THAT THE FORSAKEN MOUNTED AN *ASSAULT* AGAINST OUR GATES THAT MADE PREVIOUS ATTACKS SEEM AS NOTHING. AND NOT LONG AFTER THAT, ANOTHER *MURDER* IN THE STREETS OF OUR *CAPITAL*.

SIGHTINGS OF YOUR ESTRANGED *KIN* HAVE *GROWN*...

MONSTERS *OUTSIDE* THE WALL AND WOLVES *WITHIN*. I WOULD SAY I AM *WELL VERSED* NOW IN THE *LESSONS* OF FEAR AND LOSS. IN FACT, I'VE SUFFERED MORE THAN MY *SHARE*!

ENOUGH *TALK!* WE MUST *ACT!* WE MUST--

MAY ELUNE'S LIGHT *CALM* YOU, YOUR MAJESTY, FOR A *TIME* AT LEAST.

HAS IT *PASSED*? ARE YOU WELL?

RRRGGGHHH!!!

TO RUSH INTO BATTLE WITHOUT FULLY *UNDERSTANDING* YOUR ENEMY IS FOLLY. AND TO UNDERSTAND THIS ENEMY, DEAR KING, YOU MUST UNDERSTAND *YOURSELF*.

WELL ENOUGH FOR NOW.

WILL YOU NOT ATTEMPT THE *CEREMONY* AGAIN?

SOON, PERHAPS, BUT NOT TONIGHT. NO, I WOULD HEAR *MORE*. I WOULD *UNDERSTAND*... MORE.

TELL ME WHAT HAPPENED *NEXT*.

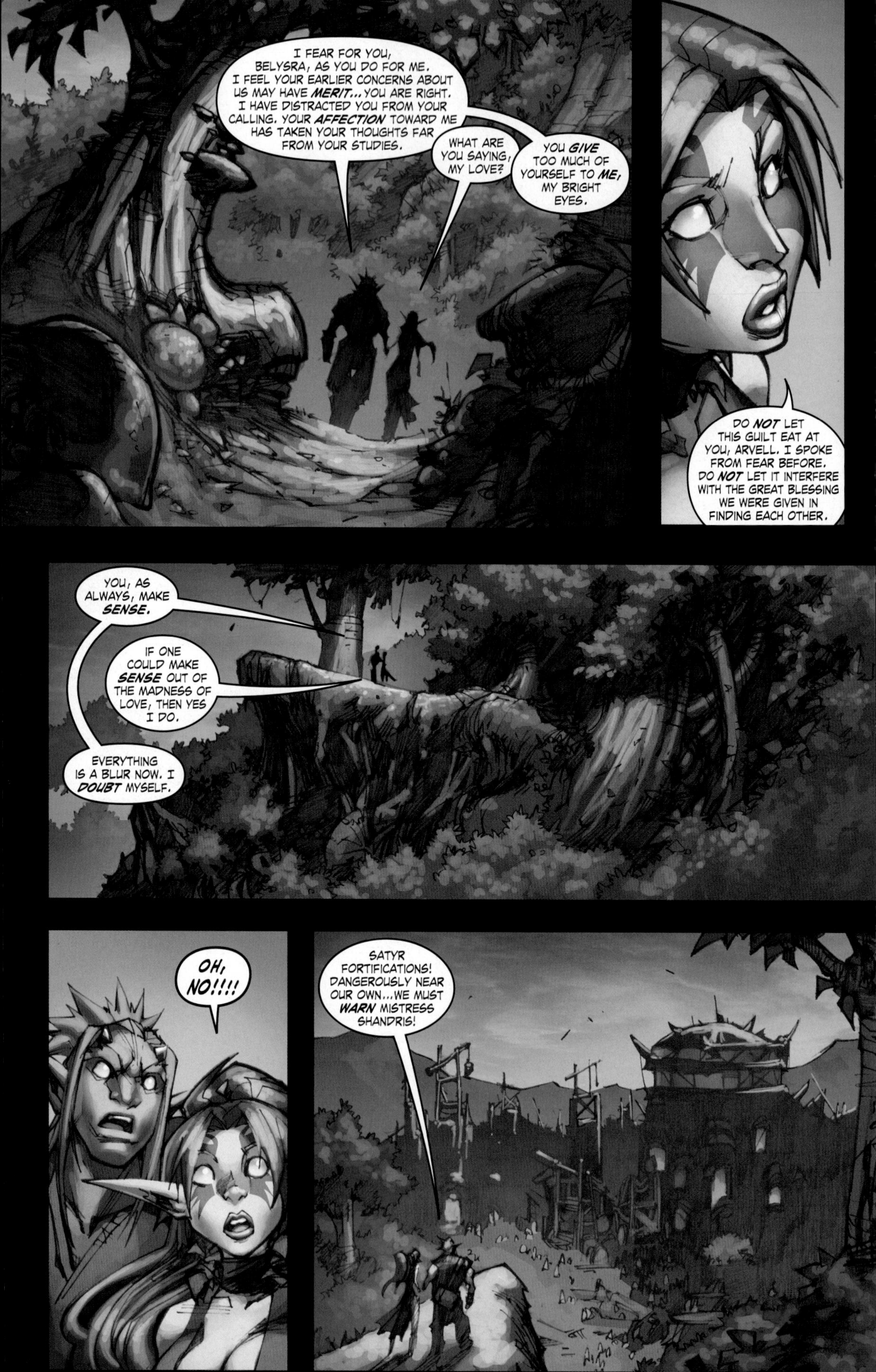

I FEAR FOR YOU, BELYSRA, AS YOU DO FOR ME. I FEEL YOUR EARLIER CONCERNS ABOUT US MAY HAVE MERIT... YOU ARE RIGHT. I HAVE DISTRACTED YOU FROM YOUR CALLING. YOUR AFFECTION TOWARD ME HAS TAKEN YOUR THOUGHTS FAR FROM YOUR STUDIES.
WHAT ARE YOU SAYING, MY LOVE?
YOU GIVE TOO MUCH OF YOURSELF TO ME, MY BRIGHT EYES.
DO NOT LET THIS GUILT EAT AT YOU, ARVELL. I SPOKE FROM FEAR BEFORE. DO NOT LET IT INTERFERE WITH THE GREAT BLESSING WE WERE GIVEN IN FINDING EACH OTHER.
YOU, AS ALWAYS, MAKE SENSE.
IF ONE COULD MAKE SENSE OUT OF THE MADNESS OF LOVE, THEN YES I DO.
EVERYTHING IS A BLUR NOW. I DOUBT MYSELF.
OH, NO!!!!
SATYR FORTIFICATIONS! DANGEROUSLY NEAR OUR OWN...WE MUST WARN MISTRESS SHANDRIS!

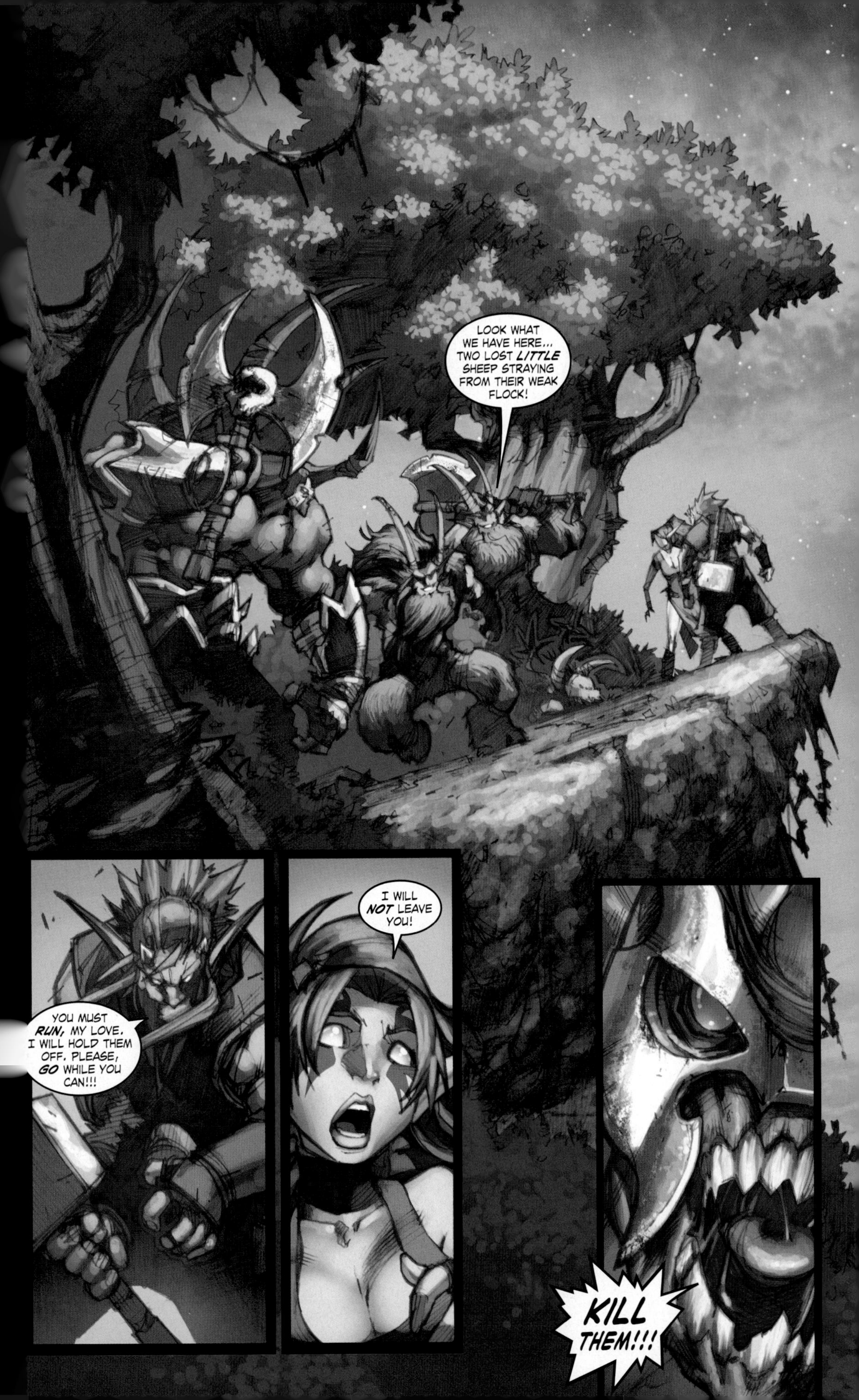
LOOK WHAT WE HAVE HERE... TWO LOST LITTLE SHEEP STRAYING FROM THEIR WEAK FLOCK!
YOU MUST RUN, MY LOVE. I WILL HOLD THEM OFF. PLEASE, GO WHILE YOU CAN!!!
I WILL NOT LEAVE YOU!
KILL THEM!!!

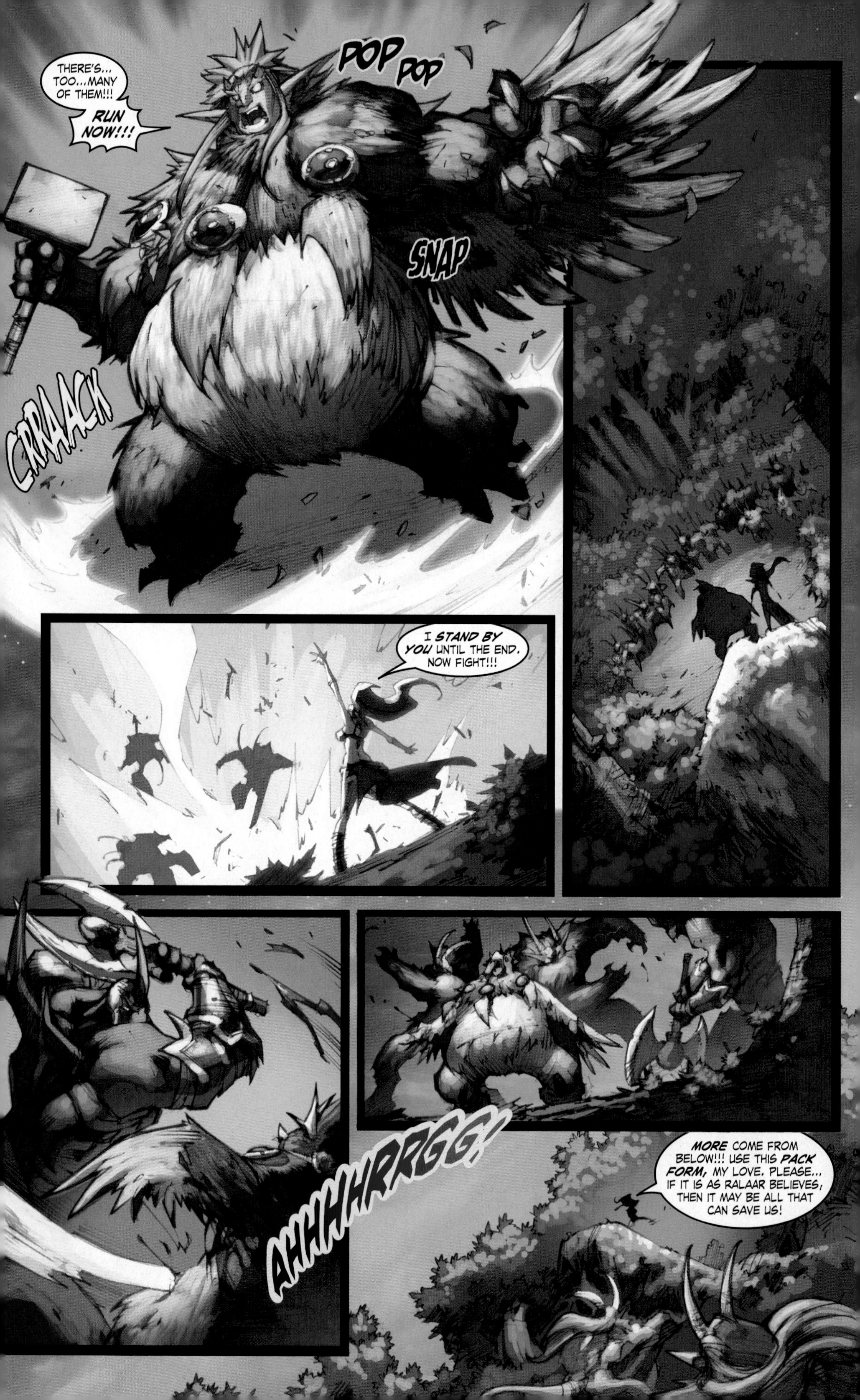
THERE'S... TOO...MANY OF THEM!!! RUN NOW!!!
POP POP
SNAP
CRRAACK
I STAND BY YOU UNTIL THE END. NOW FIGHT!!!
AHHHHRRGG!
MORE COME FROM BELOW!!! USE THIS PACK FORM, MY LOVE. PLEASE... IF IT IS AS RALAAR BELIEVES, THEN IT MAY BE ALL THAT CAN SAVE US!

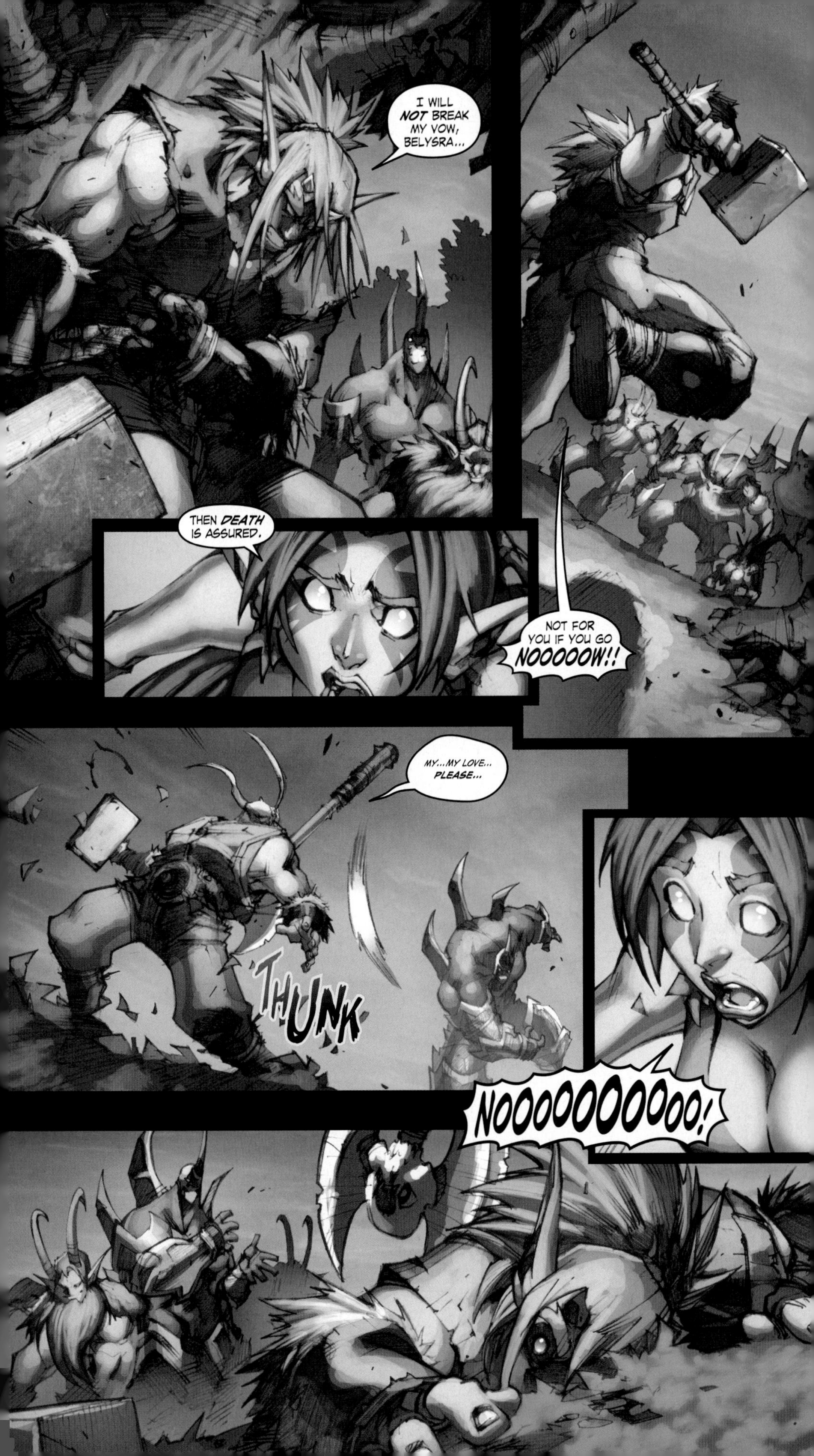
I WILL NOT BREAK MY VOW, BELYSRA...
THEN DEATH IS ASSURED.
NOT FOR YOU IF YOU GO NOOOOOW!!
MY...MY LOVE... PLEASE...
THUNK
NOOOOOOOOOO!

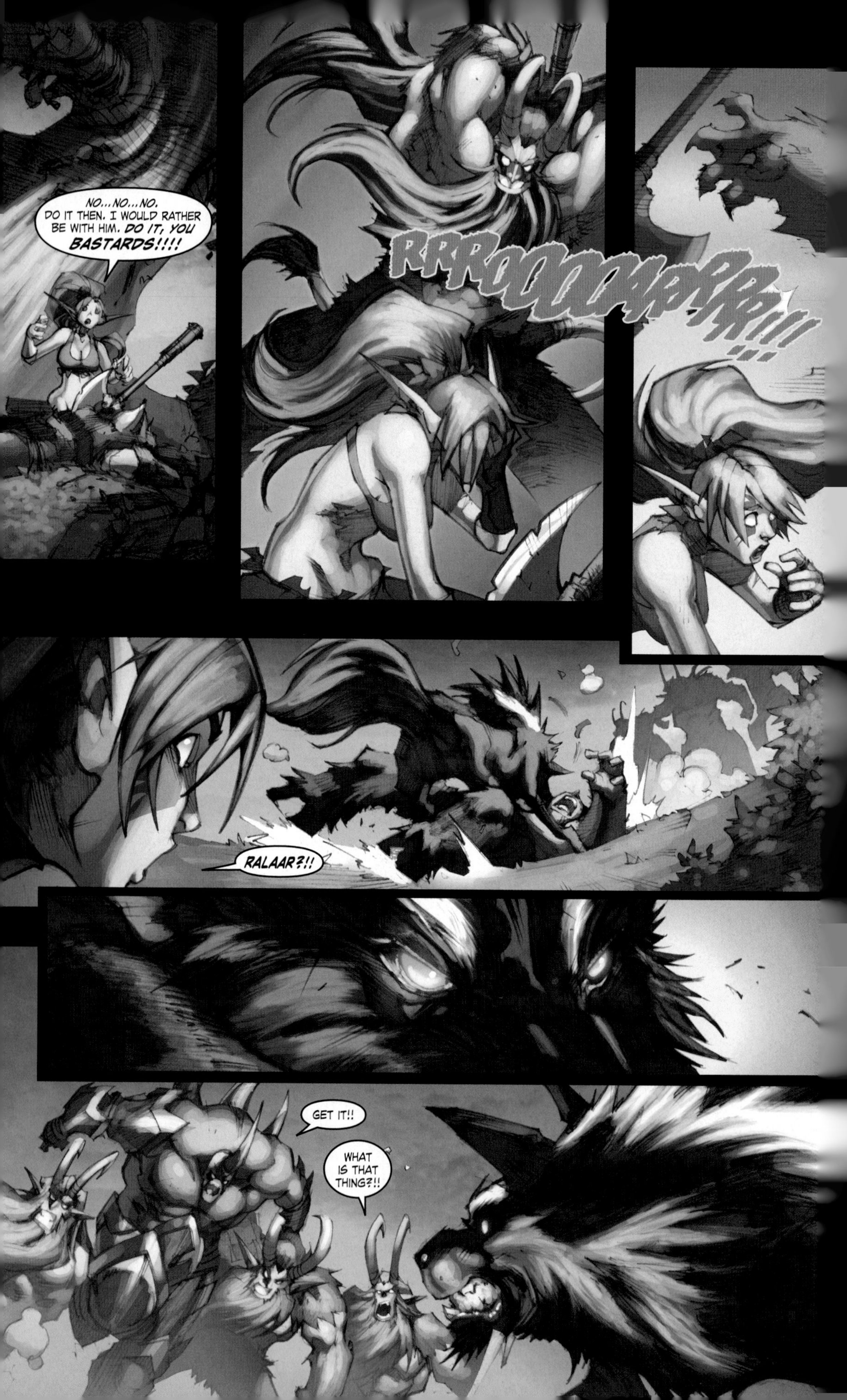
NO...NO...NO. DO IT THEN. I WOULD RATHER BE WITH HIM. DO IT, YOU BASTARDS!!!!
RRRROOOOARRRR!!!
RALAAR?!!
GET IT!!
WHAT IS THAT THING?!!

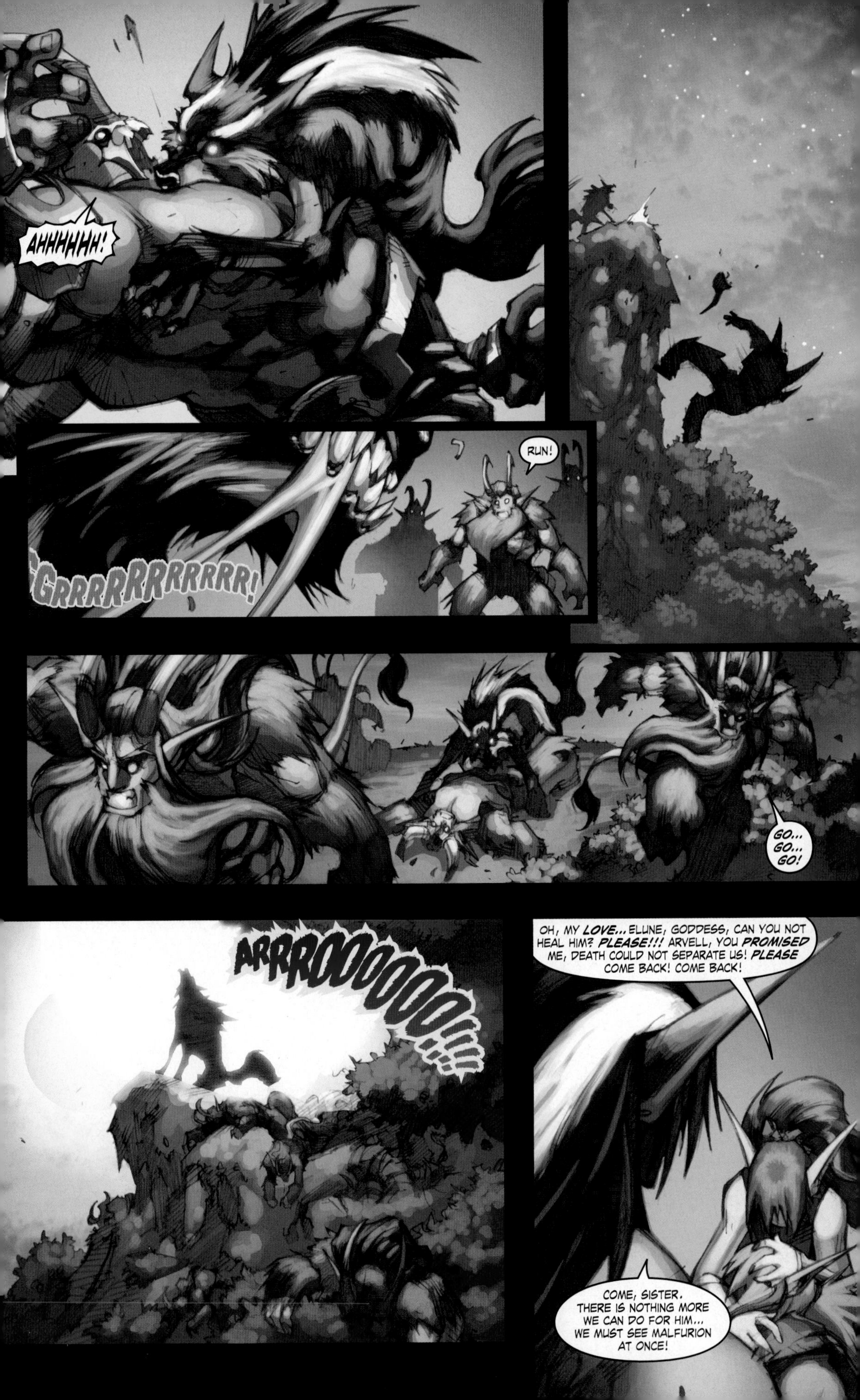
AHHHHHH!
RUN!
GRRRRRRRRRRRR!
GO... GO... GO!
ARRROOOOOOO!!!!!
OH, MY LOVE... ELUNE, GODDESS, CAN YOU NOT HEAL HIM? PLEASE!!! ARVELL, YOU PROMISED ME, DEATH COULD NOT SEPARATE US! PLEASE COME BACK! COME BACK!
COME, SISTER. THERE IS NOTHING MORE WE CAN DO FOR HIM... WE MUST SEE MALFURION AT ONCE!

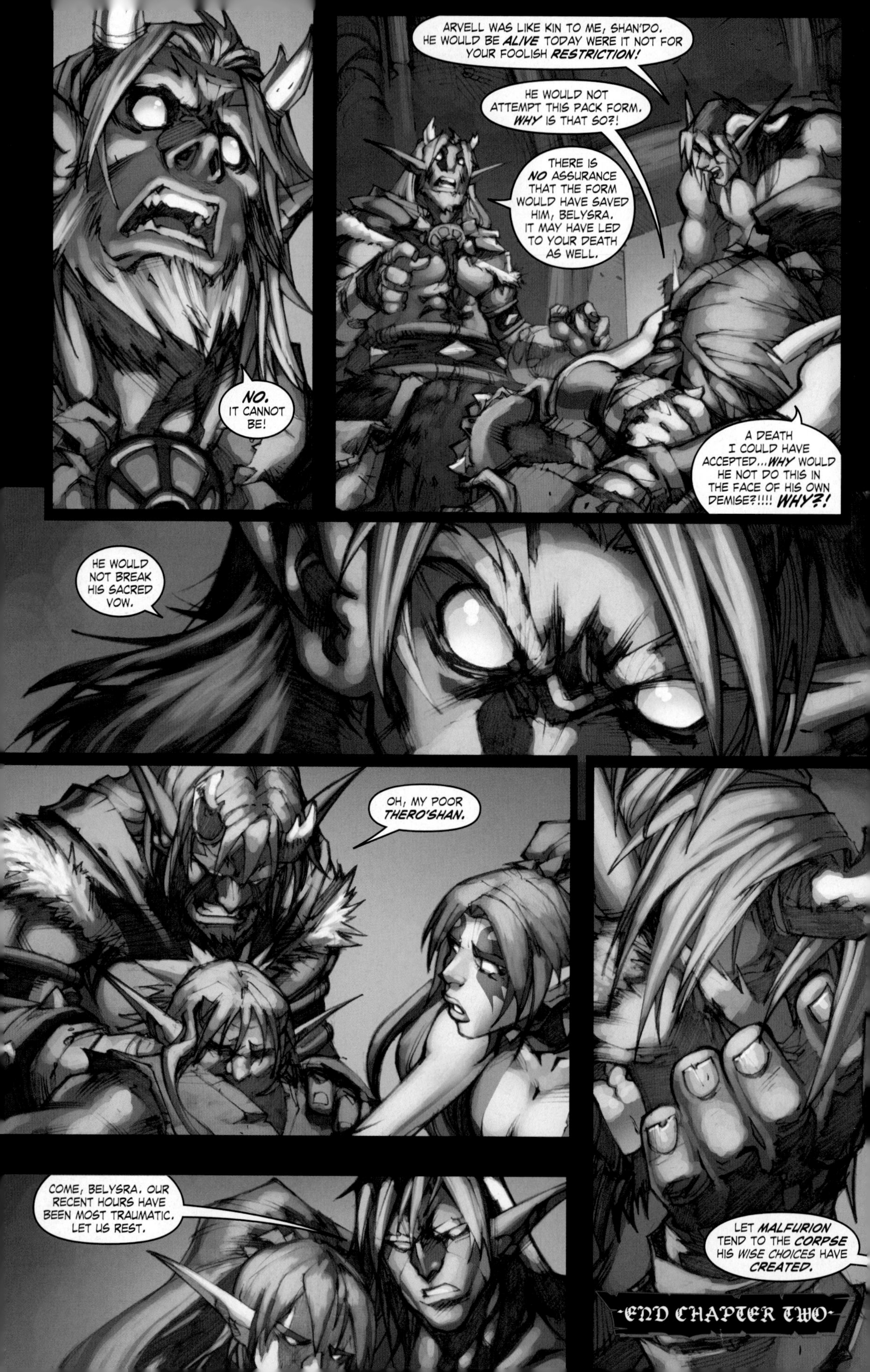

ARVELL WAS LIKE KIN TO ME, SHAN'DO. HE WOULD BE ALIVE TODAY WERE IT NOT FOR YOUR FOOLISH RESTRICTION!
HE WOULD NOT ATTEMPT THIS PACK FORM. WHY IS THAT SO?!
THERE IS NO ASSURANCE THAT THE FORM WOULD HAVE SAVED HIM, BELYSRA. IT MAY HAVE LED TO YOUR DEATH AS WELL.
NO. IT CANNOT BE!
A DEATH I COULD HAVE ACCEPTED...WHY WOULD HE NOT DO THIS IN THE FACE OF HIS OWN DEMISE?!!!! WHY?!
HE WOULD NOT BREAK HIS SACRED VOW.
OH, MY POOR THERO'SHAN.
COME, BELYSRA. OUR RECENT HOURS HAVE BEEN MOST TRAUMATIC. LET US REST.
LET MALFURION TEND TO THE CORPSE HIS WISE CHOICES HAVE CREATED.
-END CHAPTER TWO-

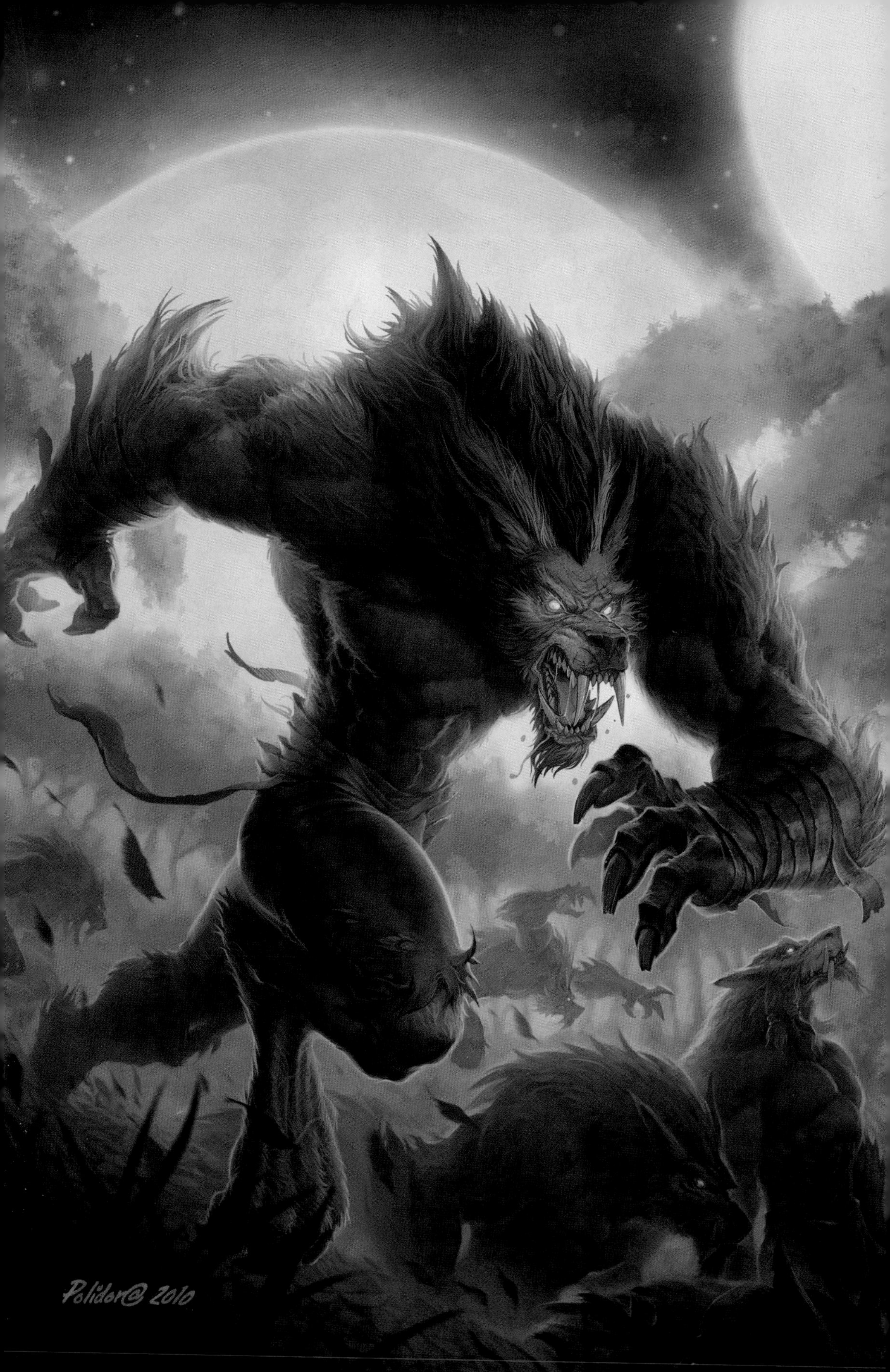
Polidora 2010

CHAPTER 3 Cover by John Polidora

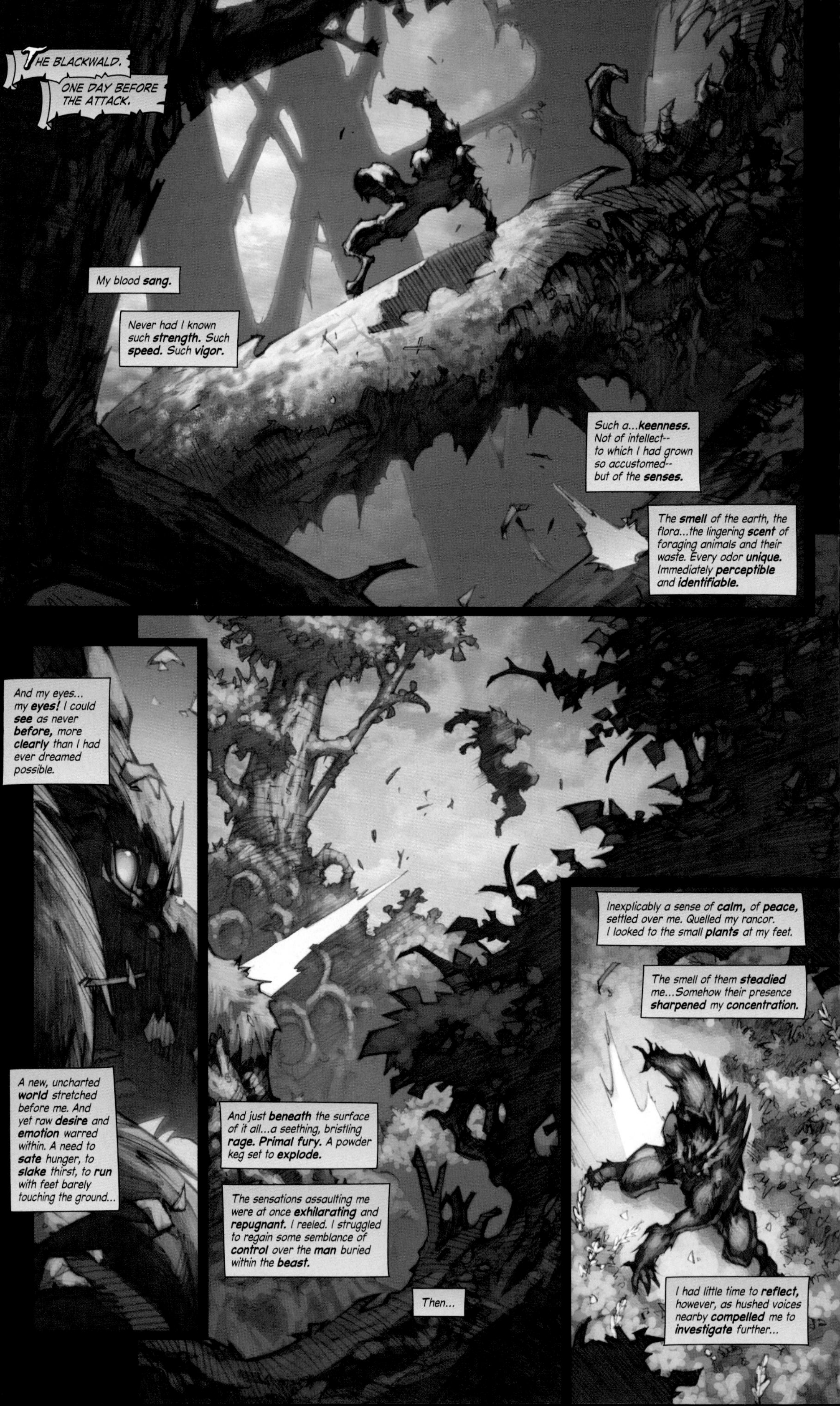

THE BLACKWALD.
ONE DAY BEFORE THE ATTACK.
My blood sang.
Never had I known such strength. Such speed. Such vigor.
Such a...keenness. Not of intellect-- to which I had grown so accustomed-- but of the senses.
The smell of the earth, the flora...the lingering scent of foraging animals and their waste. Every odor unique. Immediately perceptible and identifiable.
And my eyes... my eyes! I could see as never before, more clearly than I had ever dreamed possible.
A new, uncharted world stretched before me. And yet raw desire and emotion warred within. A need to sate hunger, to slake thirst, to run with feet barely touching the ground...
And just beneath the surface of it all...a seething, bristling rage. Primal fury. A powder keg set to explode.
The sensations assaulting me were at once exhilarating and repugnant. I reeled. I struggled to regain some semblance of control over the man buried within the beast.
Then...
Inexplicably a sense of calm, of peace, settled over me. Quelled my rancor. I looked to the small plants at my feet.
The smell of them steadied me...Somehow their presence sharpened my concentration.
I had little time to reflect, however, as hushed voices nearby compelled me to investigate further...

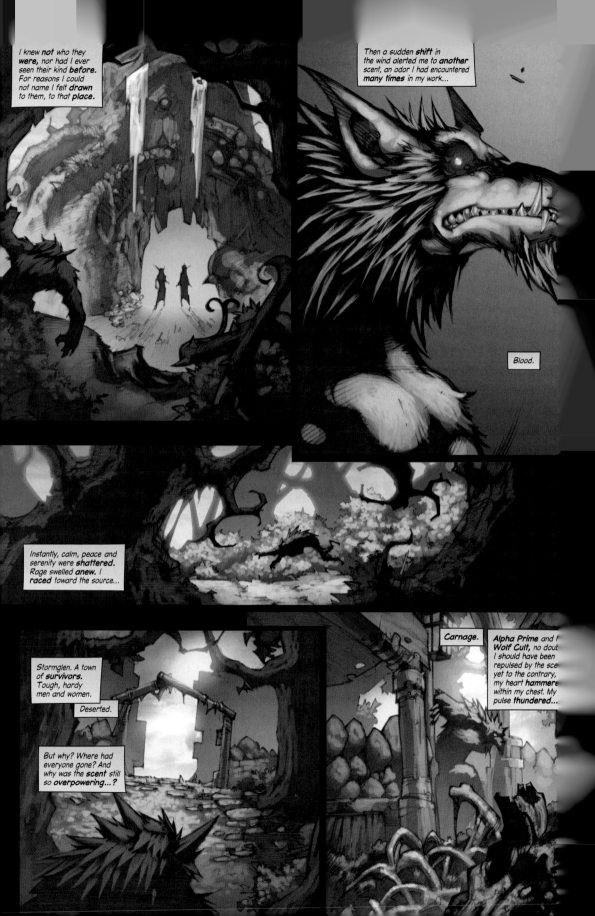

I knew **not** who they **were**, nor had I ever seen their kind **before.** For reasons I could not name I felt **drawn** to them, to that **place.**

Then a sudden **shift** in the wind alerted me to **another** scent, an odor I had encountered **many times** in my work...

Blood.

Instantly, calm, peace and serenity were **shattered.** Rage swelled **anew.** I **raced** toward the source...

Carnage.

Alpha Prime and [...] **Wolf Cult,** no doub[t...] I should have been repulsed by the sce[nt...] yet to the contrary, my heart **hammere[d]** within my chest. My pulse **thundered**...

Stormglen. A town of **survivors.** Tough, hardy men and women.

Deserted.

But why? Where had everyone gone? And why was the **scent** still so **overpowering**...?

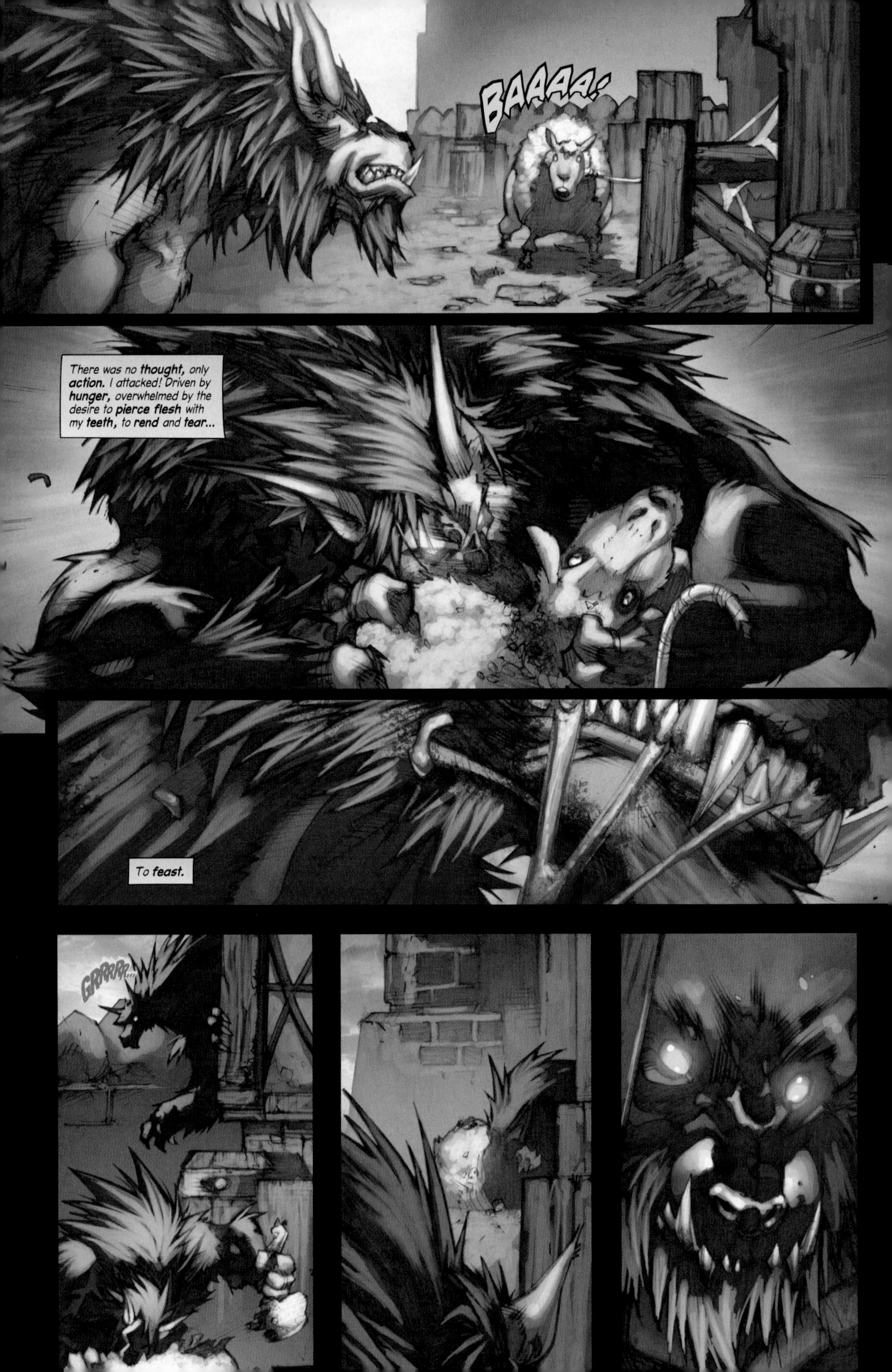
BAAAA!
There was no thought, only action. I attacked! Driven by hunger, overwhelmed by the desire to pierce flesh with my teeth, to rend and tear...
To feast.
GRRRRR...

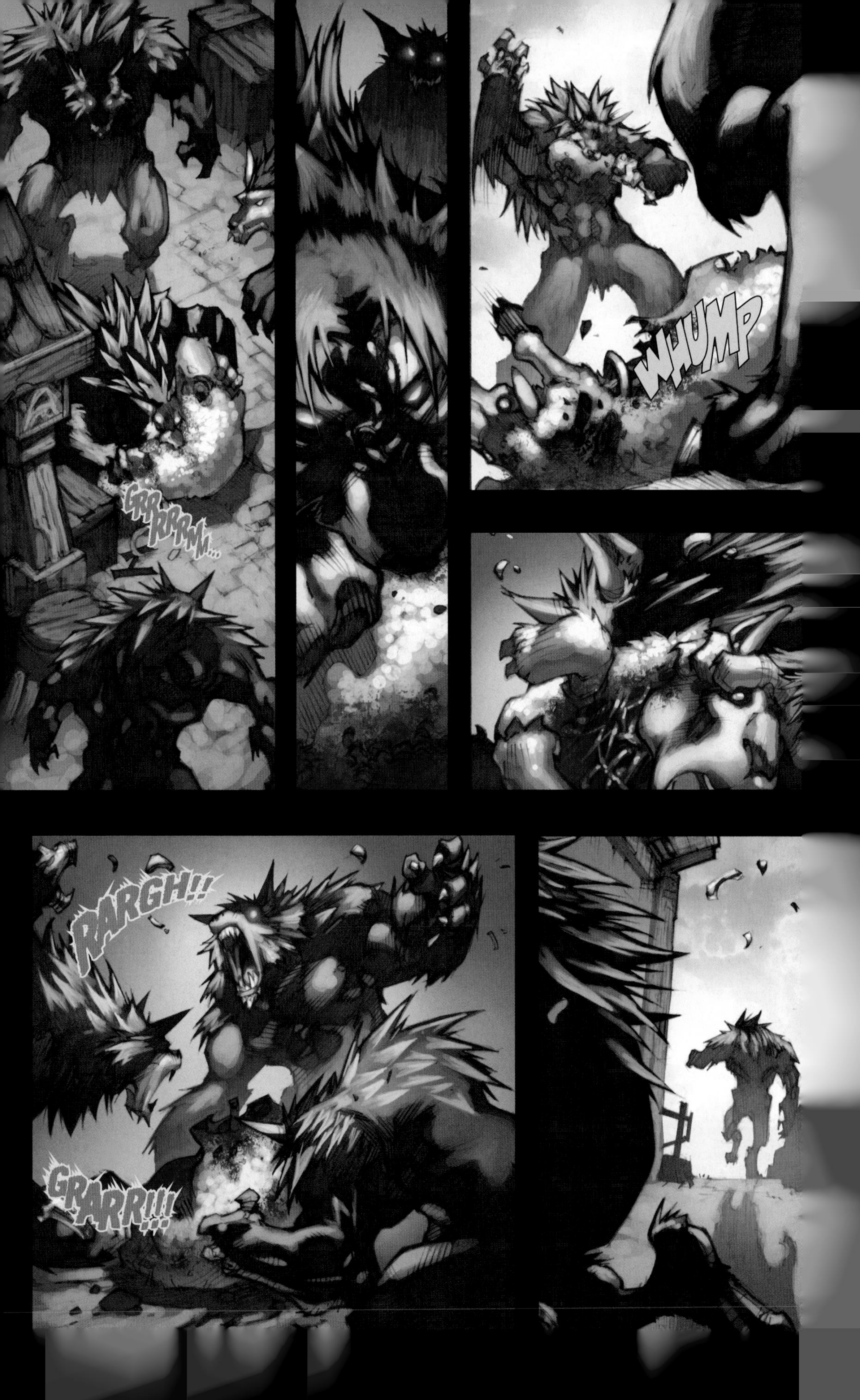

GRRRRRRM...
WHUMP
RARGH!!
GRARR!!!

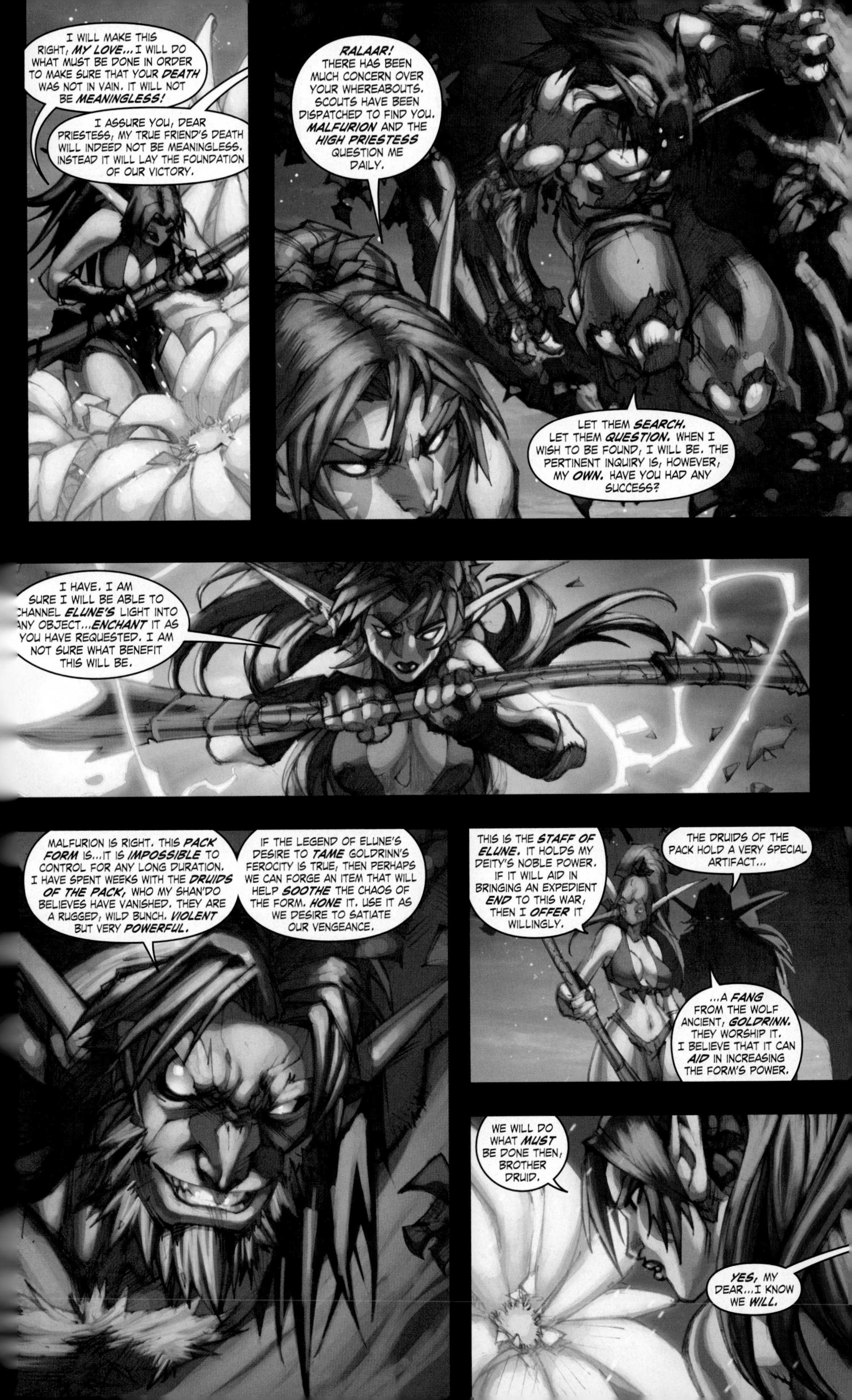
I WILL MAKE THIS RIGHT, MY LOVE... I WILL DO WHAT MUST BE DONE IN ORDER TO MAKE SURE THAT YOUR DEATH WAS NOT IN VAIN. IT WILL NOT BE MEANINGLESS!
I ASSURE YOU, DEAR PRIESTESS, MY TRUE FRIEND'S DEATH WILL INDEED NOT BE MEANINGLESS. INSTEAD IT WILL LAY THE FOUNDATION OF OUR VICTORY.
RALAAR! THERE HAS BEEN MUCH CONCERN OVER YOUR WHEREABOUTS. SCOUTS HAVE BEEN DISPATCHED TO FIND YOU. MALFURION AND THE HIGH PRIESTESS QUESTION ME DAILY.
LET THEM SEARCH. LET THEM QUESTION. WHEN I WISH TO BE FOUND, I WILL BE. THE PERTINENT INQUIRY IS, HOWEVER, MY OWN. HAVE YOU HAD ANY SUCCESS?
I HAVE. I AM SURE I WILL BE ABLE TO CHANNEL ELUNE'S LIGHT INTO ANY OBJECT...ENCHANT IT AS YOU HAVE REQUESTED. I AM NOT SURE WHAT BENEFIT THIS WILL BE.
MALFURION IS RIGHT. THIS PACK FORM IS...IT IS IMPOSSIBLE TO CONTROL FOR ANY LONG DURATION. I HAVE SPENT WEEKS WITH THE DRUIDS OF THE PACK, WHO MY SHAN'DO BELIEVES HAVE VANISHED. THEY ARE A RUGGED, WILD BUNCH. VIOLENT BUT VERY POWERFUL.
IF THE LEGEND OF ELUNE'S DESIRE TO TAME GOLDRINN'S FEROCITY IS TRUE, THEN PERHAPS WE CAN FORGE AN ITEM THAT WILL HELP SOOTHE THE CHAOS OF THE FORM. HONE IT. USE IT AS WE DESIRE TO SATIATE OUR VENGEANCE.
THIS IS THE STAFF OF ELUNE. IT HOLDS MY DEITY'S NOBLE POWER. IF IT WILL AID IN BRINGING AN EXPEDIENT END TO THIS WAR, THEN I OFFER IT WILLINGLY.
THE DRUIDS OF THE PACK HOLD A VERY SPECIAL ARTIFACT...
...A FANG FROM THE WOLF ANCIENT, GOLDRINN. THEY WORSHIP IT. I BELIEVE THAT IT CAN AID IN INCREASING THE FORM'S POWER.
WE WILL DO WHAT MUST BE DONE THEN, BROTHER DRUID.
YES, MY DEAR...I KNOW WE WILL.

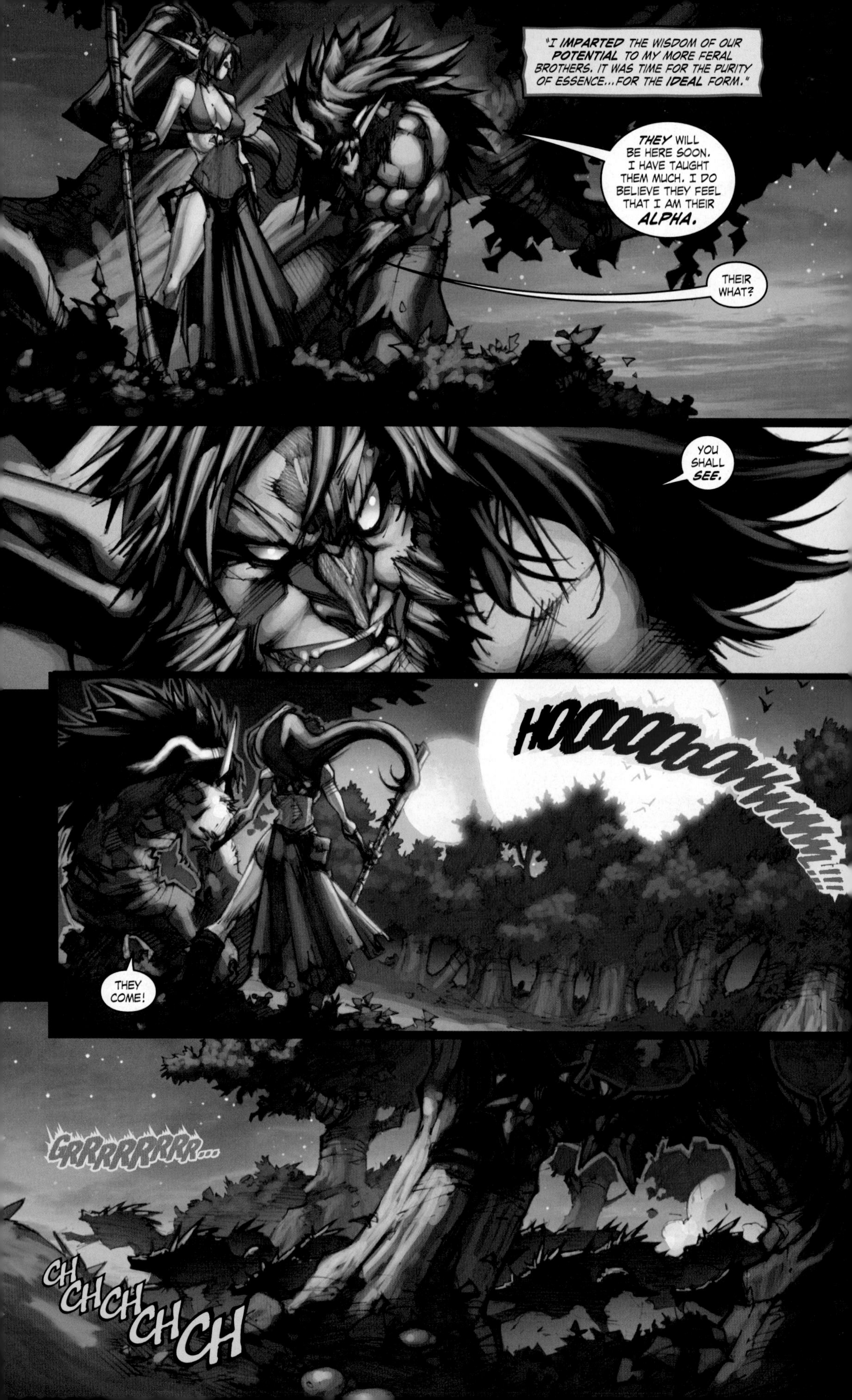
"I IMPARTED THE WISDOM OF OUR POTENTIAL TO MY MORE FERAL BROTHERS. IT WAS TIME FOR THE PURITY OF ESSENCE...FOR THE IDEAL FORM."
THEY WILL BE HERE SOON. I HAVE TAUGHT THEM MUCH. I DO BELIEVE THEY FEEL THAT I AM THEIR ALPHA.
THEIR WHAT?
YOU SHALL SEE.
HOOOOOOOWWWWL!!!
THEY COME!
GRRRRRRRR...
CH CH CH CH CH CH

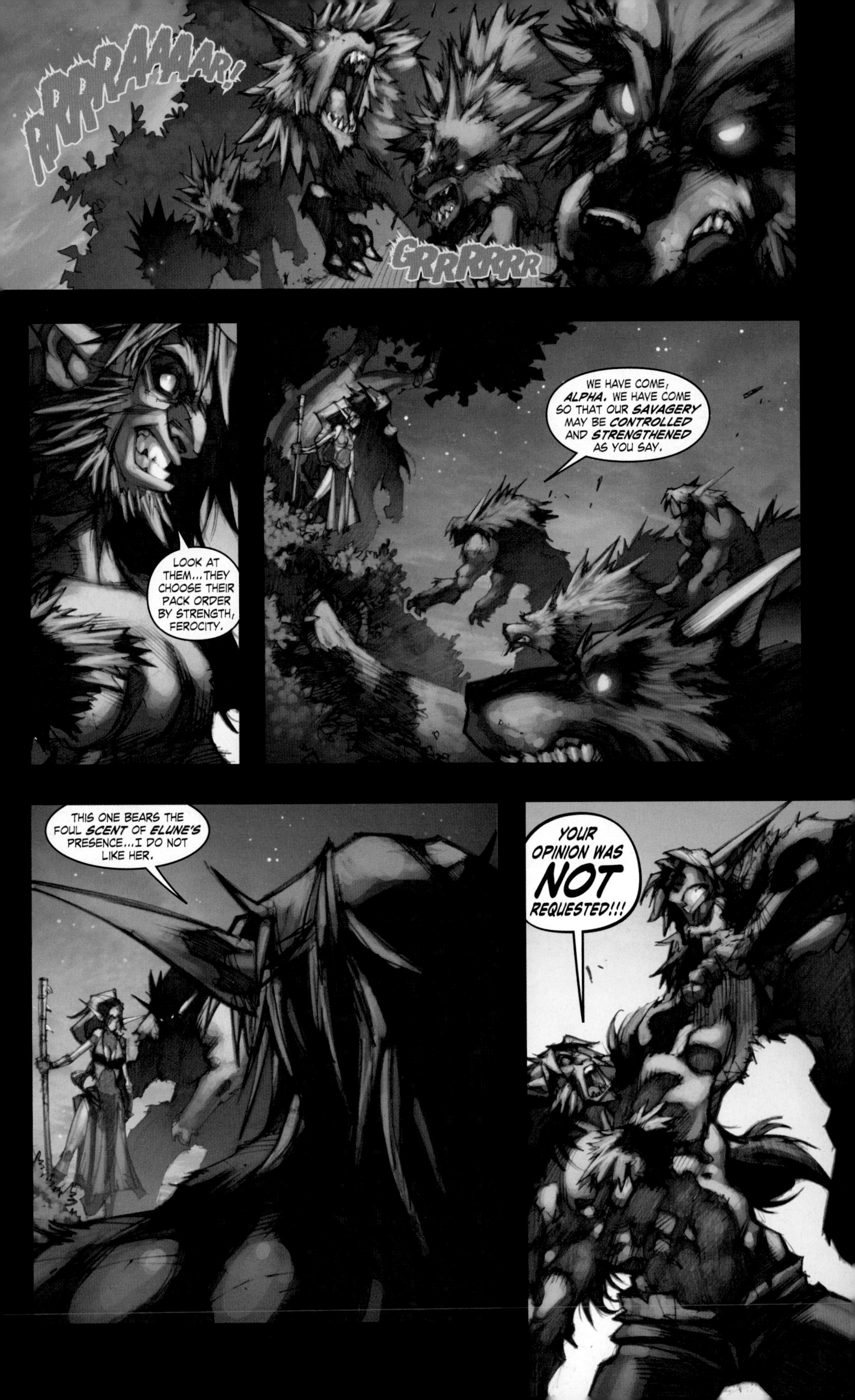
RRRRAAAAR!
GRRRRRRR
LOOK AT THEM...THEY CHOOSE THEIR PACK ORDER BY STRENGTH, FEROCITY.
WE HAVE COME, ALPHA. WE HAVE COME SO THAT OUR SAVAGERY MAY BE CONTROLLED AND STRENGTHENED AS YOU SAY.
THIS ONE BEARS THE FOUL SCENT OF ELUNE'S PRESENCE...I DO NOT LIKE HER.
YOUR OPINION WAS NOT REQUESTED!!!

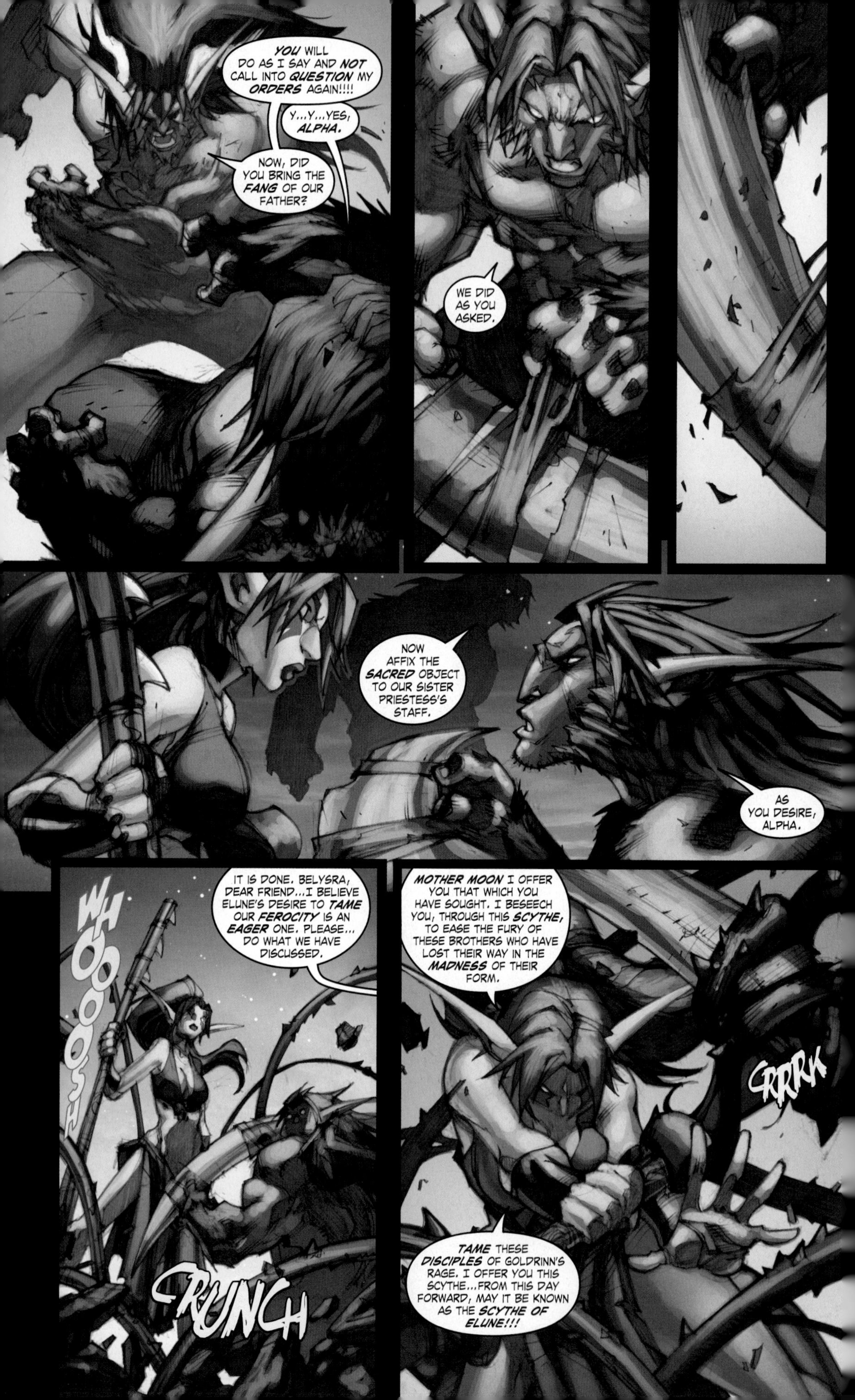
YOU WILL DO AS I SAY AND NOT CALL INTO QUESTION MY ORDERS AGAIN!!!!
Y...Y...YES, ALPHA.
NOW, DID YOU BRING THE FANG OF OUR FATHER?
WE DID AS YOU ASKED.
NOW AFFIX THE SACRED OBJECT TO OUR SISTER PRIESTESS'S STAFF.
AS YOU DESIRE, ALPHA.
WHOOOOSH
IT IS DONE. BELYSRA, DEAR FRIEND...I BELIEVE ELUNE'S DESIRE TO TAME OUR FEROCITY IS AN EAGER ONE. PLEASE... DO WHAT WE HAVE DISCUSSED.
MOTHER MOON I OFFER YOU THAT WHICH YOU HAVE SOUGHT. I BESEECH YOU, THROUGH THIS SCYTHE, TO EASE THE FURY OF THESE BROTHERS WHO HAVE LOST THEIR WAY IN THE MADNESS OF THEIR FORM.
CRRRK
TAME THESE DISCIPLES OF GOLDRINN'S RAGE. I OFFER YOU THIS SCYTHE...FROM THIS DAY FORWARD, MAY IT BE KNOWN AS THE SCYTHE OF ELUNE!!!
CRUNCH

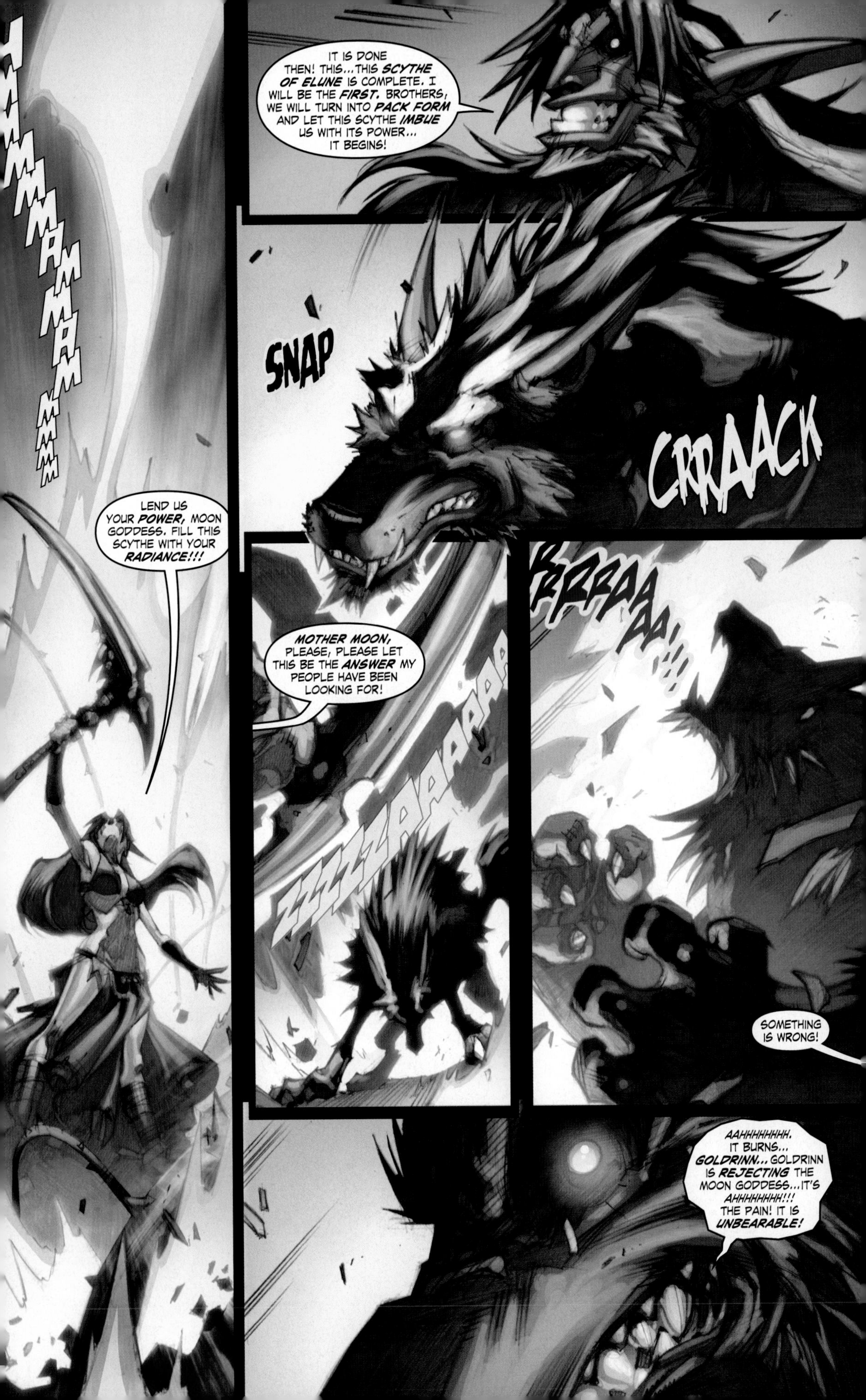
HMMMMMMMMMMMMMMMMMMM
IT IS DONE THEN! THIS...THIS SCYTHE OF ELUNE IS COMPLETE. I WILL BE THE FIRST. BROTHERS, WE WILL TURN INTO PACK FORM AND LET THIS SCYTHE IMBUE US WITH ITS POWER... IT BEGINS!
SNAP
CRRAACK
LEND US YOUR POWER, MOON GODDESS. FILL THIS SCYTHE WITH YOUR RADIANCE!!!
MOTHER MOON, PLEASE, PLEASE LET THIS BE THE ANSWER MY PEOPLE HAVE BEEN LOOKING FOR!
ZZZZZAAAAAAAAAA
RRRAAAAA!!!
SOMETHING IS WRONG!
AAHHHHHHHHH. IT BURNS... GOLDRINN... GOLDRINN IS REJECTING THE MOON GODDESS...IT'S AHHHHHHHHH!!! THE PAIN! IT IS UNBEARABLE!

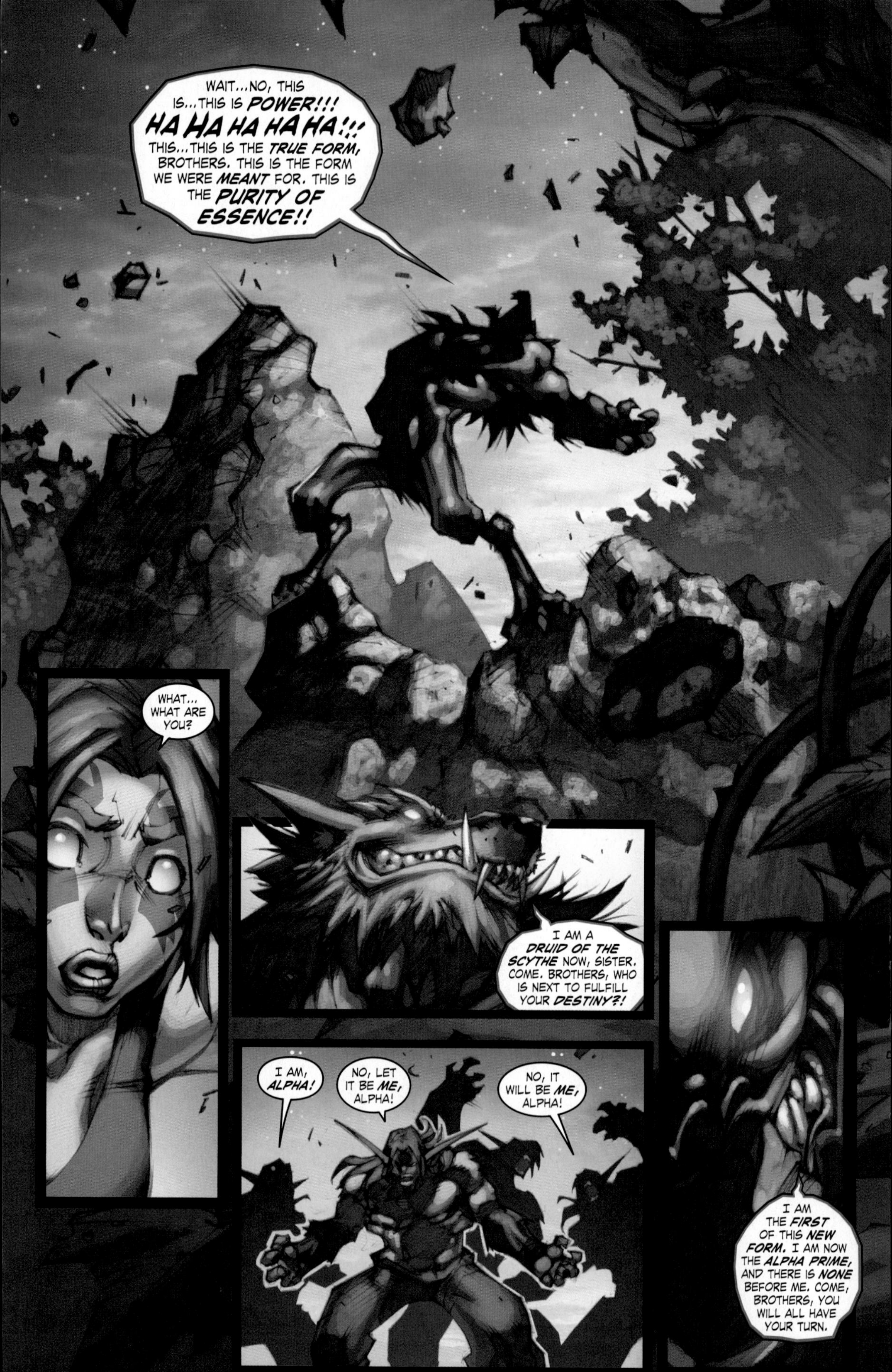
WAIT...NO, THIS IS...THIS IS POWER!!! HA HA HA HA HA!!! THIS...THIS IS THE TRUE FORM, BROTHERS. THIS IS THE FORM WE WERE MEANT FOR. THIS IS THE PURITY OF ESSENCE!!
WHAT... WHAT ARE YOU?
I AM A DRUID OF THE SCYTHE NOW, SISTER. COME. BROTHERS, WHO IS NEXT TO FULFILL YOUR DESTINY?!
I AM, ALPHA!
NO, LET IT BE ME, ALPHA!
NO, IT WILL BE ME, ALPHA!
I AM THE FIRST OF THIS NEW FORM. I AM NOW THE ALPHA PRIME, AND THERE IS NONE BEFORE ME. COME, BROTHERS, YOU WILL ALL HAVE YOUR TURN.

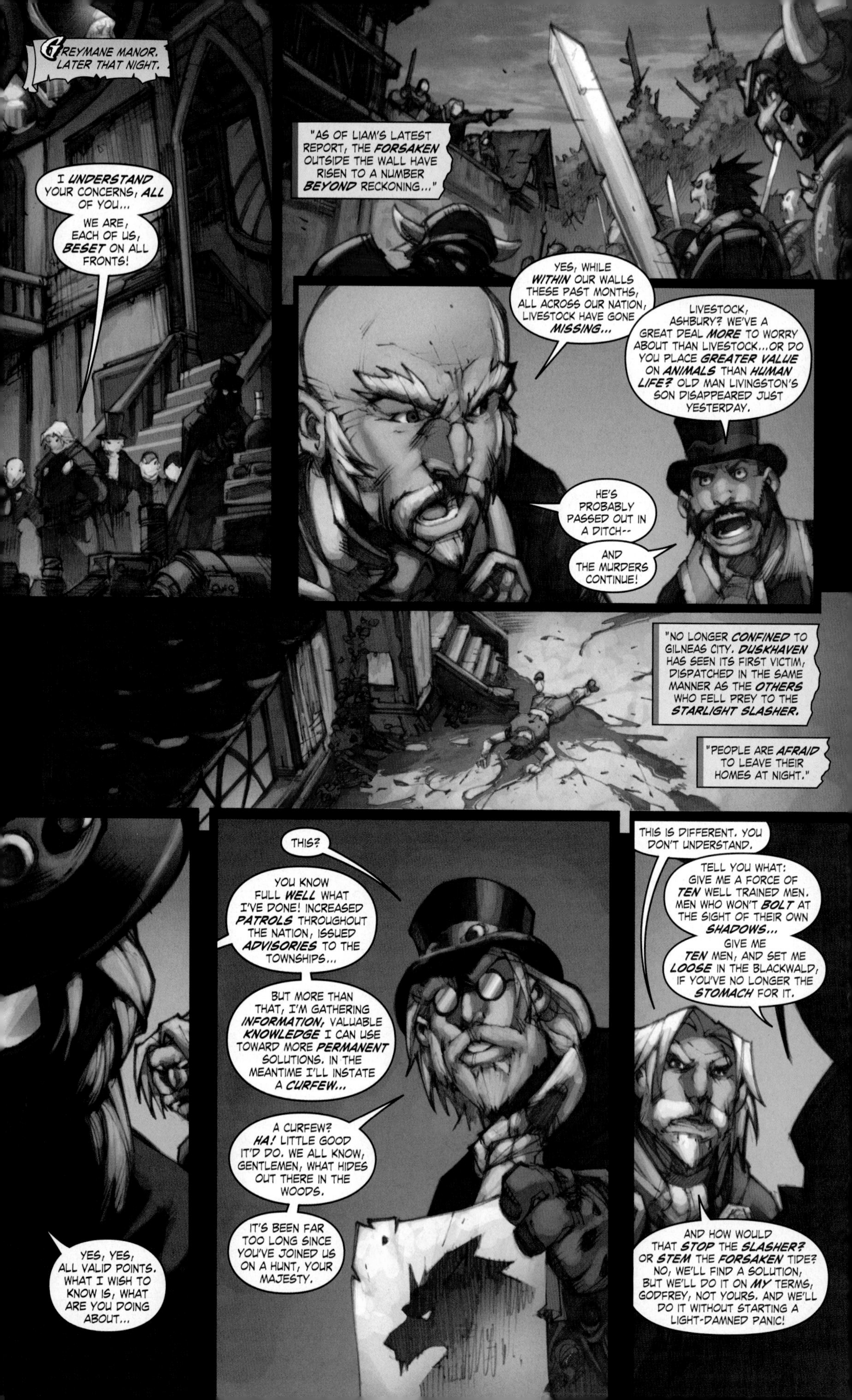
GREYMANE MANOR. LATER THAT NIGHT.
I UNDERSTAND YOUR CONCERNS, ALL OF YOU...
WE ARE, EACH OF US, BESET ON ALL FRONTS!
"AS OF LIAM'S LATEST REPORT, THE FORSAKEN OUTSIDE THE WALL HAVE RISEN TO A NUMBER BEYOND RECKONING..."
YES, WHILE WITHIN OUR WALLS THESE PAST MONTHS, ALL ACROSS OUR NATION, LIVESTOCK HAVE GONE MISSING...
LIVESTOCK, ASHBURY? WE'VE A GREAT DEAL MORE TO WORRY ABOUT THAN LIVESTOCK...OR DO YOU PLACE GREATER VALUE ON ANIMALS THAN HUMAN LIFE? OLD MAN LIVINGSTON'S SON DISAPPEARED JUST YESTERDAY.
HE'S PROBABLY PASSED OUT IN A DITCH--
AND THE MURDERS CONTINUE!
"NO LONGER CONFINED TO GILNEAS CITY. DUSKHAVEN HAS SEEN ITS FIRST VICTIM, DISPATCHED IN THE SAME MANNER AS THE OTHERS WHO FELL PREY TO THE STARLIGHT SLASHER.
"PEOPLE ARE AFRAID TO LEAVE THEIR HOMES AT NIGHT."
YES, YES, ALL VALID POINTS. WHAT I WISH TO KNOW IS, WHAT ARE YOU DOING ABOUT...
THIS?
YOU KNOW FULL WELL WHAT I'VE DONE! INCREASED PATROLS THROUGHOUT THE NATION, ISSUED ADVISORIES TO THE TOWNSHIPS...
BUT MORE THAN THAT, I'M GATHERING INFORMATION, VALUABLE KNOWLEDGE I CAN USE TOWARD MORE PERMANENT SOLUTIONS. IN THE MEANTIME I'LL INSTATE A CURFEW...
A CURFEW? HA! LITTLE GOOD IT'D DO. WE ALL KNOW, GENTLEMEN, WHAT HIDES OUT THERE IN THE WOODS.
IT'S BEEN FAR TOO LONG SINCE YOU'VE JOINED US ON A HUNT, YOUR MAJESTY.
THIS IS DIFFERENT. YOU DON'T UNDERSTAND.
TELL YOU WHAT: GIVE ME A FORCE OF TEN WELL TRAINED MEN. MEN WHO WON'T BOLT AT THE SIGHT OF THEIR OWN SHADOWS...
GIVE ME TEN MEN, AND SET ME LOOSE IN THE BLACKWALD, IF YOU'VE NO LONGER THE STOMACH FOR IT.
AND HOW WOULD THAT STOP THE SLASHER? OR STEM THE FORSAKEN TIDE? NO, WE'LL FIND A SOLUTION, BUT WE'LL DO IT ON MY TERMS, GODFREY, NOT YOURS. AND WE'LL DO IT WITHOUT STARTING A LIGHT-DAMNED PANIC!

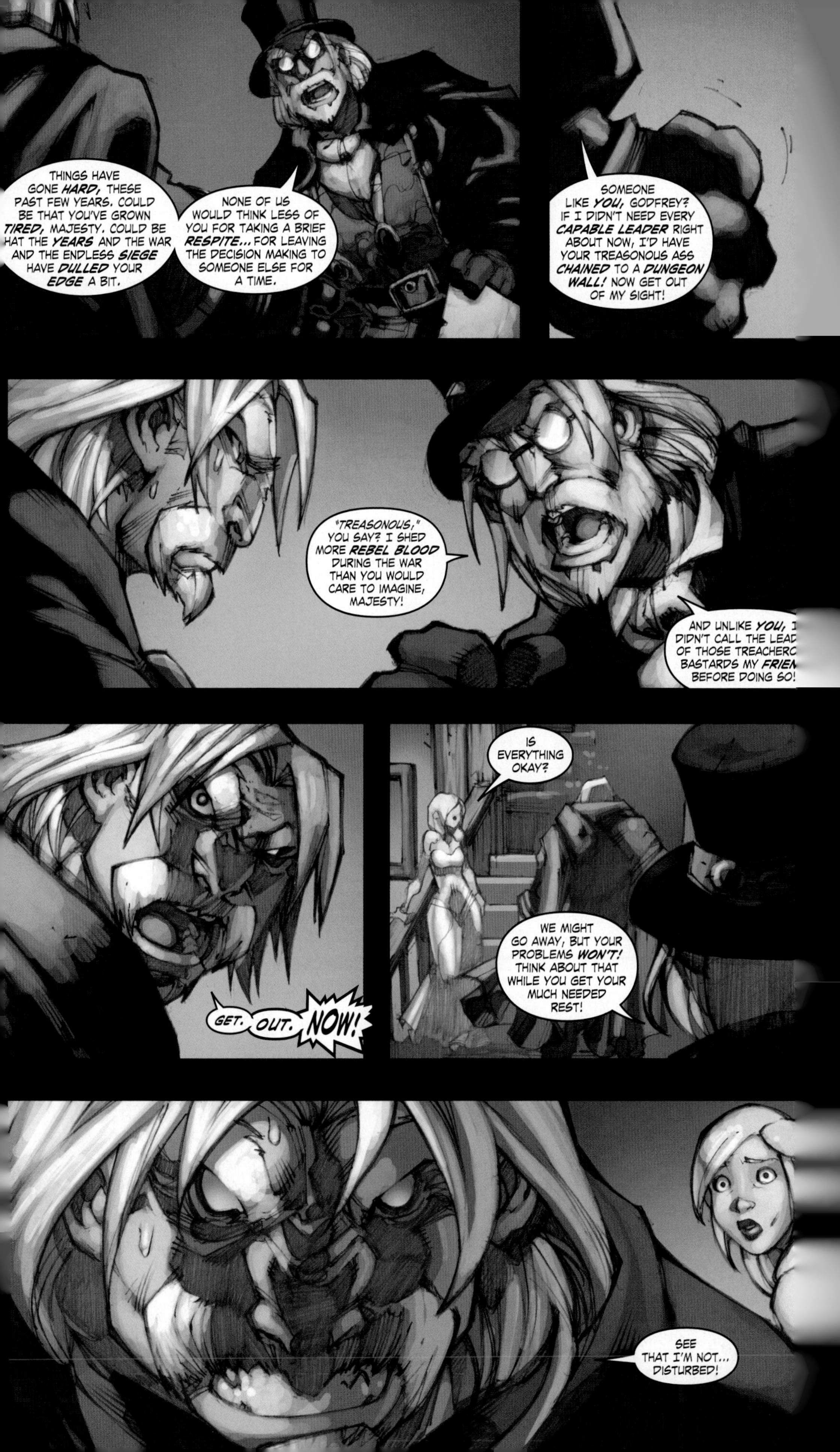
THINGS HAVE GONE HARD, THESE PAST FEW YEARS. COULD BE THAT YOU'VE GROWN TIRED, MAJESTY. COULD BE HAT THE YEARS AND THE WAR AND THE ENDLESS SIEGE HAVE DULLED YOUR EDGE A BIT.
NONE OF US WOULD THINK LESS OF YOU FOR TAKING A BRIEF RESPITE... FOR LEAVING THE DECISION MAKING TO SOMEONE ELSE FOR A TIME.
SOMEONE LIKE YOU, GODFREY? IF I DIDN'T NEED EVERY CAPABLE LEADER RIGHT ABOUT NOW, I'D HAVE YOUR TREASONOUS ASS CHAINED TO A DUNGEON WALL! NOW GET OUT OF MY SIGHT!
"TREASONOUS," YOU SAY? I SHED MORE REBEL BLOOD DURING THE WAR THAN YOU WOULD CARE TO IMAGINE, MAJESTY!
AND UNLIKE YOU, I DIDN'T CALL THE LEAD OF THOSE TREACHERO BASTARDS MY FRIEN BEFORE DOING SO!
GET. OUT. NOW!
IS EVERYTHING OKAY?
WE MIGHT GO AWAY, BUT YOUR PROBLEMS WON'T! THINK ABOUT THAT WHILE YOU GET YOUR MUCH NEEDED REST!
SEE THAT I'M NOT... DISTURBED!

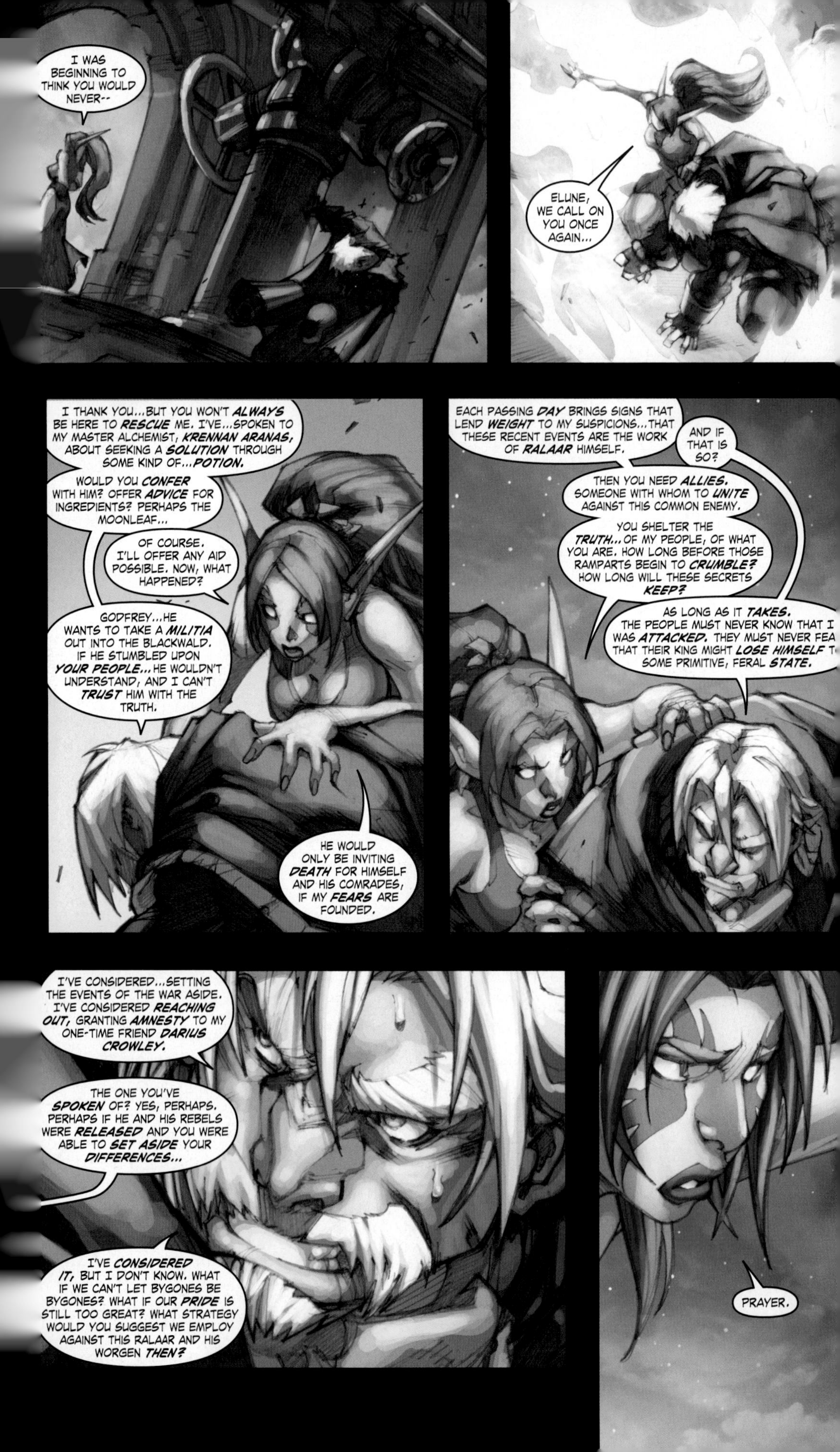
I WAS BEGINNING TO THINK YOU WOULD NEVER--
ELUNE, WE CALL ON YOU ONCE AGAIN...
I THANK YOU...BUT YOU WON'T ALWAYS BE HERE TO RESCUE ME. I'VE...SPOKEN TO MY MASTER ALCHEMIST, KRENNAN ARANAS, ABOUT SEEKING A SOLUTION THROUGH SOME KIND OF...POTION.
WOULD YOU CONFER WITH HIM? OFFER ADVICE FOR INGREDIENTS? PERHAPS THE MOONLEAF...
OF COURSE. I'LL OFFER ANY AID POSSIBLE. NOW, WHAT HAPPENED?
GODFREY...HE WANTS TO TAKE A MILITIA OUT INTO THE BLACKWALD. IF HE STUMBLED UPON YOUR PEOPLE...HE WOULDN'T UNDERSTAND, AND I CAN'T TRUST HIM WITH THE TRUTH.
HE WOULD ONLY BE INVITING DEATH FOR HIMSELF AND HIS COMRADES, IF MY FEARS ARE FOUNDED.
EACH PASSING DAY BRINGS SIGNS THAT LEND WEIGHT TO MY SUSPICIONS...THAT THESE RECENT EVENTS ARE THE WORK OF RALAAR HIMSELF.
AND IF THAT IS SO?
THEN YOU NEED ALLIES. SOMEONE WITH WHOM TO UNITE AGAINST THIS COMMON ENEMY.
YOU SHELTER THE TRUTH...OF MY PEOPLE, OF WHAT YOU ARE. HOW LONG BEFORE THOSE RAMPARTS BEGIN TO CRUMBLE? HOW LONG WILL THESE SECRETS KEEP?
AS LONG AS IT TAKES. THE PEOPLE MUST NEVER KNOW THAT I WAS ATTACKED. THEY MUST NEVER FEA THAT THEIR KING MIGHT LOSE HIMSELF T SOME PRIMITIVE, FERAL STATE.
I'VE CONSIDERED...SETTING THE EVENTS OF THE WAR ASIDE. I'VE CONSIDERED REACHING OUT, GRANTING AMNESTY TO MY ONE-TIME FRIEND DARIUS CROWLEY.
THE ONE YOU'VE SPOKEN OF? YES, PERHAPS. PERHAPS IF HE AND HIS REBELS WERE RELEASED AND YOU WERE ABLE TO SET ASIDE YOUR DIFFERENCES...
I'VE CONSIDERED IT, BUT I DON'T KNOW. WHAT IF WE CAN'T LET BYGONES BE BYGONES? WHAT IF OUR PRIDE IS STILL TOO GREAT? WHAT STRATEGY WOULD YOU SUGGEST WE EMPLOY AGAINST THIS RALAAR AND HIS WORGEN THEN?
PRAYER.

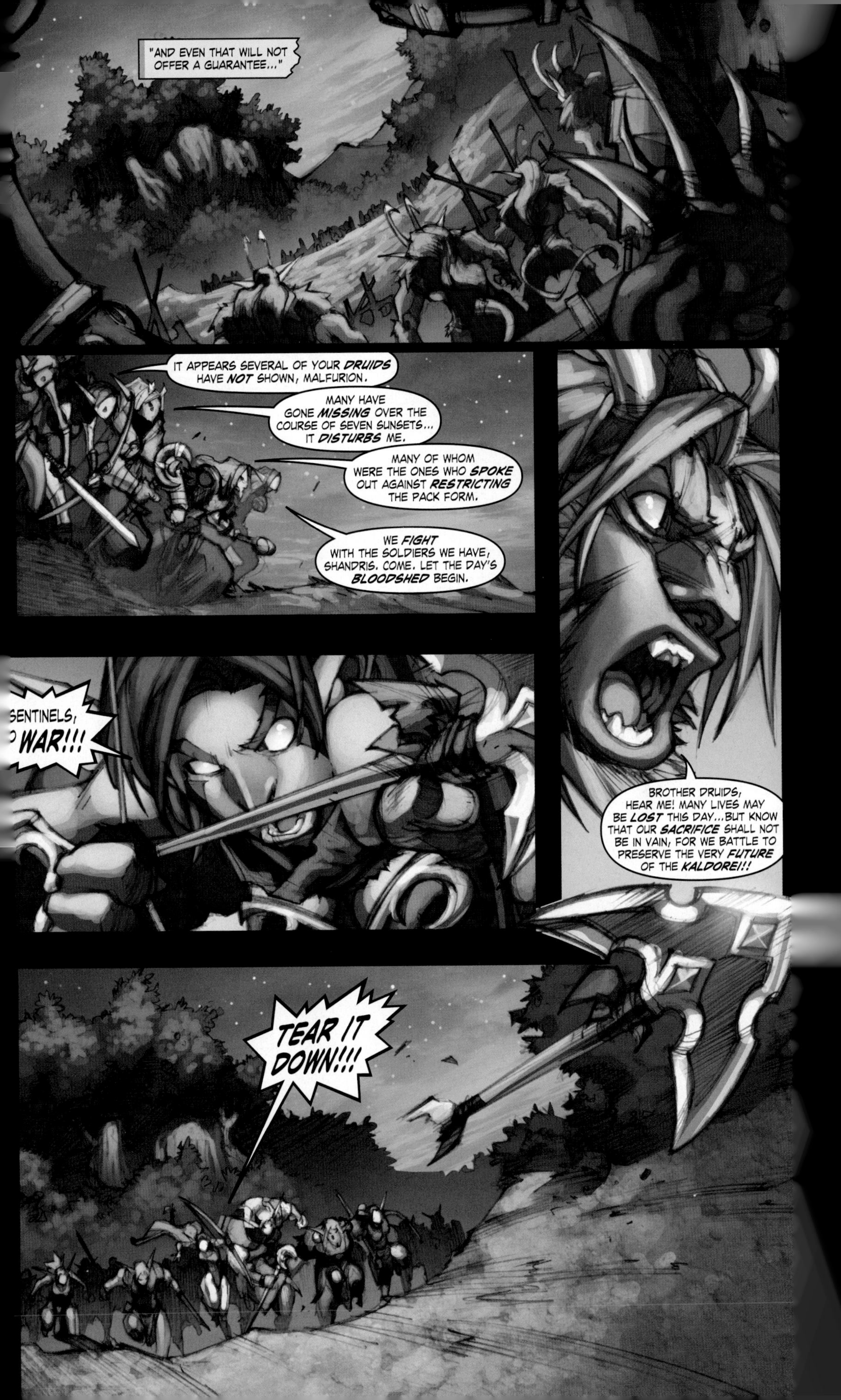
"AND EVEN THAT WILL NOT OFFER A GUARANTEE..."
IT APPEARS SEVERAL OF YOUR DRUIDS HAVE NOT SHOWN, MALFURION.
MANY HAVE GONE MISSING OVER THE COURSE OF SEVEN SUNSETS... IT DISTURBS ME.
MANY OF WHOM WERE THE ONES WHO SPOKE OUT AGAINST RESTRICTING THE PACK FORM.
WE FIGHT WITH THE SOLDIERS WE HAVE, SHANDRIS. COME. LET THE DAY'S BLOODSHED BEGIN.
BROTHER DRUIDS, HEAR ME! MANY LIVES MAY BE LOST THIS DAY...BUT KNOW THAT OUR SACRIFICE SHALL NOT BE IN VAIN, FOR WE BATTLE TO PRESERVE THE VERY FUTURE OF THE KALDORE!!!
SENTINELS, WAR!!!
TEAR IT DOWN!!!

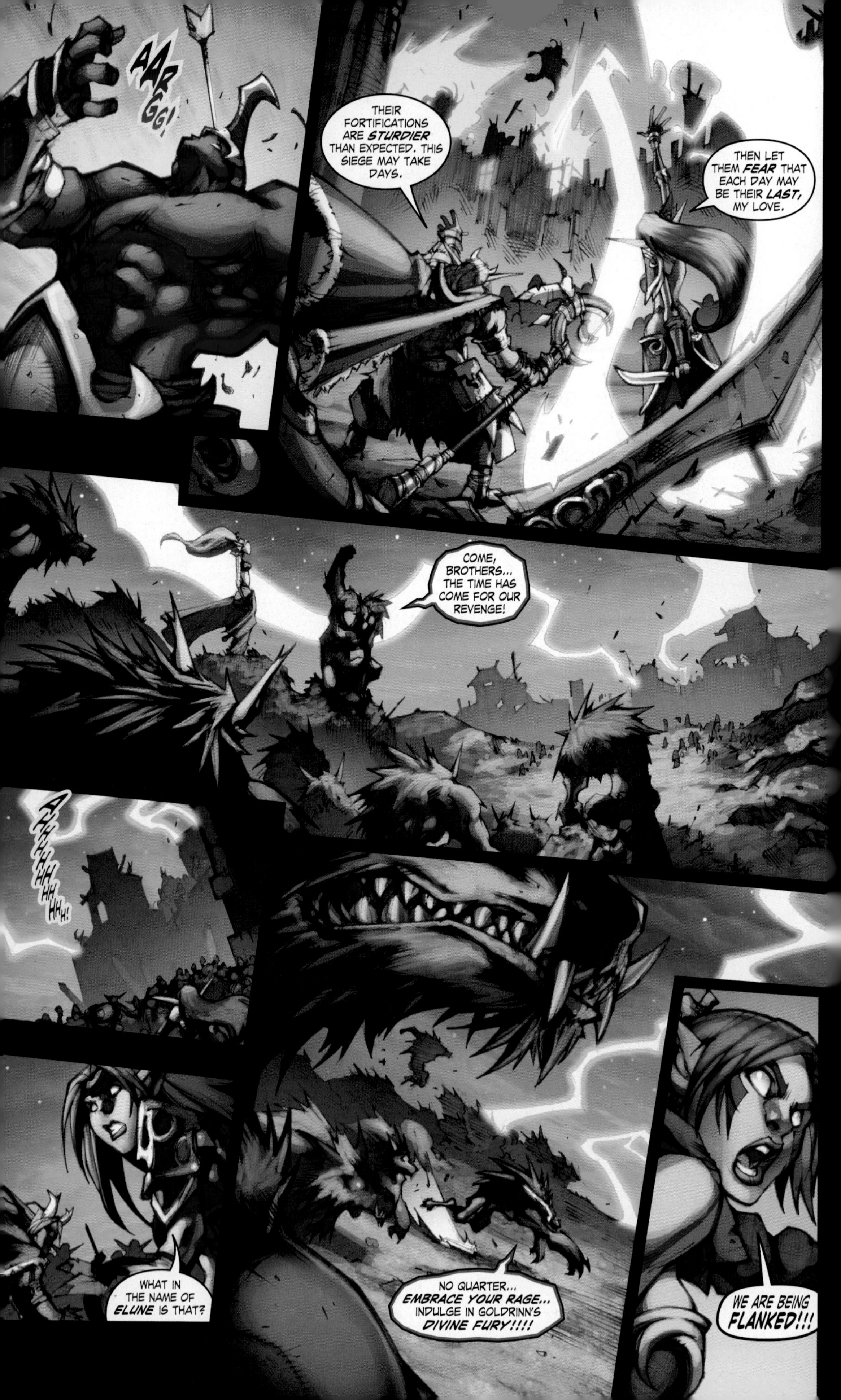
AARGG!
THEIR FORTIFICATIONS ARE STURDIER THAN EXPECTED. THIS SIEGE MAY TAKE DAYS.
THEN LET THEM FEAR THAT EACH DAY MAY BE THEIR LAST, MY LOVE.
COME, BROTHERS... THE TIME HAS COME FOR OUR REVENGE!
AHHHHHHHHHH!!
WHAT IN THE NAME OF ELUNE IS THAT?
NO QUARTER... EMBRACE YOUR RAGE... INDULGE IN GOLDRINN'S DIVINE FURY!!!!
WE ARE BEING FLANKED!!!

RRAAARRRR!

WHAT ARE THOSE CREATURES??!

AHHHHHHHH!!!

AHHHHAHHHHAHHHHHH!

"THEY *TORE* INTO THE SATYRS WITH *FEROCITY* UNPARALLELED. THESE CREATURES...THESE DRUIDS OF THE SCYTHE...THESE WORGEN WERE A *FORCE* UNLIKE ANY OTHER, *TERRIFYINGLY* UNSTOPPABLE."

THEY ARE *ATTACKING* THE *SATYRS*, NOT US...SISTERS, JOIN THEM!

"WATCHING THE SATYRS' *BLOOD SPILL*, WATCHING THEIR FORTIFICATIONS *SHATTER*... I FELT A *SATISFACTION* IN *VENGEANCE*... I FELT THE RELIEF OF THE *FOOLISH*.

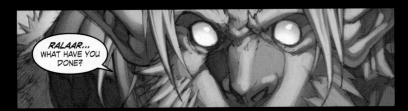

RALAAR... WHAT HAVE YOU DONE?

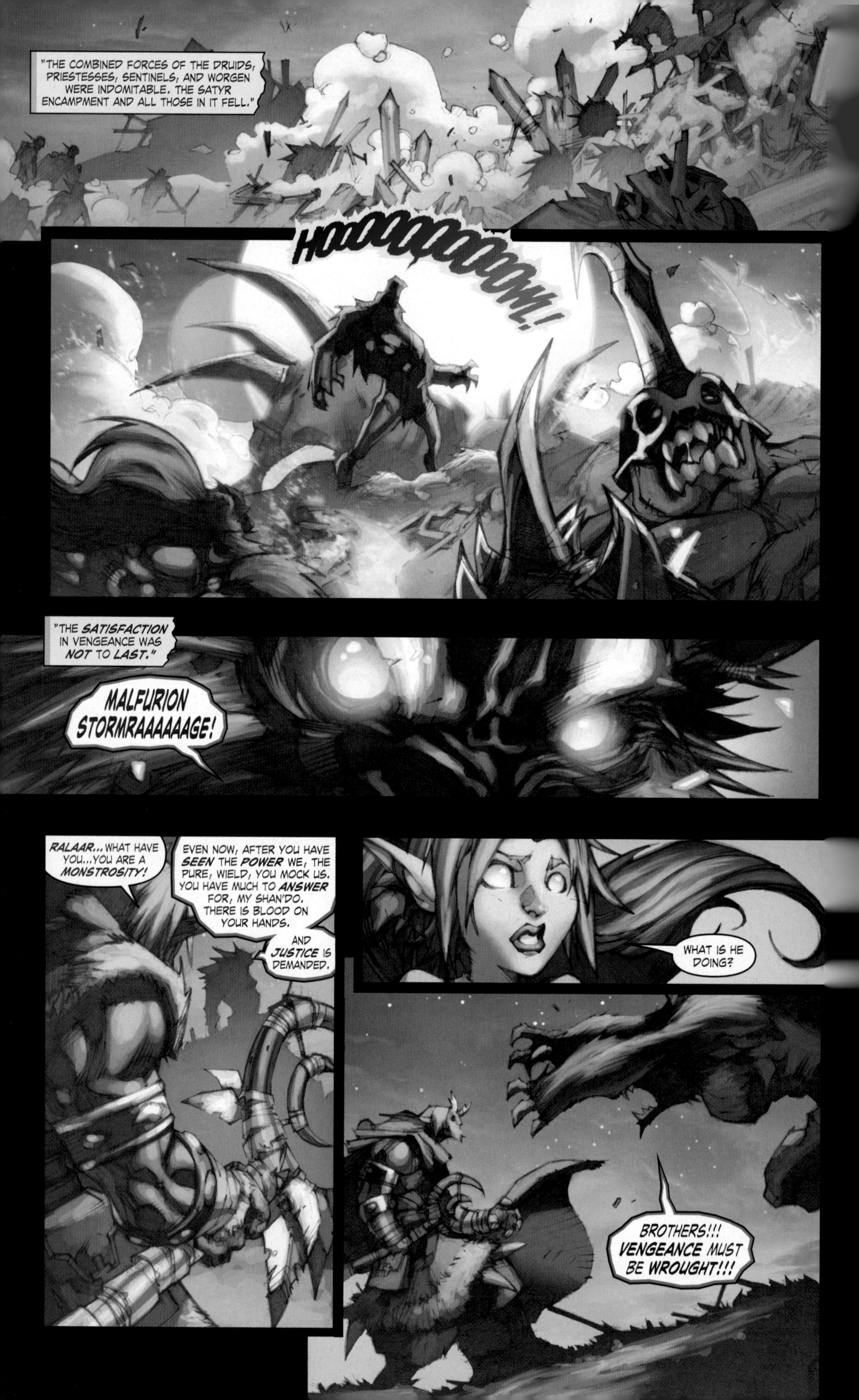
"THE COMBINED FORCES OF THE DRUIDS, PRIESTESSES, SENTINELS, AND WORGEN WERE INDOMITABLE. THE SATYR ENCAMPMENT AND ALL THOSE IN IT FELL."
HOOOOOOOOOOWL!
"THE SATISFACTION IN VENGEANCE WAS NOT TO LAST."
MALFURION STORMRAAAAAAGE!
RALAAR... WHAT HAVE YOU...YOU ARE A MONSTROSITY!
EVEN NOW, AFTER YOU HAVE SEEN THE POWER WE, THE PURE, WIELD, YOU MOCK US. YOU HAVE MUCH TO ANSWER FOR, MY SHAN'DO. THERE IS BLOOD ON YOUR HANDS.
AND JUSTICE IS DEMANDED.
WHAT IS HE DOING?
BROTHERS!!! VENGEANCE MUST BE WROUGHT!!!

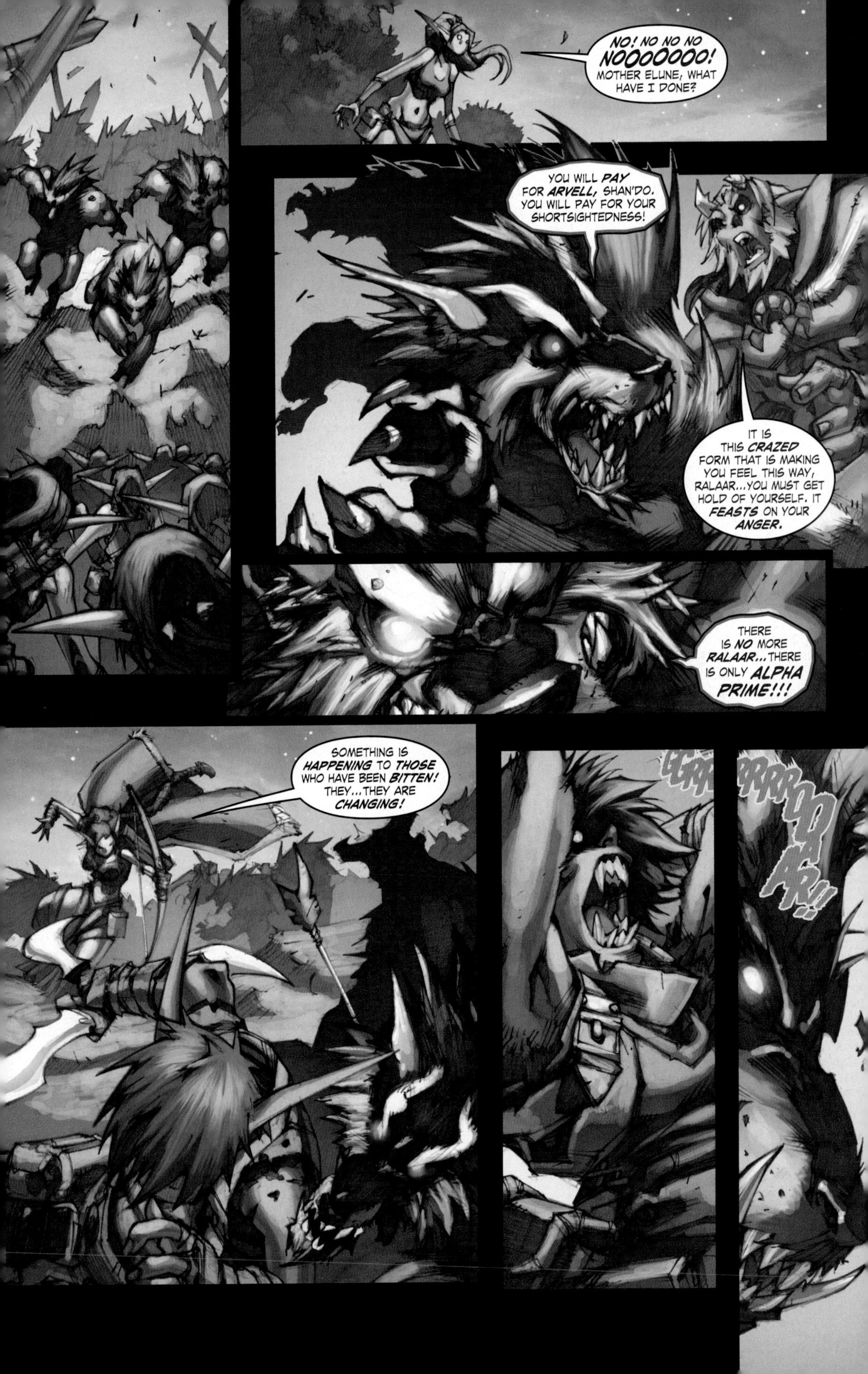
NO! NO NO NO NOOOOOOO! MOTHER ELUNE, WHAT HAVE I DONE?
YOU WILL PAY FOR ARVELL, SHAN'DO. YOU WILL PAY FOR YOUR SHORTSIGHTEDNESS!
IT IS THIS CRAZED FORM THAT IS MAKING YOU FEEL THIS WAY, RALAAR...YOU MUST GET HOLD OF YOURSELF. IT FEASTS ON YOUR ANGER.
THERE IS NO MORE RALAAR...THERE IS ONLY ALPHA PRIME!!!
SOMETHING IS HAPPENING TO THOSE WHO HAVE BEEN BITTEN! THEY...THEY ARE CHANGING!
GGRRRRRRROOAAR!!

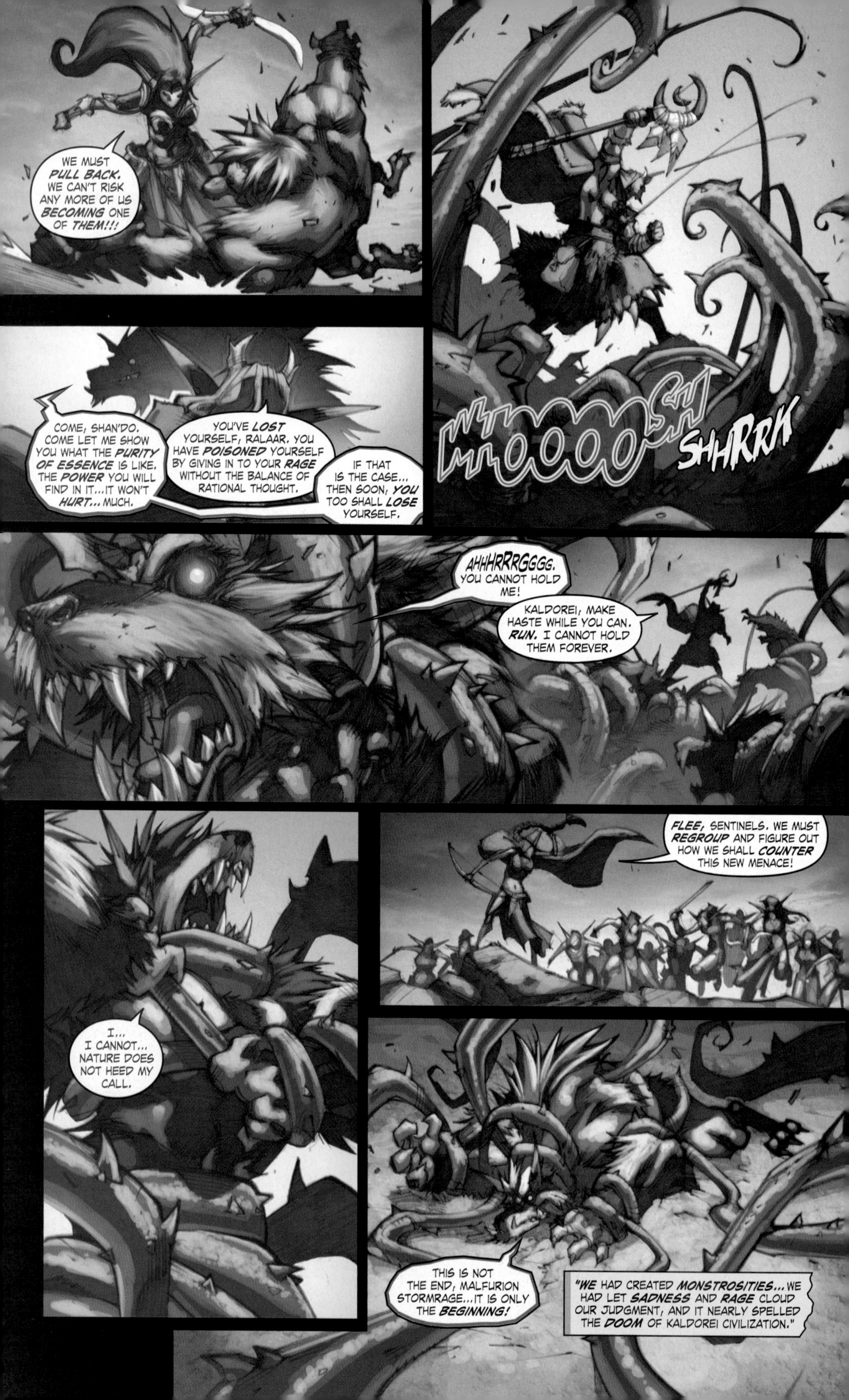

WE MUST PULL BACK. WE CAN'T RISK ANY MORE OF US BECOMING ONE OF THEM!!!
WHOOOOOSH
SHHRRK
COME, SHAN'DO. COME LET ME SHOW YOU WHAT THE PURITY OF ESSENCE IS LIKE. THE POWER YOU WILL FIND IN IT...IT WON'T HURT... MUCH.
YOU'VE LOST YOURSELF, RALAAR. YOU HAVE POISONED YOURSELF BY GIVING IN TO YOUR RAGE WITHOUT THE BALANCE OF RATIONAL THOUGHT.
IF THAT IS THE CASE... THEN SOON, YOU TOO SHALL LOSE YOURSELF.
AHHHRRRGGGG. YOU CANNOT HOLD ME!
KALDOREI, MAKE HASTE WHILE YOU CAN. RUN. I CANNOT HOLD THEM FOREVER.
I... I CANNOT... NATURE DOES NOT HEED MY CALL.
FLEE, SENTINELS. WE MUST REGROUP AND FIGURE OUT HOW WE SHALL COUNTER THIS NEW MENACE!
THIS IS NOT THE END, MALFURION STORMRAGE...IT IS ONLY THE BEGINNING!
"WE HAD CREATED MONSTROSITIES... WE HAD LET SADNESS AND RAGE CLOUD OUR JUDGMENT, AND IT NEARLY SPELLED THE DOOM OF KALDOREI CIVILIZATION."

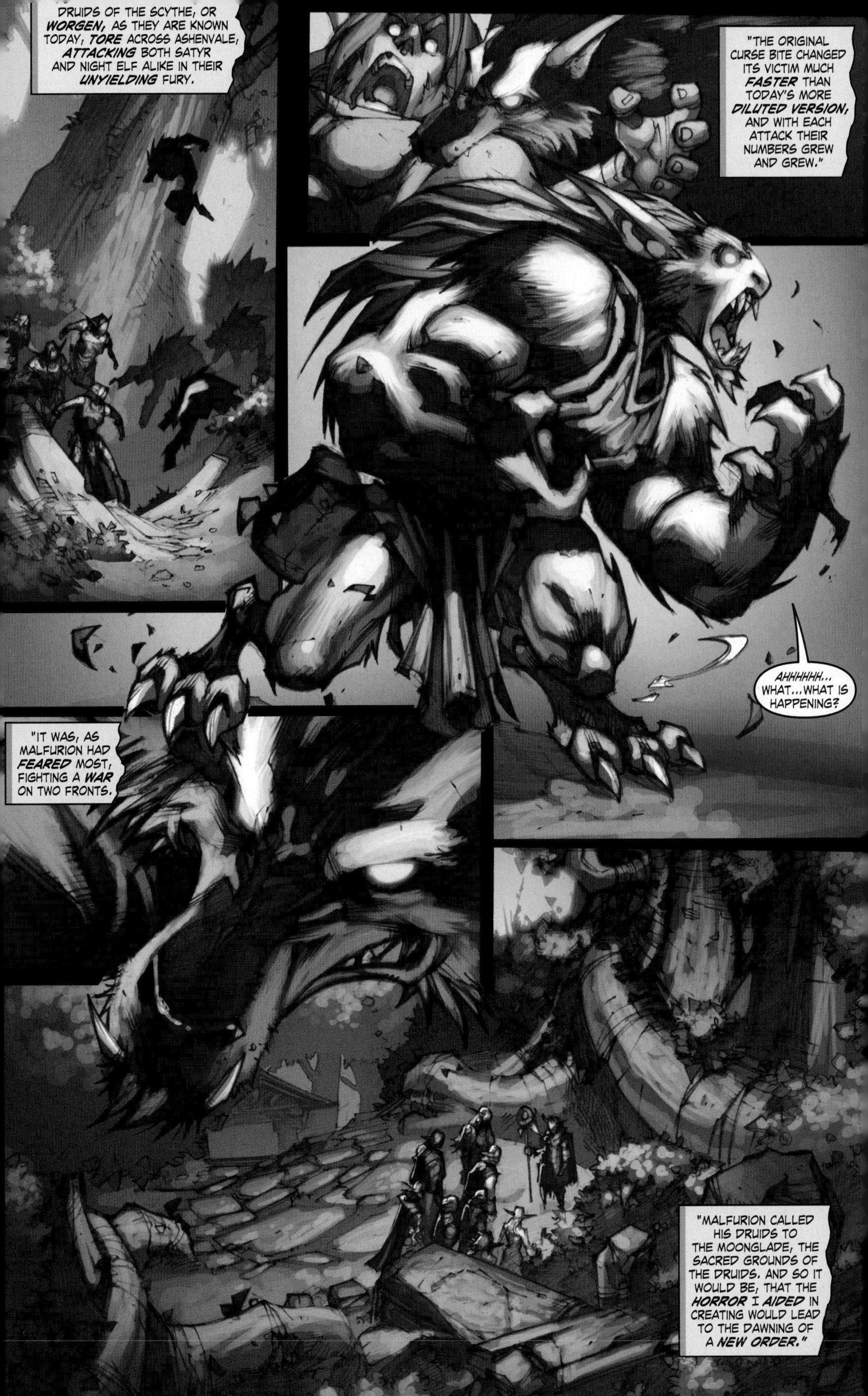
DRUIDS OF THE SCYTHE, OR WORGEN, AS THEY ARE KNOWN TODAY, TORE ACROSS ASHENVALE, ATTACKING BOTH SATYR AND NIGHT ELF ALIKE IN THEIR UNYIELDING FURY.
"THE ORIGINAL CURSE BITE CHANGED ITS VICTIM MUCH FASTER THAN TODAY'S MORE DILUTED VERSION, AND WITH EACH ATTACK THEIR NUMBERS GREW AND GREW."
AHHHHHH... WHAT...WHAT IS HAPPENING?
"IT WAS, AS MALFURION HAD FEARED MOST, FIGHTING A WAR ON TWO FRONTS.
"MALFURION CALLED HIS DRUIDS TO THE MOONGLADE, THE SACRED GROUNDS OF THE DRUIDS. AND SO IT WOULD BE, THAT THE HORROR I AIDED IN CREATING WOULD LEAD TO THE DAWNING OF A NEW ORDER."

...IF THESE *DRUIDS OF THE SCYTHE* HAVE SHOWN US ANYTHING, BROTHERS, IT IS THAT OUR GREAT *POWER* COMES WITH A *PRICE.*

WE MUST *ESTABLISH* A WAY FOR OUR *PRACTICE.* WE HAVE EXPERIMENTED LONG ENOUGH TO KNOW THE *TRUTHS* OF EACH FORM.

I HAVE CONSULTED WITH *CENARIUS,* AND IT IS WITH HIS BLESSING THAT I ESTABLISH *THE CENARION CIRCLE.*

THEN IT SHALL BE SO, BROTHER MALFURION. LET THIS NEW ORDER *GUIDE* US TRUTHFULLY.

AN ORDER THAT WILL DO ALL IT CAN TO *PROTECT* NATURE AND ESTABLISH A *TRADITION* OF DRUIDISM. IT WILL ENSURE THAT TRAGEDIES LIKE THIS, MISUSES OF OUR GREAT *CONNECTION* WITH *NATURE,* WILL NEVER HAPPEN AGAIN.

HEAR, HEAR!

BUT, SHAN'DO...WHAT OF THE DRUIDS OF THE SCYTHE? THESE *ABOMINATIONS* MUST BE *DESTROYED.* THEY HAVE MISUSED THE TEACHINGS OF CENARIUS AND BECOME THE MOST *SAVAGE* OF EVILS.

NARALEX, I UNDERSTAND YOUR *ANGER.* BUT THEY ARE STILL OUR BROTHERS, AND THEIR INTENT WAS A NOBLE ONE. THEY HAVE BECOME *MISGUIDED,* FLAWED, AND *CONSUMED* BY GOLDRINN'S GREAT FURY. SHOULD WE *DESTROY* THEM BECAUSE OF THIS?

SHAN'DO... WHAT OTHER OPTION DO WE HAVE?

I INTEND TO USE THE *SCYTHE OF ELUNE* AGAINST THEM.

YOU SEE, THE *SPIRIT* OF GOLDRINN, LIKE THE SPIRITS OF ALL *ANCIENTS,* RESIDES IN THE *EMERALD DREAM.* IT IS MY UNDERSTANDING THAT THE SCYTHE CAN *TEAR* THROUGH THE BOUNDARY THAT *DIVIDES* HIS *FANG* FROM HIS *SPIRIT.*

IN DOING SO WE WILL *BANISH* THESE WAYWARD DRUIDS TO THE *WILD REALM...* THERE IS A *TREE* THAT *SOOTHES* THE FERAL NATURE OF MANY OF THESE ANIMAL FORMS WITHIN THE DREAM.

"IT IS CALLED *DARAL'NIR.*

"AND IT WILL *SEDATE* THEIR RAGE AND BRING AN END TO THIS *MADNESS.*"

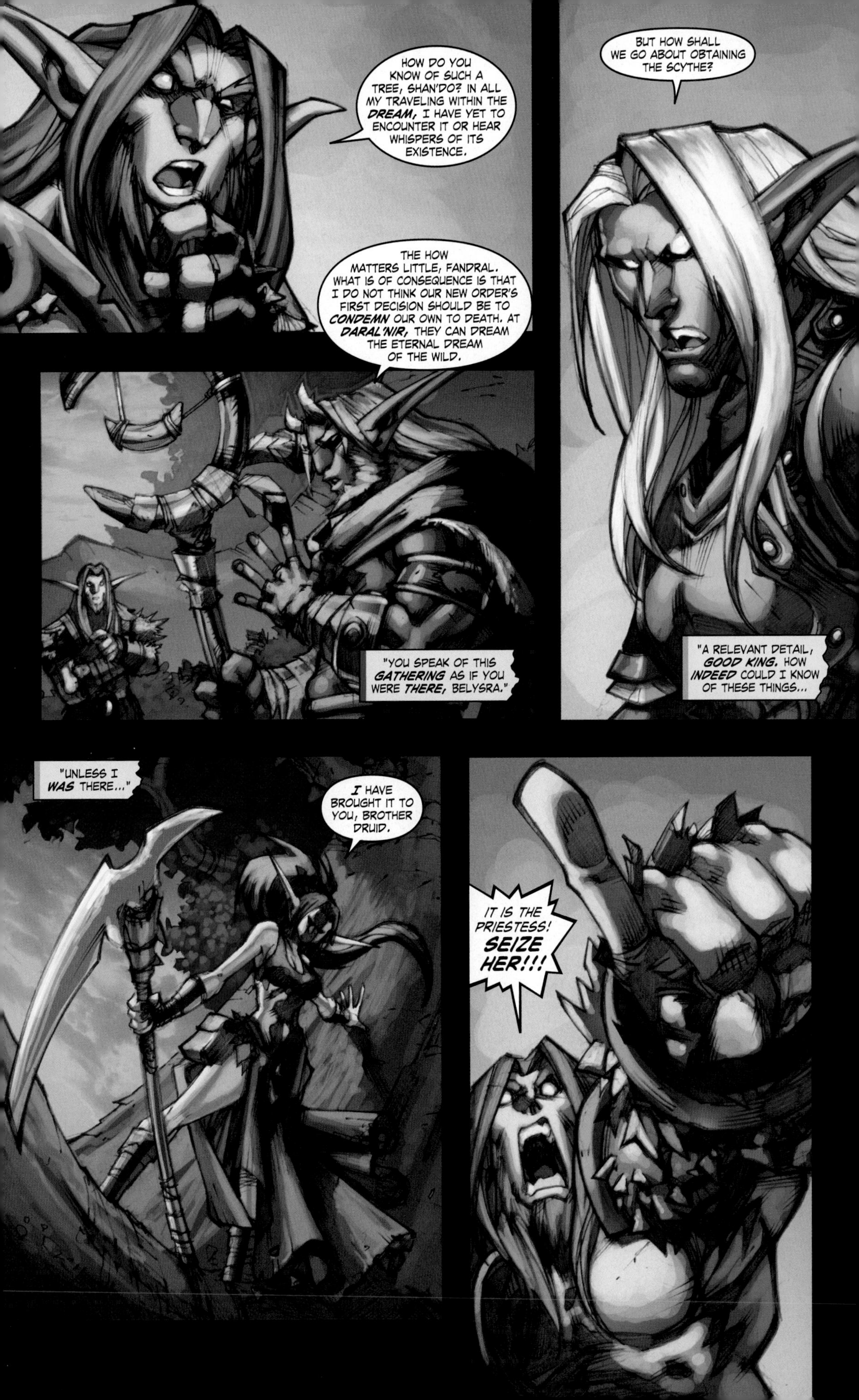

HOW DO YOU KNOW OF SUCH A TREE, SHAN'DO? IN ALL MY TRAVELING WITHIN THE *DREAM,* I HAVE YET TO ENCOUNTER IT OR HEAR WHISPERS OF ITS EXISTENCE.
THE HOW MATTERS LITTLE, FANDRAL. WHAT IS OF CONSEQUENCE IS THAT I DO NOT THINK OUR NEW ORDER'S FIRST DECISION SHOULD BE TO *CONDEMN* OUR OWN TO DEATH. AT *DARAL'NIR,* THEY CAN DREAM THE ETERNAL DREAM OF THE WILD.
BUT HOW SHALL WE GO ABOUT OBTAINING THE SCYTHE?
"YOU SPEAK OF THIS *GATHERING* AS IF YOU WERE *THERE,* BELYSRA."
"A RELEVANT DETAIL, *GOOD KING.* HOW *INDEED* COULD I KNOW OF THESE THINGS...
"UNLESS I *WAS* THERE..."
I HAVE BROUGHT IT TO YOU, BROTHER DRUID.
IT IS THE PRIESTESS! **SEIZE HER!!!**

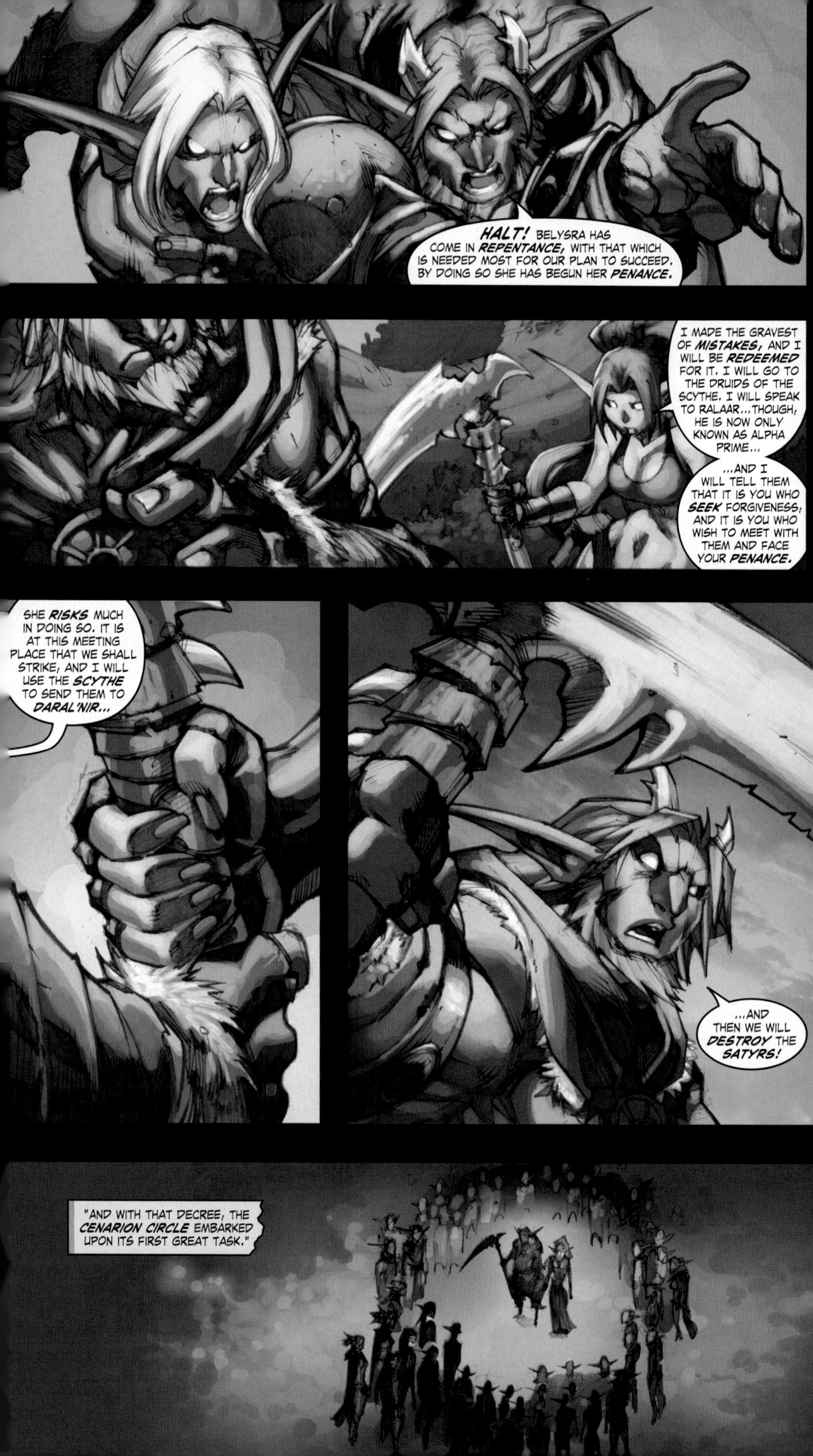
HALT! BELYSRA HAS COME IN REPENTANCE, WITH THAT WHICH IS NEEDED MOST FOR OUR PLAN TO SUCCEED. BY DOING SO SHE HAS BEGUN HER PENANCE.
I MADE THE GRAVEST OF MISTAKES, AND I WILL BE REDEEMED FOR IT. I WILL GO TO THE DRUIDS OF THE SCYTHE. I WILL SPEAK TO RALAAR...THOUGH, HE IS NOW ONLY KNOWN AS ALPHA PRIME...
...AND I WILL TELL THEM THAT IT IS YOU WHO SEEK FORGIVENESS, AND IT IS YOU WHO WISH TO MEET WITH THEM AND FACE YOUR PENANCE.
SHE RISKS MUCH IN DOING SO. IT IS AT THIS MEETING PLACE THAT WE SHALL STRIKE, AND I WILL USE THE SCYTHE TO SEND THEM TO DARAL'NIR...
...AND THEN WE WILL DESTROY THE SATYRS!
"AND WITH THAT DECREE, THE CENARION CIRCLE EMBARKED UPON ITS FIRST GREAT TASK."

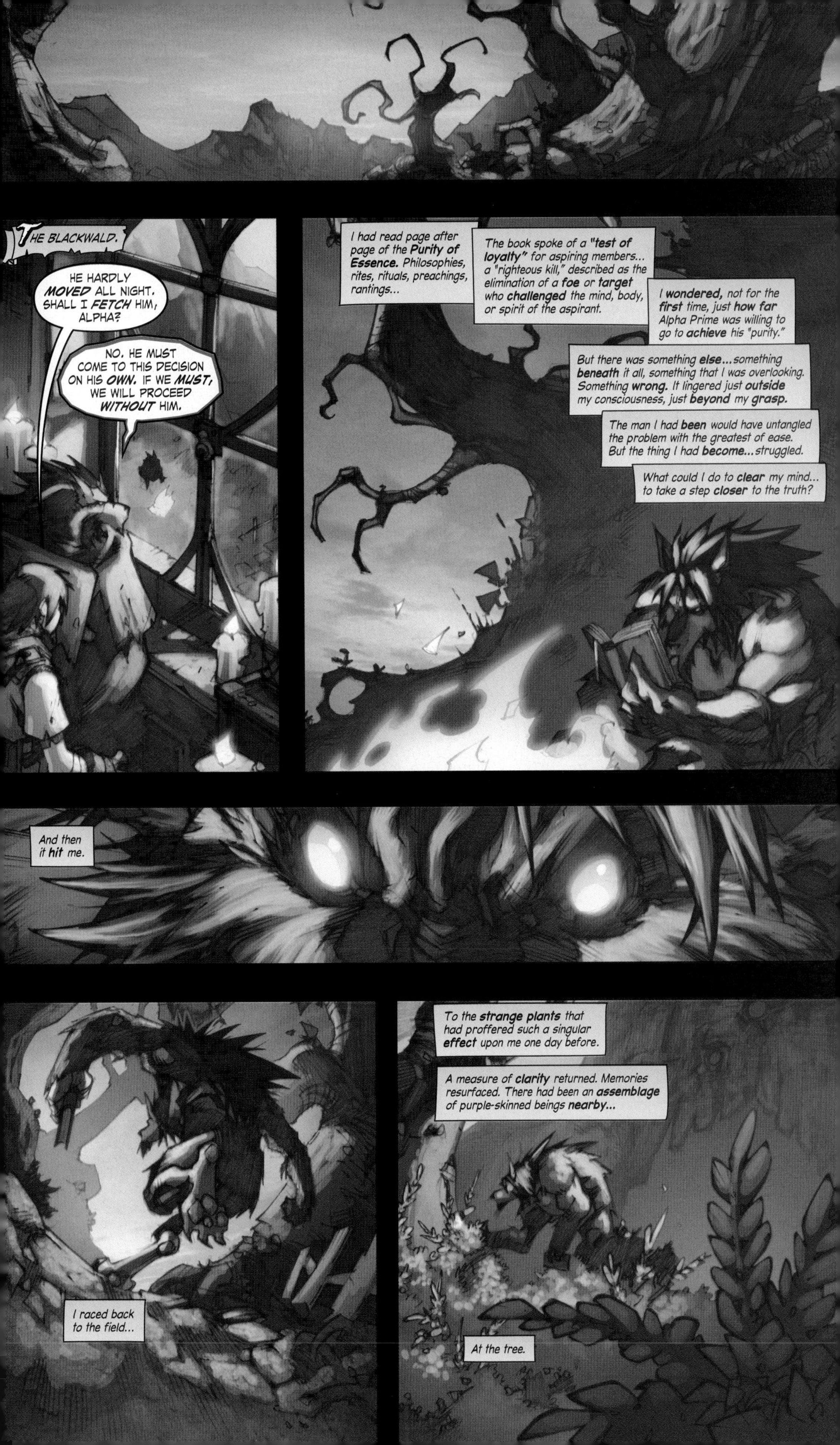
THE BLACKWALD.
HE HARDLY MOVED ALL NIGHT. SHALL I FETCH HIM, ALPHA?
NO. HE MUST COME TO THIS DECISION ON HIS OWN. IF WE MUST, WE WILL PROCEED WITHOUT HIM.
I had read page after page of the Purity of Essence. Philosophies, rites, rituals, preachings, rantings...
The book spoke of a "test of loyalty" for aspiring members... a "righteous kill," described as the elimination of a foe or target who challenged the mind, body, or spirit of the aspirant.
I wondered, not for the first time, just how far Alpha Prime was willing to go to achieve his "purity."
But there was something else... something beneath it all, something that I was overlooking. Something wrong. It lingered just outside my consciousness, just beyond my grasp.
The man I had been would have untangled the problem with the greatest of ease. But the thing I had become... struggled.
What could I do to clear my mind... to take a step closer to the truth?
And then it hit me.
I raced back to the field...
To the strange plants that had proffered such a singular effect upon me one day before.
A measure of clarity returned. Memories resurfaced. There had been an assemblage of purple-skinned beings nearby...
At the tree.

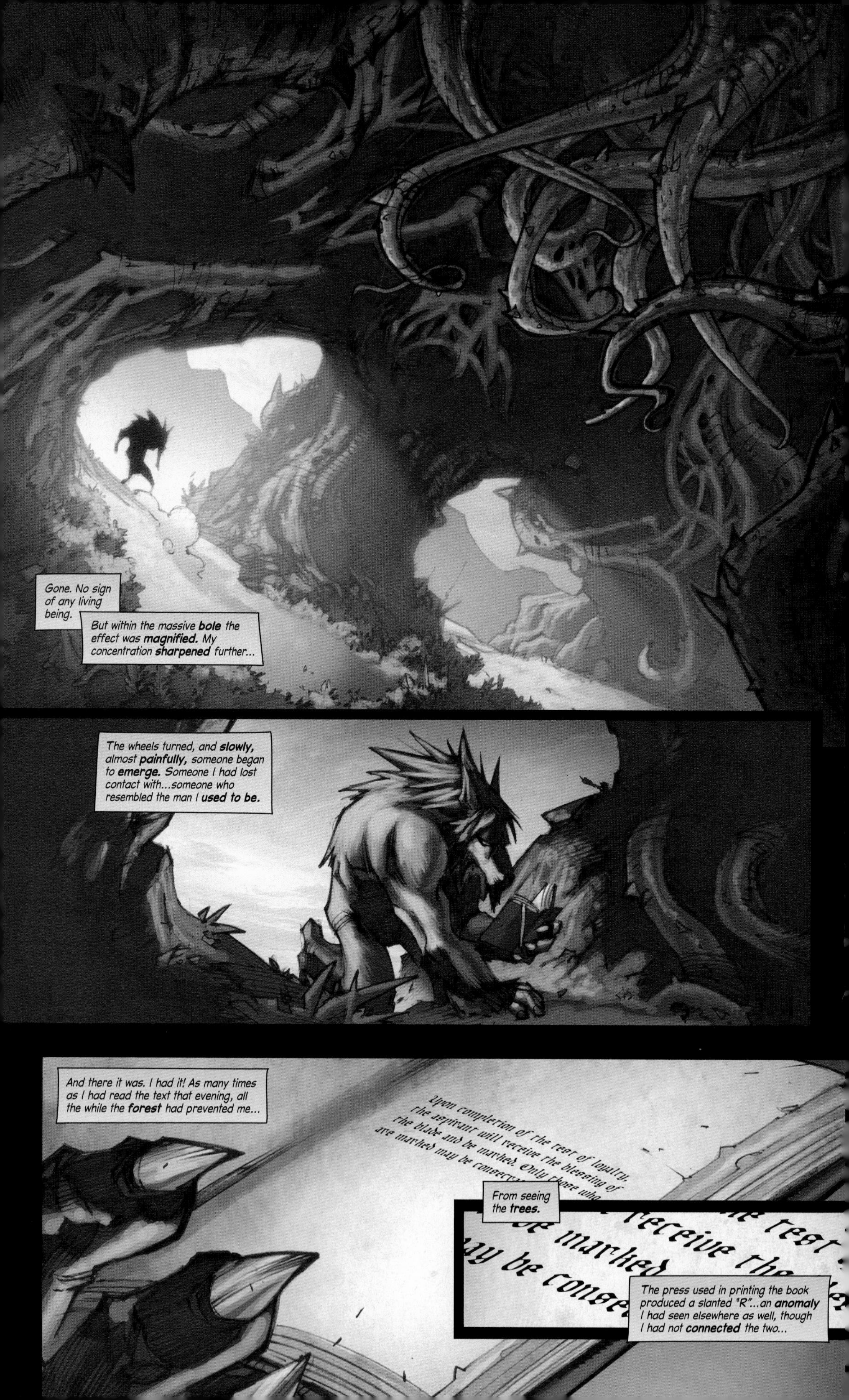
Gone. No sign of any living being.
But within the massive **bole** the effect was **magnified.** My concentration **sharpened** further...
The wheels turned, and **slowly,** almost **painfully,** someone began to **emerge.** Someone I had lost contact with...someone who resembled the man I **used to be.**
And there it was. I had it! As many times as I had read the text that evening, all the while the **forest** had prevented me...
Upon completion of the test of loyalty,
the aspirant will receive the blessing of
the blade and be marked.
From seeing the **trees.**
The press used in printing the book produced a slanted "R"...an **anomaly** I had seen elsewhere as well, though I had not **connected** the two...

CHAPTER 4 Cover by Glenn Rane

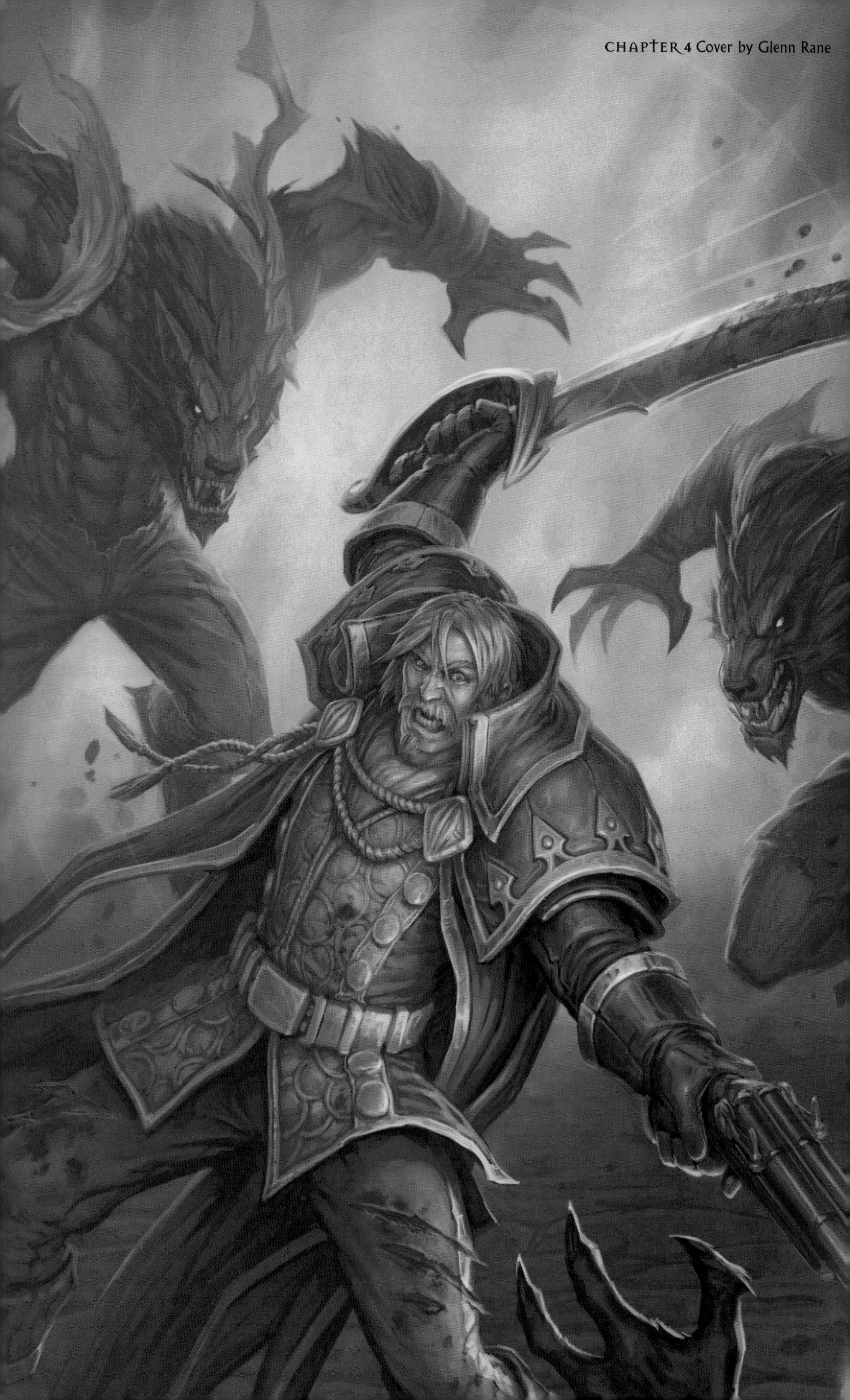

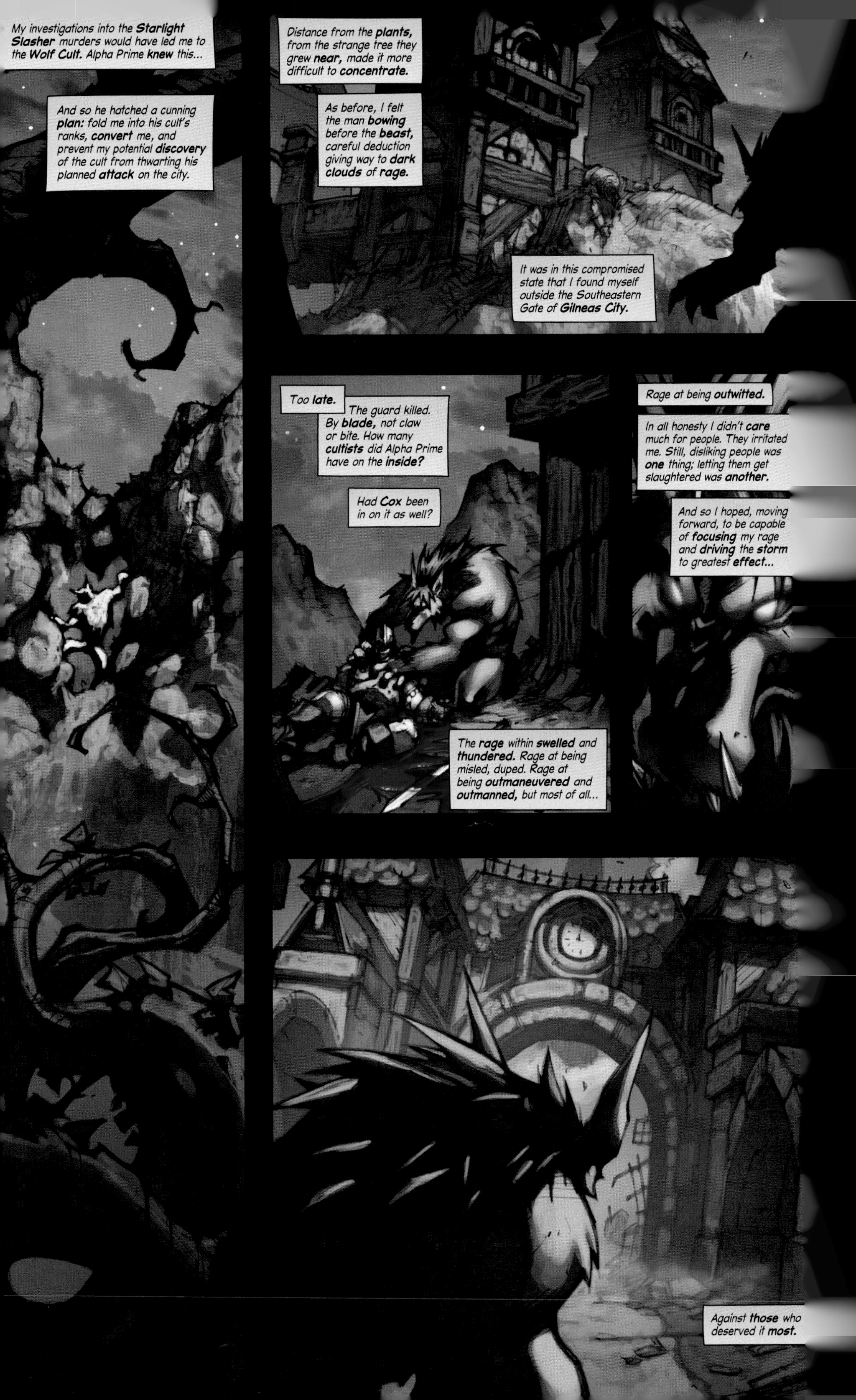
My investigations into the Starlight Slasher murders would have led me to the Wolf Cult. Alpha Prime knew this...
And so he hatched a cunning plan: fold me into his cult's ranks, convert me, and prevent my potential discovery of the cult from thwarting his planned attack on the city.
Distance from the plants, from the strange tree they grew near, made it more difficult to concentrate.
As before, I felt the man bowing before the beast, careful deduction giving way to dark clouds of rage.
It was in this compromised state that I found myself outside the Southeastern Gate of Gilneas City.
Too late.
The guard killed. By blade, not claw or bite. How many cultists did Alpha Prime have on the inside?
Had Cox been in on it as well?
The rage within swelled and thundered. Rage at being misled, duped. Rage at being outmaneuvered and outmanned, but most of all...
Rage at being outwitted.
In all honesty I didn't care much for people. They irritated me. Still, disliking people was one thing; letting them get slaughtered was another.
And so I hoped, moving forward, to be capable of focusing my rage and driving the storm to greatest effect...
Against those who deserved it most.

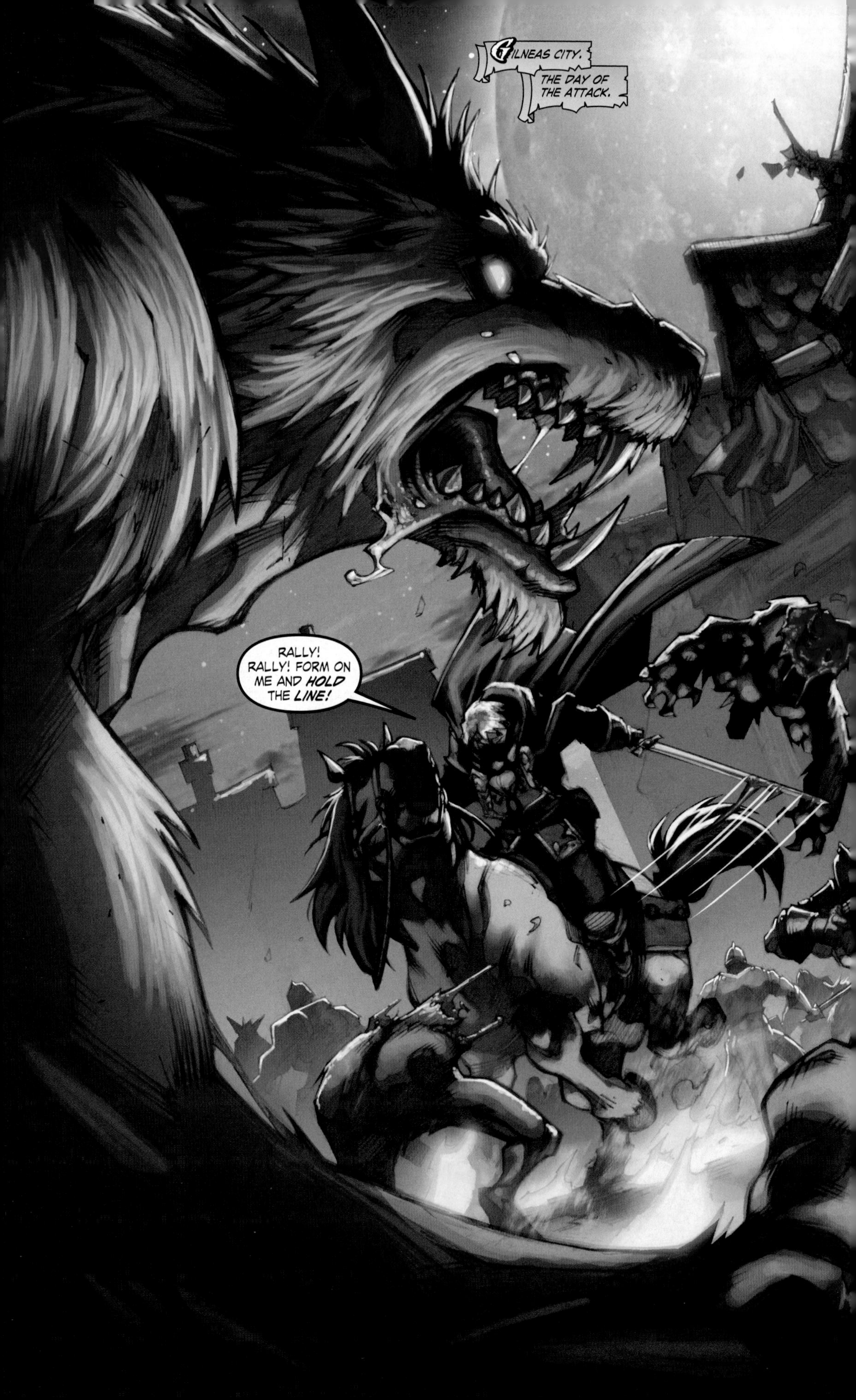
GILNEAS CITY.
THE DAY OF THE ATTACK.
RALLY! RALLY! FORM ON ME AND HOLD THE LINE!

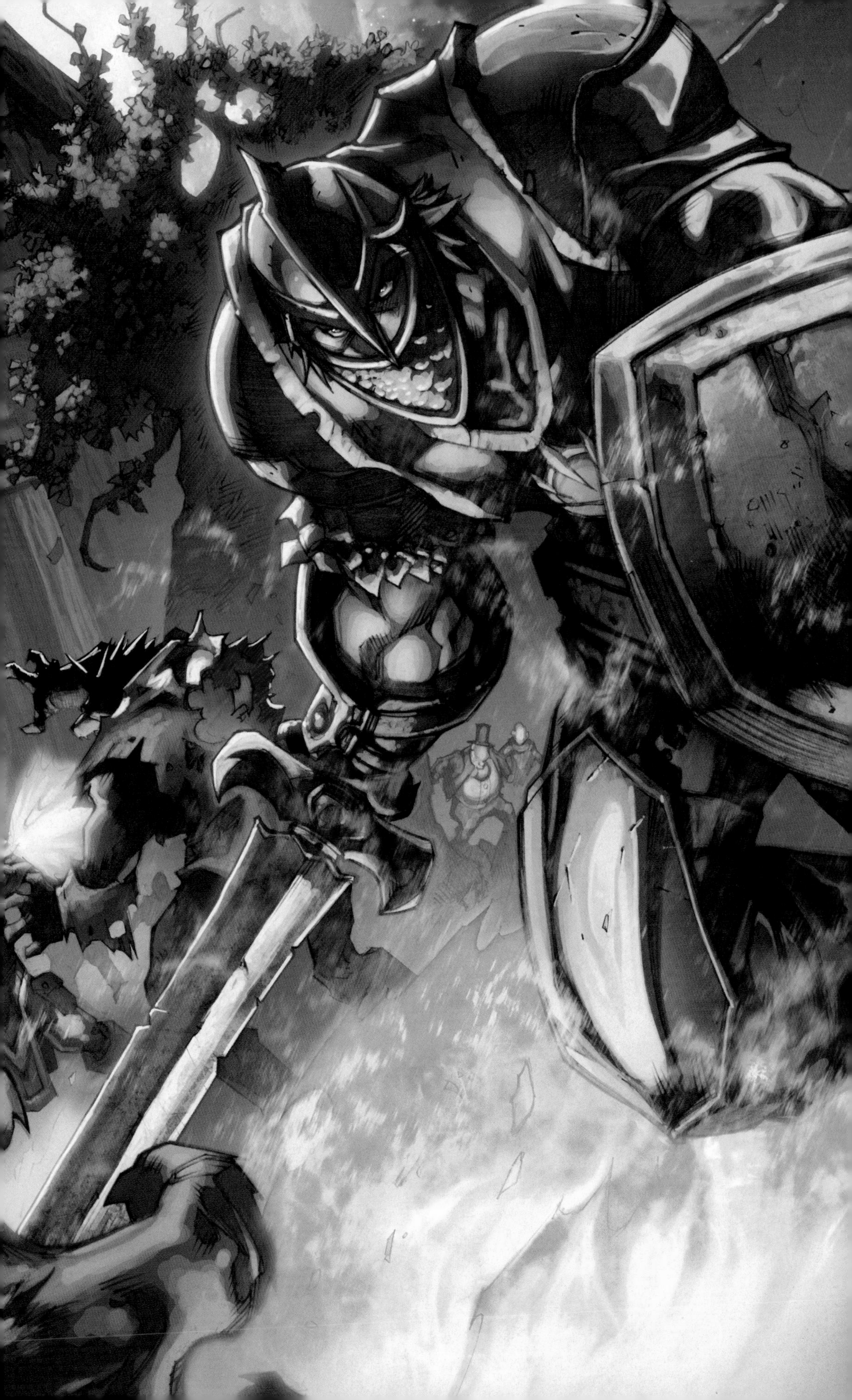

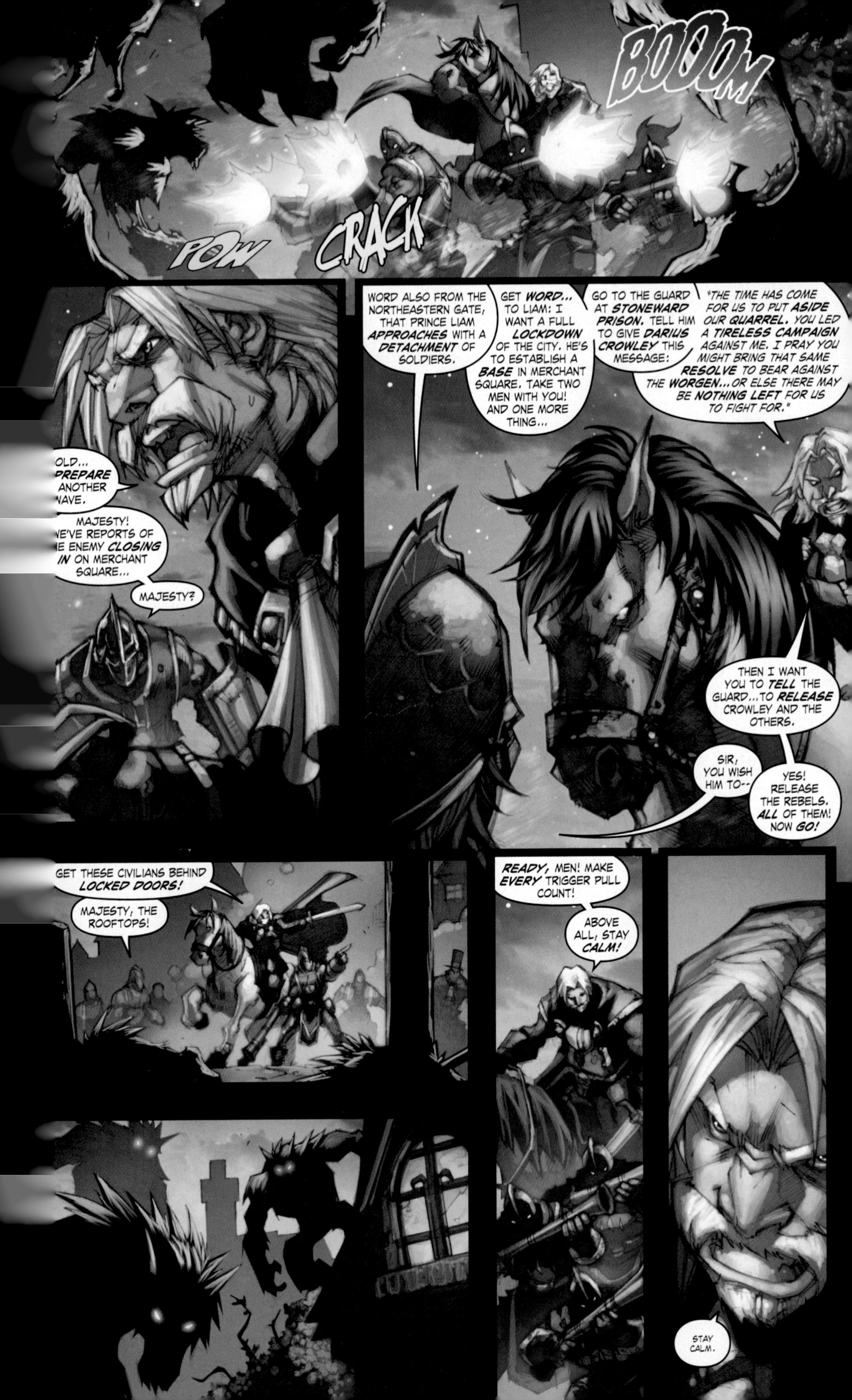
BOOOM
POW
CRACK
...OLD... ...PREPARE ...ANOTHER ...WAVE.
MAJESTY! ...WE'VE REPORTS OF ...E ENEMY CLOSING IN ON MERCHANT SQUARE...
MAJESTY?
WORD ALSO FROM THE NORTHEASTERN GATE, THAT PRINCE LIAM APPROACHES WITH A DETACHMENT OF SOLDIERS.
GET WORD... TO LIAM: I WANT A FULL LOCKDOWN OF THE CITY. HE'S TO ESTABLISH A BASE IN MERCHANT SQUARE. TAKE TWO MEN WITH YOU! AND ONE MORE THING...
GO TO THE GUARD AT STONEWARD PRISON. TELL HIM TO GIVE DARIUS CROWLEY THIS MESSAGE:
"THE TIME HAS COME FOR US TO PUT ASIDE OUR QUARREL. YOU LED A TIRELESS CAMPAIGN AGAINST ME. I PRAY YOU MIGHT BRING THAT SAME RESOLVE TO BEAR AGAINST THE WORGEN...OR ELSE THERE MAY BE NOTHING LEFT FOR US TO FIGHT FOR."
THEN I WANT YOU TO TELL THE GUARD...TO RELEASE CROWLEY AND THE OTHERS.
SIR, YOU WISH HIM TO--
YES! RELEASE THE REBELS. ALL OF THEM! NOW GO!
GET THESE CIVILIANS BEHIND LOCKED DOORS!
MAJESTY, THE ROOFTOPS!
READY, MEN! MAKE EVERY TRIGGER PULL COUNT!
ABOVE ALL, STAY CALM!
STAY CALM.

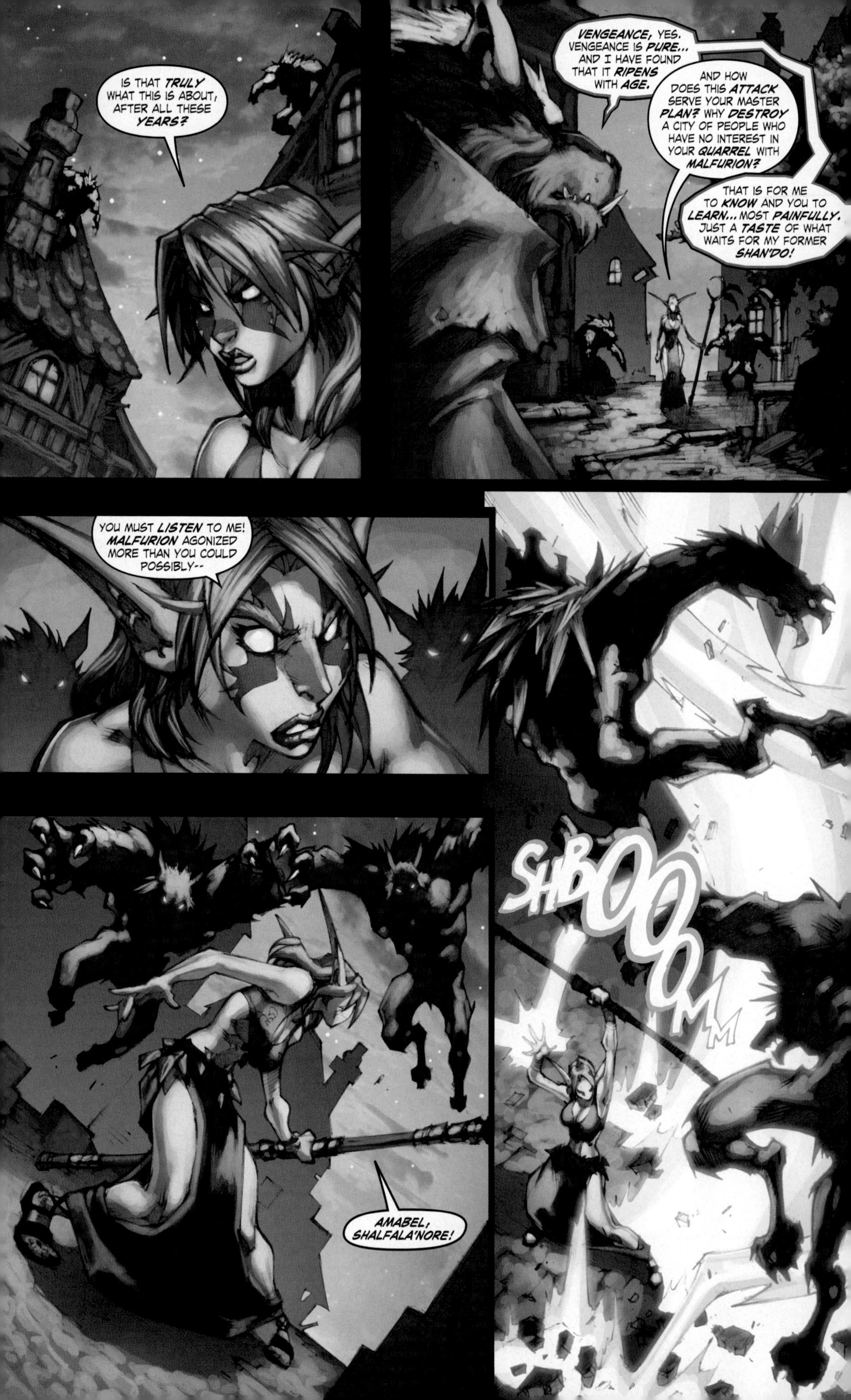
IS THAT TRULY WHAT THIS IS ABOUT, AFTER ALL THESE YEARS?
VENGEANCE, YES. VENGEANCE IS PURE... AND I HAVE FOUND THAT IT RIPENS WITH AGE.
AND HOW DOES THIS ATTACK SERVE YOUR MASTER PLAN? WHY DESTROY A CITY OF PEOPLE WHO HAVE NO INTEREST IN YOUR QUARREL WITH MALFURION?
THAT IS FOR ME TO KNOW AND YOU TO LEARN... MOST PAINFULLY. JUST A TASTE OF WHAT WAITS FOR MY FORMER SHAN'DO!
YOU MUST LISTEN TO ME! MALFURION AGONIZED MORE THAN YOU COULD POSSIBLY--
AMABEL, SHALFALA'NORE!
SHBOOOOMM

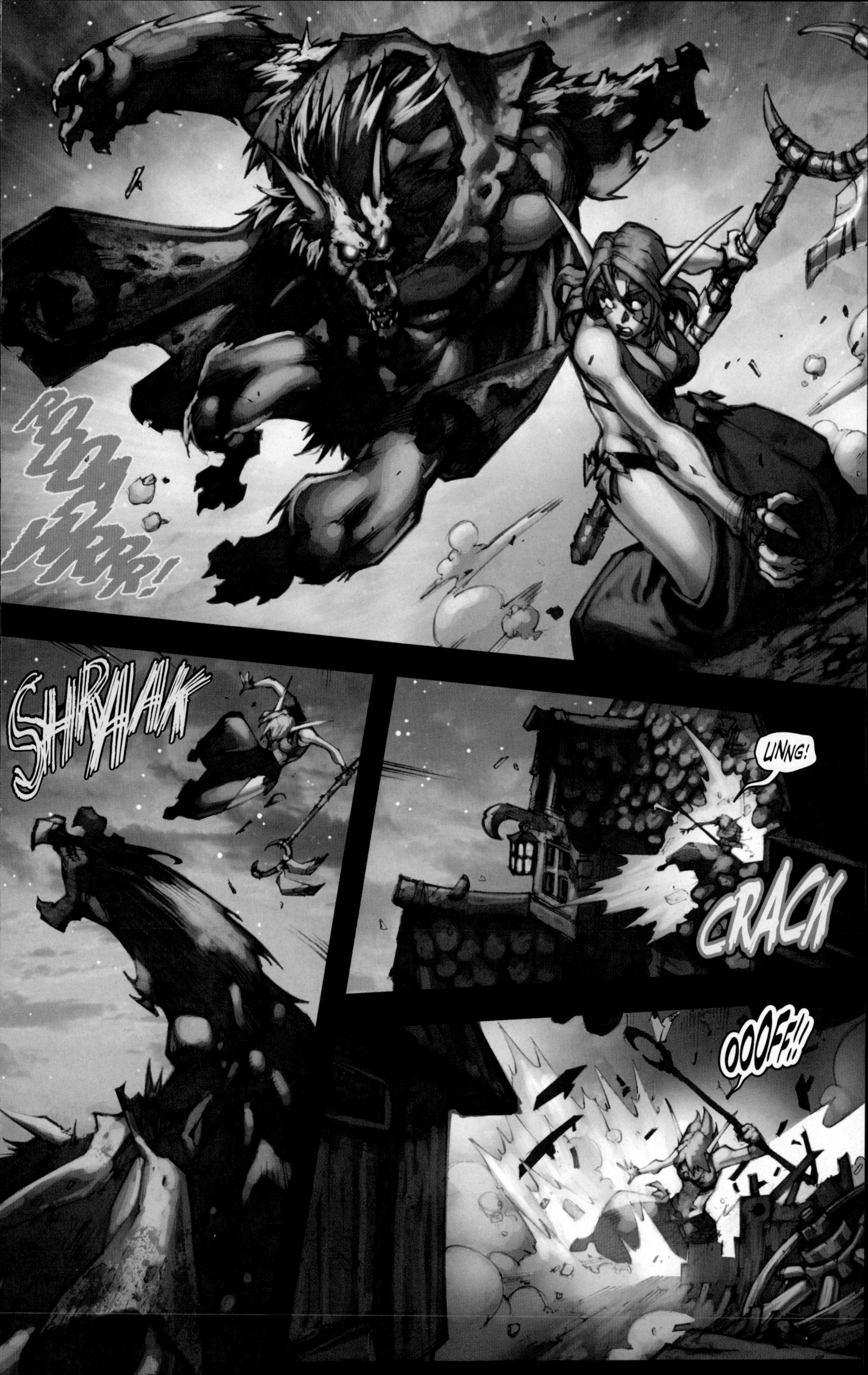
ROOOAHRRR!
SHRAAK
UNNG!
CRACK
OOOFF!!

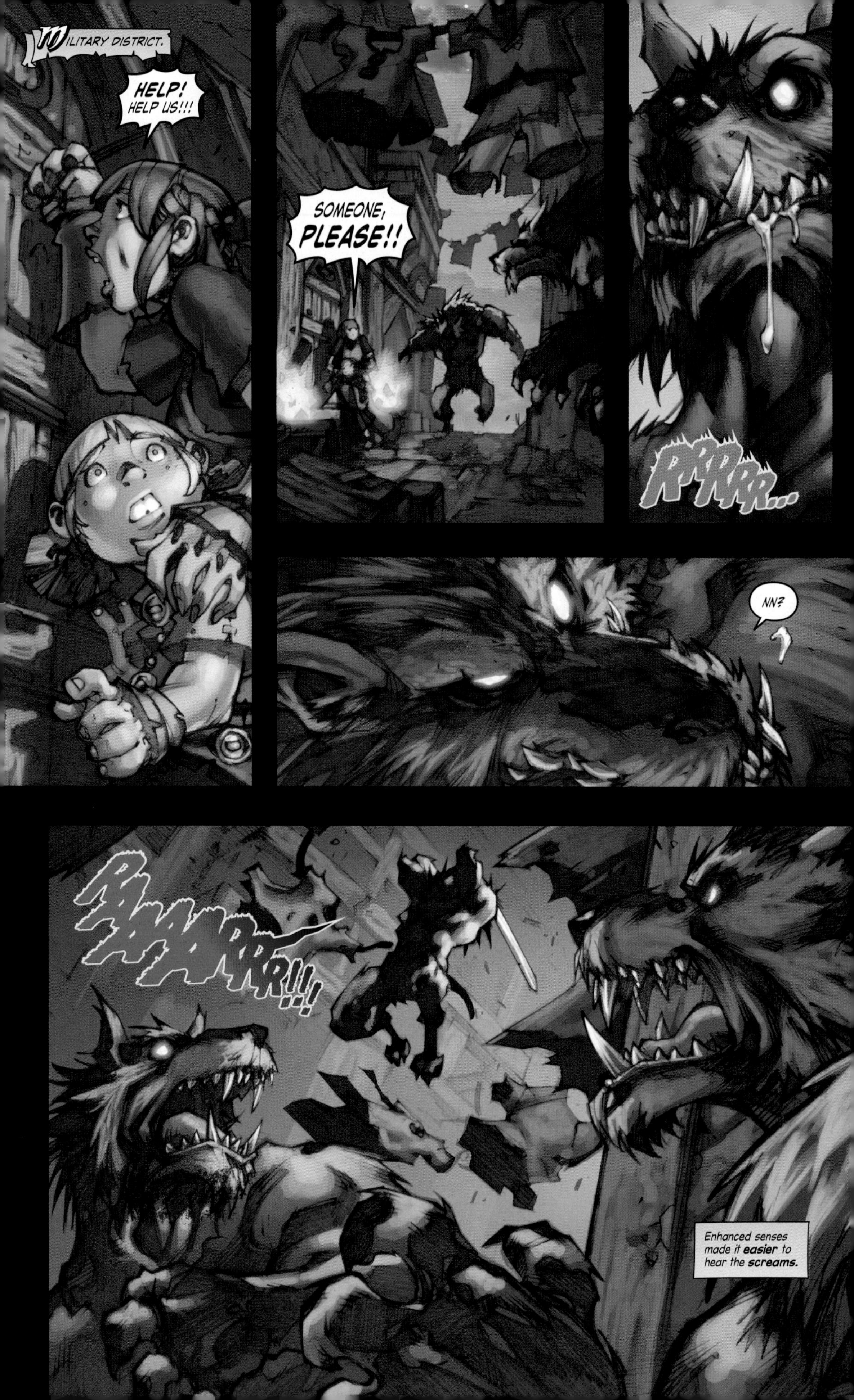
MILITARY DISTRICT.
HELP! HELP US!!!
SOMEONE, PLEASE!!
RRRRRR...
NN?
RAAARRRRRR!!!
Enhanced senses made it easier to hear the screams.

SLUNKT

A *fallen* officer's *sword* dispatched the *first* of them.

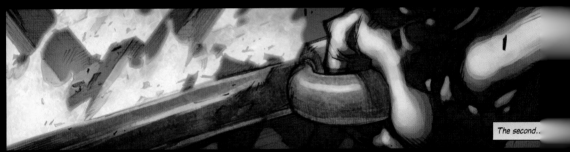

The second...

KUSSHHH

RAAAGGGHH!!

Met a much more *painful* demise.

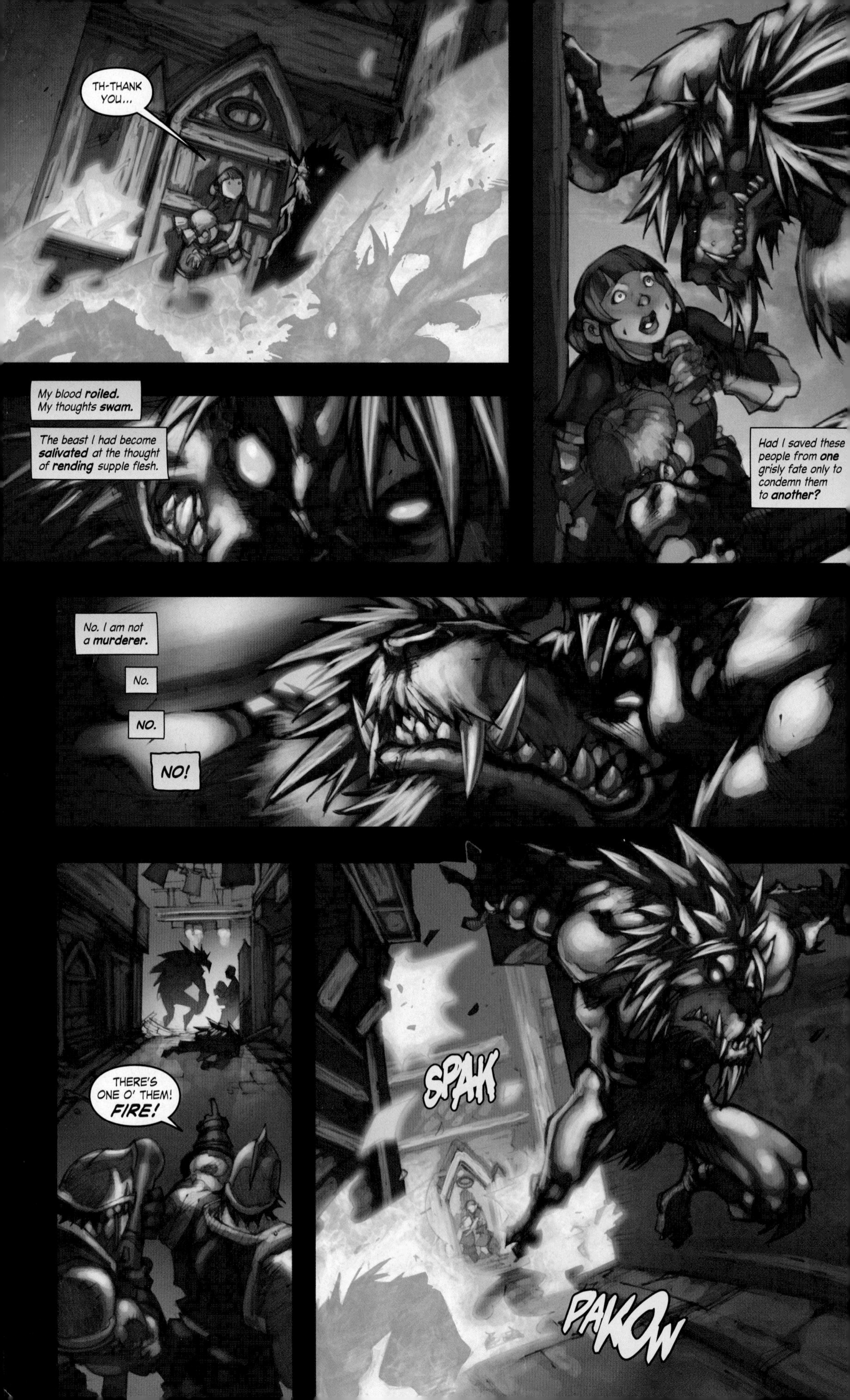

TH-THANK YOU...
My blood roiled. My thoughts swam.
The beast I had become salivated at the thought of rending supple flesh.
Had I saved these people from one grisly fate only to condemn them to another?
No. I am not a murderer.
No.
NO.
NO!
THERE'S ONE O' THEM! FIRE!
SPAK
PAKOW

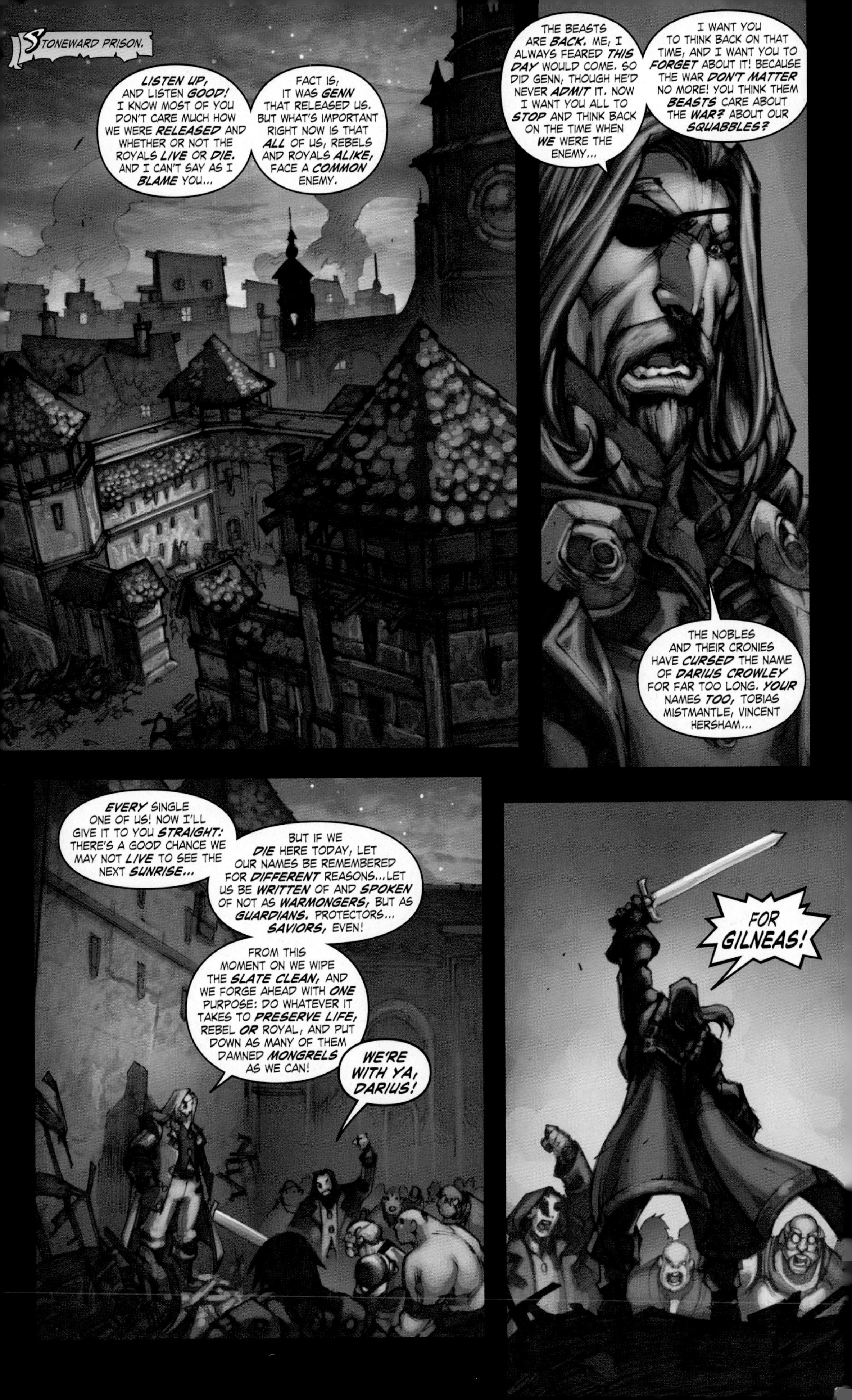
STONEWARD PRISON.
LISTEN UP, AND LISTEN GOOD! I KNOW MOST OF YOU DON'T CARE MUCH HOW WE WERE RELEASED AND WHETHER OR NOT THE ROYALS LIVE OR DIE. AND I CAN'T SAY AS I BLAME YOU...
FACT IS, IT WAS GENN THAT RELEASED US. BUT WHAT'S IMPORTANT RIGHT NOW IS THAT ALL OF US, REBELS AND ROYALS ALIKE, FACE A COMMON ENEMY.
THE BEASTS ARE BACK. ME, I ALWAYS FEARED THIS DAY WOULD COME. SO DID GENN, THOUGH HE'D NEVER ADMIT IT. NOW I WANT YOU ALL TO STOP AND THINK BACK ON THE TIME WHEN WE WERE THE ENEMY...
I WANT YOU TO THINK BACK ON THAT TIME, AND I WANT YOU TO FORGET ABOUT IT! BECAUSE THE WAR DON'T MATTER NO MORE! YOU THINK THEM BEASTS CARE ABOUT THE WAR? ABOUT OUR SQUABBLES?
THE NOBLES AND THEIR CRONIES HAVE CURSED THE NAME OF DARIUS CROWLEY FOR FAR TOO LONG. YOUR NAMES TOO, TOBIAS MISTMANTLE, VINCENT HERSHAM...
EVERY SINGLE ONE OF US! NOW I'LL GIVE IT TO YOU STRAIGHT: THERE'S A GOOD CHANCE WE MAY NOT LIVE TO SEE THE NEXT SUNRISE...
BUT IF WE DIE HERE TODAY, LET OUR NAMES BE REMEMBERED FOR DIFFERENT REASONS...LET US BE WRITTEN OF AND SPOKEN OF NOT AS WARMONGERS, BUT AS GUARDIANS. PROTECTORS... SAVIORS, EVEN!
FROM THIS MOMENT ON WE WIPE THE SLATE CLEAN, AND WE FORGE AHEAD WITH ONE PURPOSE: DO WHATEVER IT TAKES TO PRESERVE LIFE, REBEL OR ROYAL, AND PUT DOWN AS MANY OF THEM DAMNED MONGRELS AS WE CAN!
WE'RE WITH YA, DARIUS!
FOR GILNEAS!

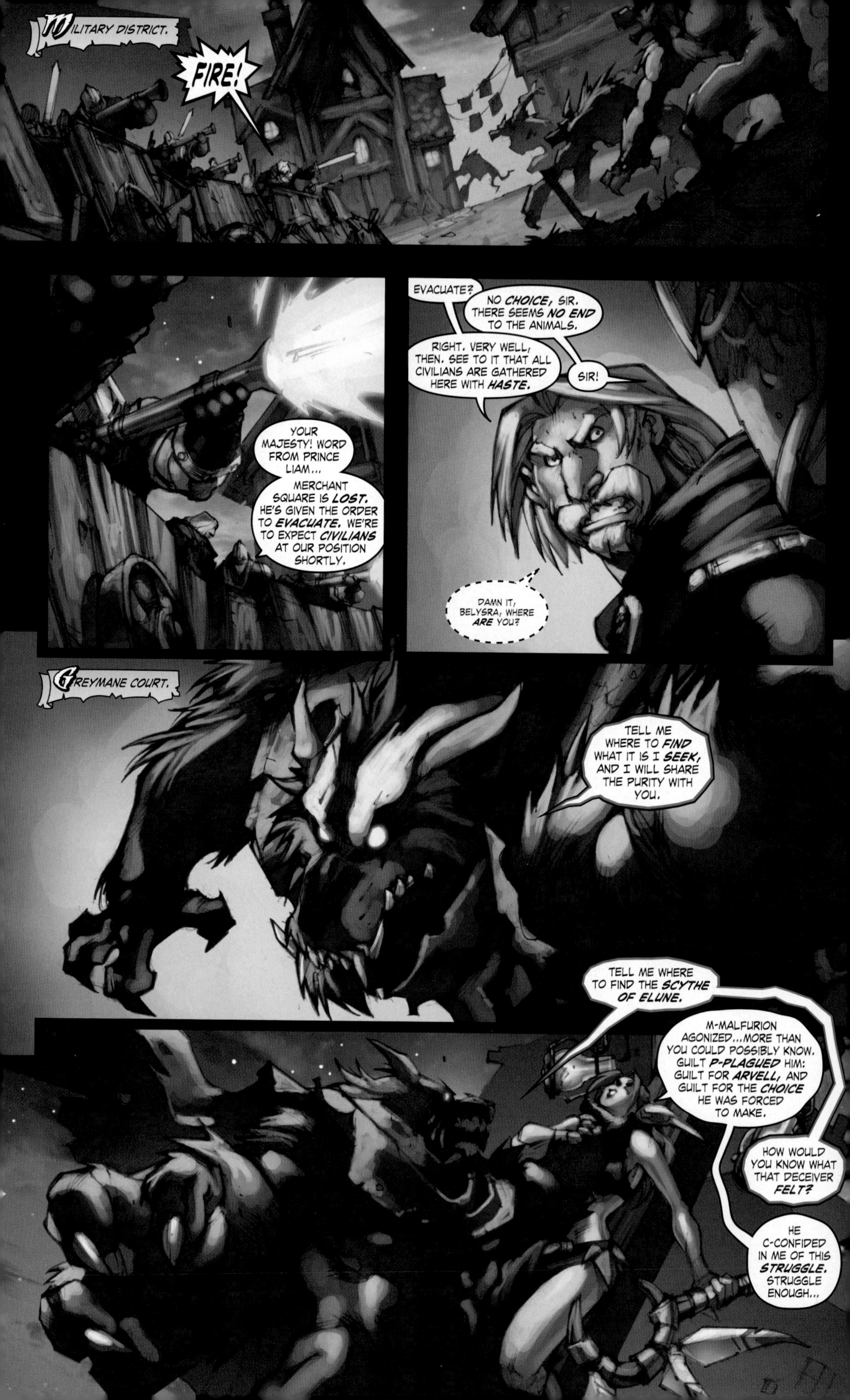
MILITARY DISTRICT.
FIRE!
YOUR MAJESTY! WORD FROM PRINCE LIAM...
MERCHANT SQUARE IS LOST. HE'S GIVEN THE ORDER TO EVACUATE. WE'RE TO EXPECT CIVILIANS AT OUR POSITION SHORTLY.
EVACUATE?
NO CHOICE, SIR. THERE SEEMS NO END TO THE ANIMALS.
RIGHT. VERY WELL, THEN. SEE TO IT THAT ALL CIVILIANS ARE GATHERED HERE WITH HASTE.
SIR!
DAMN IT, BELYSRA, WHERE ARE YOU?
GREYMANE COURT.
TELL ME WHERE TO FIND WHAT IT IS I SEEK, AND I WILL SHARE THE PURITY WITH YOU.
TELL ME WHERE TO FIND THE SCYTHE OF ELUNE.
M-MALFURION AGONIZED...MORE THAN YOU COULD POSSIBLY KNOW. GUILT P-PLAGUED HIM: GUILT FOR ARVELL, AND GUILT FOR THE CHOICE HE WAS FORCED TO MAKE.
HOW WOULD YOU KNOW WHAT THAT DECEIVER FELT?
HE C-CONFIDED IN ME OF THIS STRUGGLE. STRUGGLE ENOUGH...

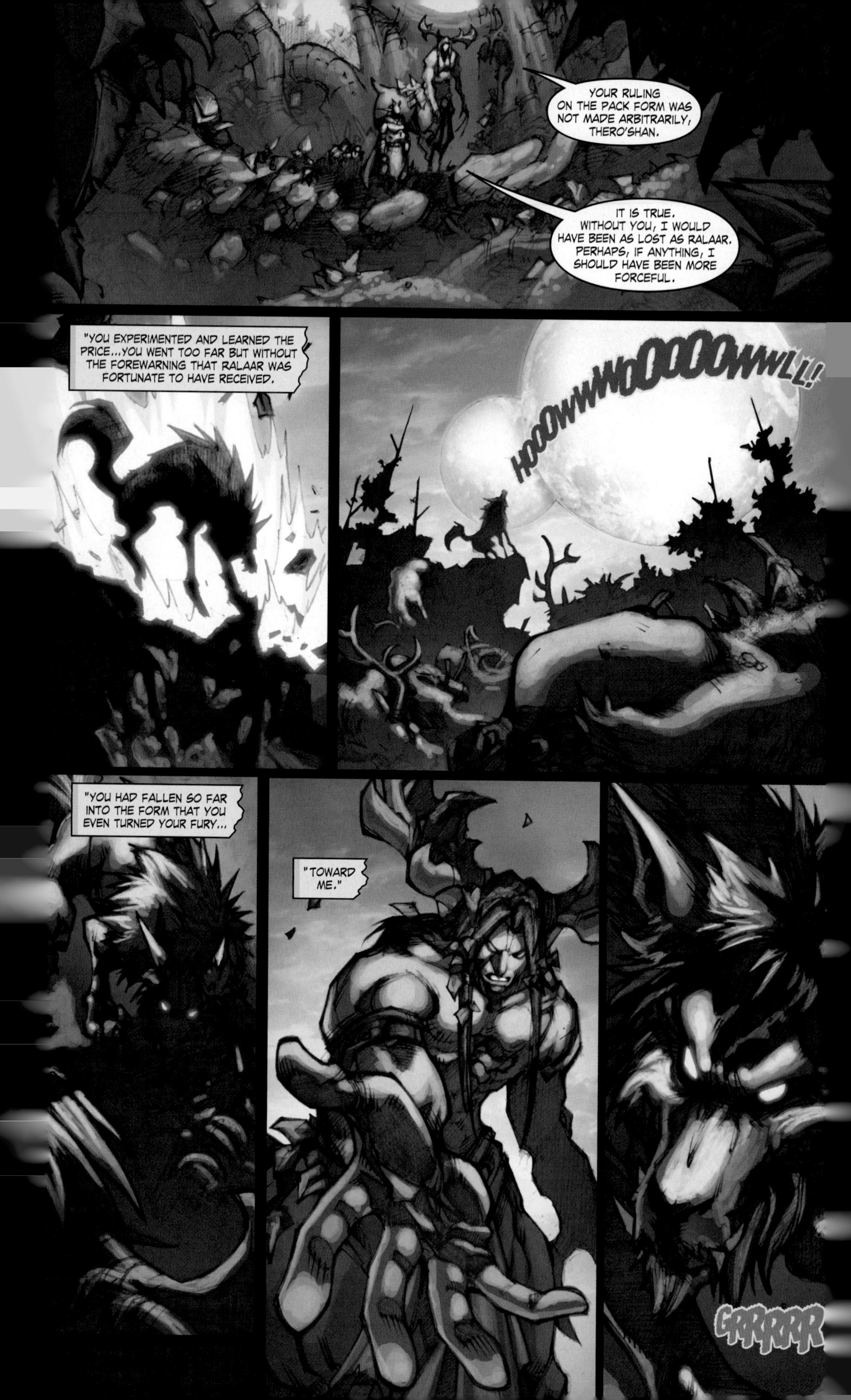
YOUR RULING ON THE PACK FORM WAS NOT MADE ARBITRARILY, THERO'SHAN.
IT IS TRUE. WITHOUT YOU, I WOULD HAVE BEEN AS LOST AS RALAAR. PERHAPS, IF ANYTHING, I SHOULD HAVE BEEN MORE FORCEFUL.
"YOU EXPERIMENTED AND LEARNED THE PRICE...YOU WENT TOO FAR BUT WITHOUT THE FOREWARNING THAT RALAAR WAS FORTUNATE TO HAVE RECEIVED.
HOOOWWWOOOOOOWWLL!
"YOU HAD FALLEN SO FAR INTO THE FORM THAT YOU EVEN TURNED YOUR FURY...
"TOWARD ME."
GRRRRRR

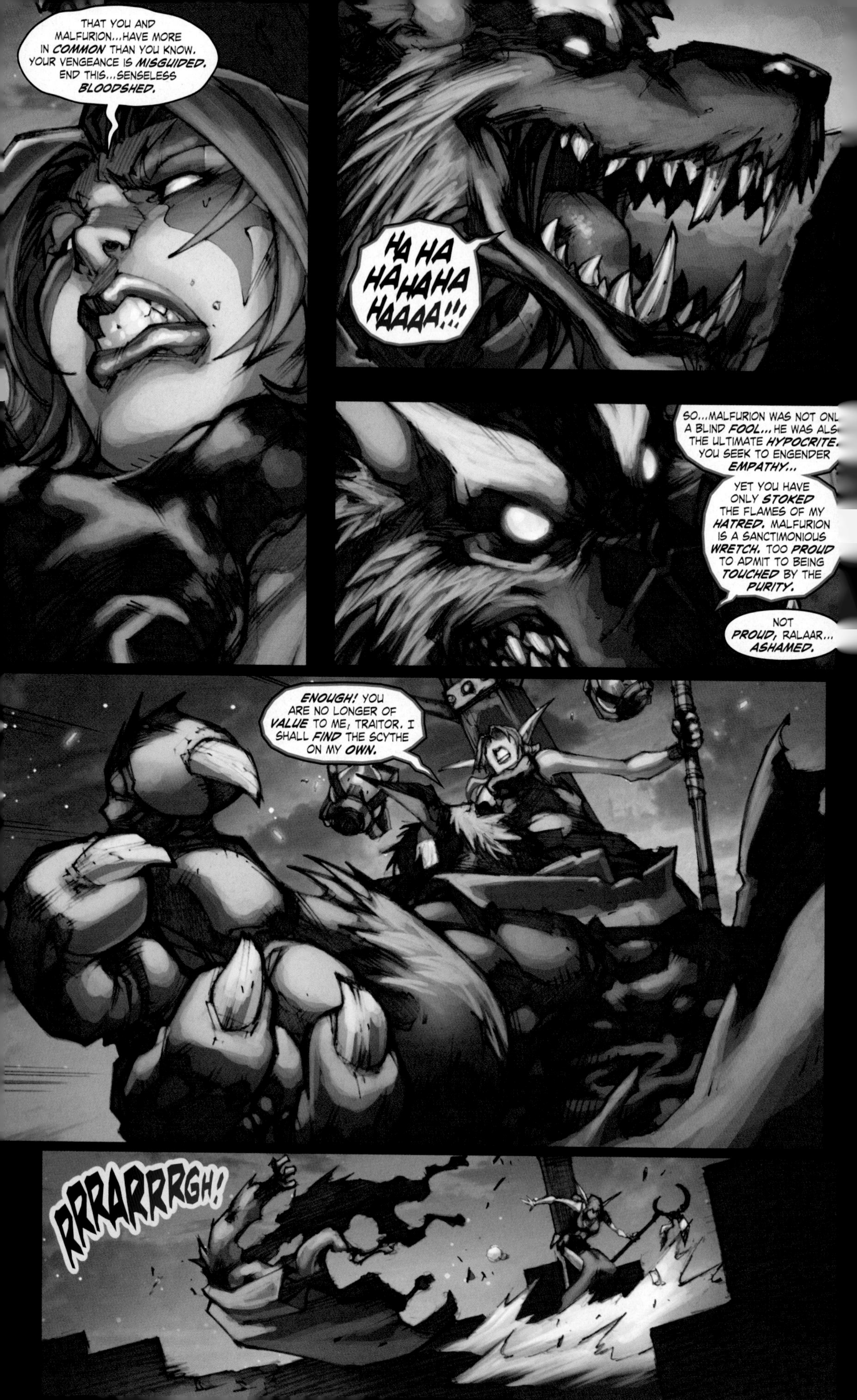
THAT YOU AND MALFURION...HAVE MORE IN COMMON THAN YOU KNOW. YOUR VENGEANCE IS MISGUIDED. END THIS...SENSELESS BLOODSHED.
HA HA HAHAHA HAAAA!!!
SO...MALFURION WAS NOT ONL A BLIND FOOL...HE WAS ALS THE ULTIMATE HYPOCRITE. YOU SEEK TO ENGENDER EMPATHY...
YET YOU HAVE ONLY STOKED THE FLAMES OF MY HATRED. MALFURION IS A SANCTIMONIOUS WRETCH. TOO PROUD TO ADMIT TO BEING TOUCHED BY THE PURITY.
NOT PROUD, RALAAR... ASHAMED.
ENOUGH! YOU ARE NO LONGER OF VALUE TO ME, TRAITOR. I SHALL FIND THE SCYTHE ON MY OWN.
RRRARRRGH!

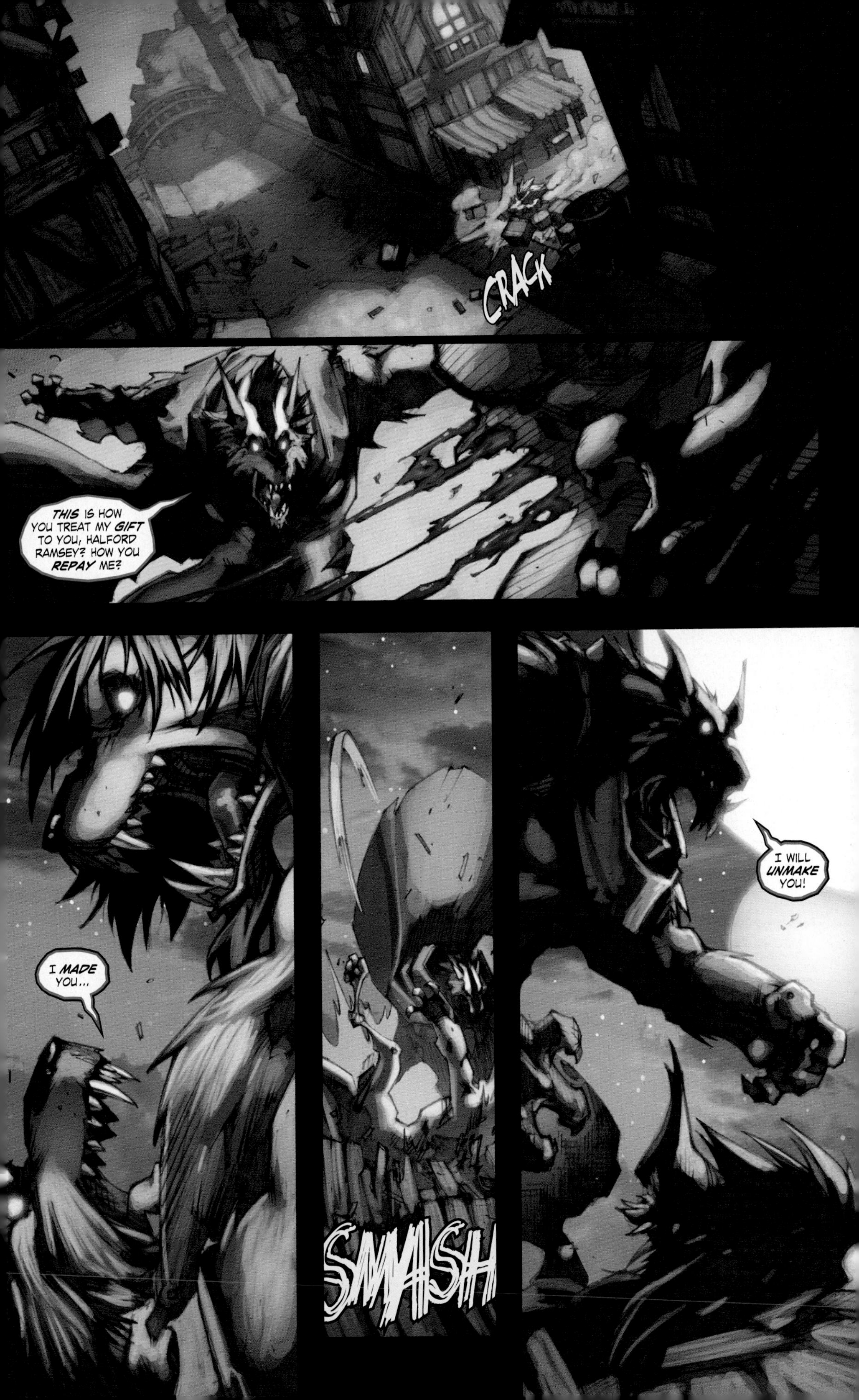
CRACK
THIS IS HOW YOU TREAT MY GIFT TO YOU, HALFORD RAMSEY? HOW YOU REPAY ME?
I MADE YOU...
SMASH
I WILL UNMAKE YOU!

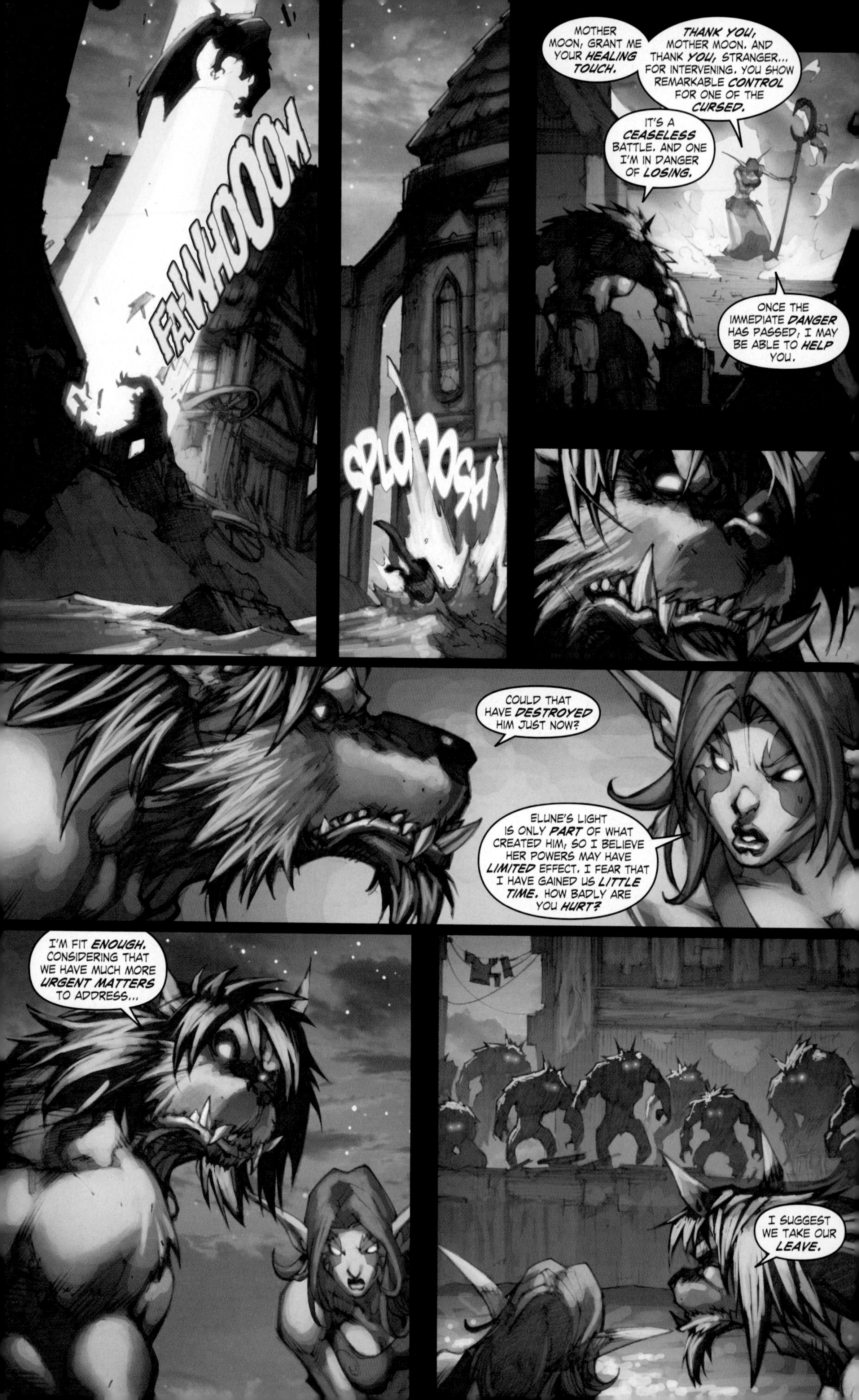
FA-WHOOOM
SPLOOOSH
MOTHER MOON, GRANT ME YOUR HEALING TOUCH.
THANK YOU, MOTHER MOON. AND THANK YOU, STRANGER... FOR INTERVENING. YOU SHOW REMARKABLE CONTROL FOR ONE OF THE CURSED.
IT'S A CEASELESS BATTLE. AND ONE I'M IN DANGER OF LOSING.
ONCE THE IMMEDIATE DANGER HAS PASSED, I MAY BE ABLE TO HELP YOU.
COULD THAT HAVE DESTROYED HIM JUST NOW?
ELUNE'S LIGHT IS ONLY PART OF WHAT CREATED HIM, SO I BELIEVE HER POWERS MAY HAVE LIMITED EFFECT. I FEAR THAT I HAVE GAINED US LITTLE TIME. HOW BADLY ARE YOU HURT?
I'M FIT ENOUGH. CONSIDERING THAT WE HAVE MUCH MORE URGENT MATTERS TO ADDRESS...
I SUGGEST WE TAKE OUR LEAVE.

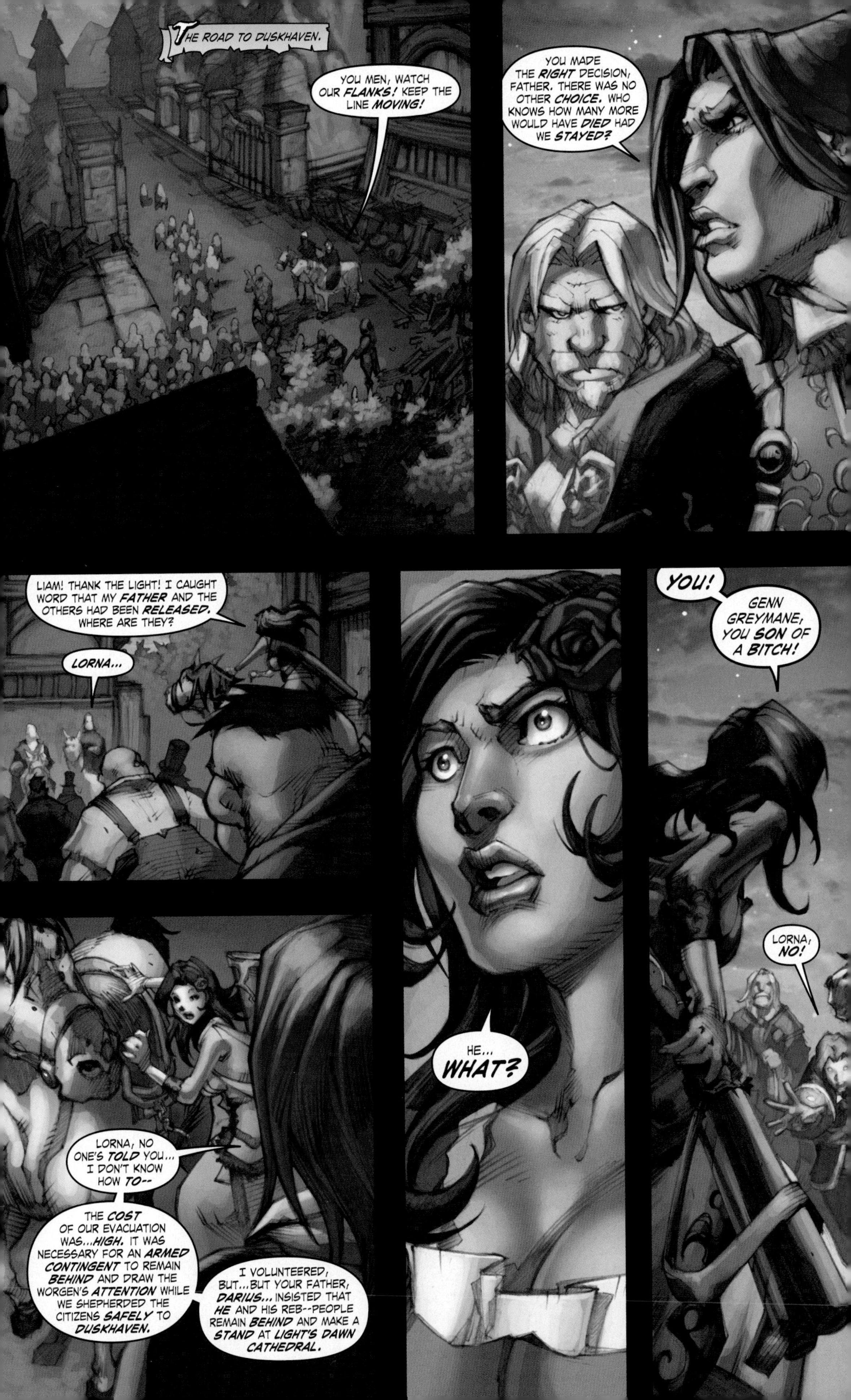
THE ROAD TO DUSKHAVEN.
YOU MEN, WATCH OUR FLANKS! KEEP THE LINE MOVING!
YOU MADE THE RIGHT DECISION, FATHER. THERE WAS NO OTHER CHOICE. WHO KNOWS HOW MANY MORE WOULD HAVE DIED HAD WE STAYED?
LIAM! THANK THE LIGHT! I CAUGHT WORD THAT MY FATHER AND THE OTHERS HAD BEEN RELEASED. WHERE ARE THEY?
LORNA...
LORNA, NO ONE'S TOLD YOU... I DON'T KNOW HOW TO--
THE COST OF OUR EVACUATION WAS...HIGH. IT WAS NECESSARY FOR AN ARMED CONTINGENT TO REMAIN BEHIND AND DRAW THE WORGEN'S ATTENTION WHILE WE SHEPHERDED THE CITIZENS SAFELY TO DUSKHAVEN.
I VOLUNTEERED, BUT...BUT YOUR FATHER, DARIUS... INSISTED THAT HE AND HIS REB--PEOPLE REMAIN BEHIND AND MAKE A STAND AT LIGHT'S DAWN CATHEDRAL.
HE... WHAT?
YOU!
GENN GREYMANE, YOU SON OF A BITCH!
LORNA, NO!

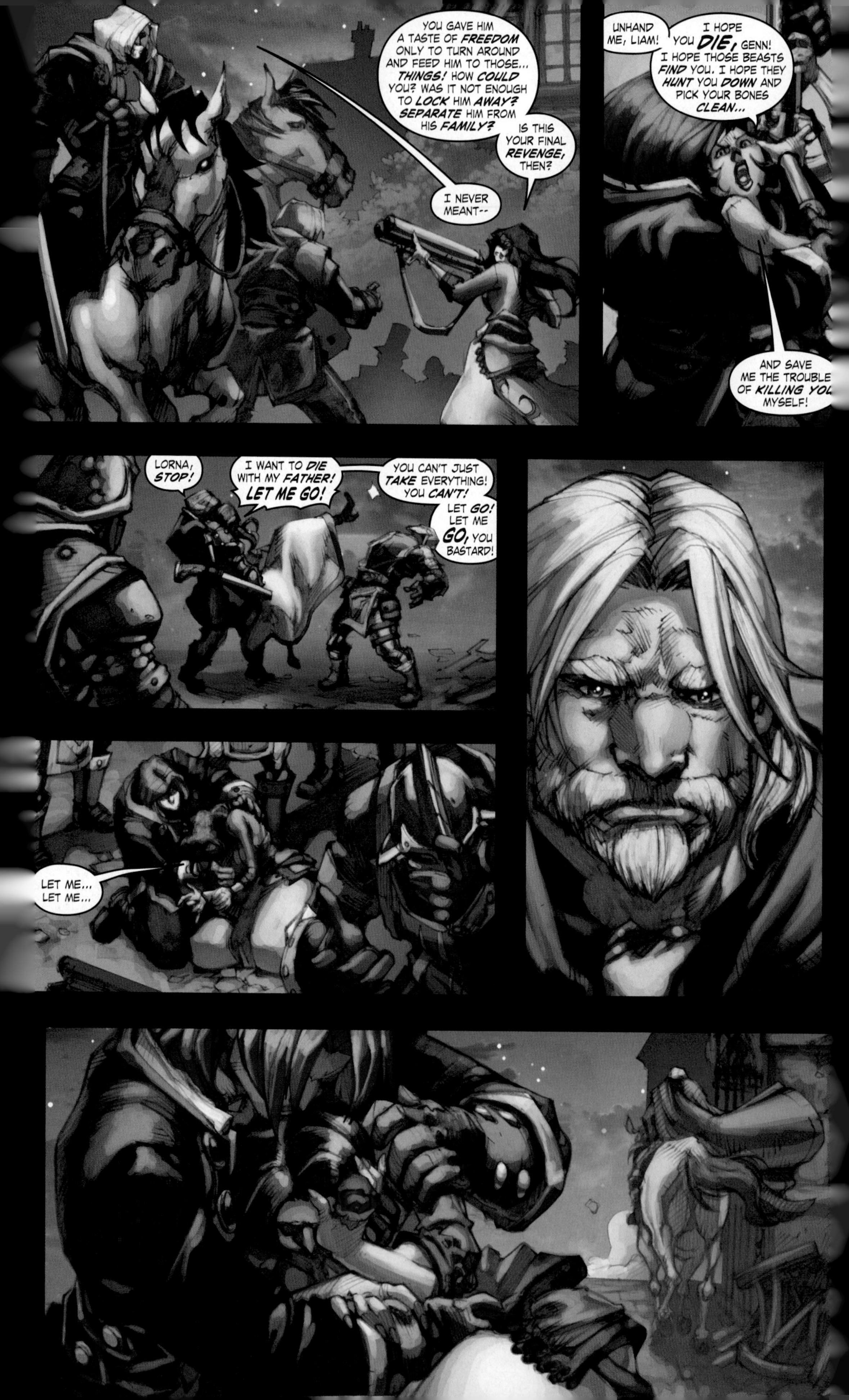
YOU GAVE HIM A TASTE OF FREEDOM ONLY TO TURN AROUND AND FEED HIM TO THOSE... THINGS! HOW COULD YOU? WAS IT NOT ENOUGH TO LOCK HIM AWAY? SEPARATE HIM FROM HIS FAMILY?
IS THIS YOUR FINAL REVENGE, THEN?
I NEVER MEANT--
UNHAND ME, LIAM!
I HOPE YOU DIE, GENN! I HOPE THOSE BEASTS FIND YOU. I HOPE THEY HUNT YOU DOWN AND PICK YOUR BONES CLEAN...
AND SAVE ME THE TROUBLE OF KILLING YOU MYSELF!
LORNA, STOP!
I WANT TO DIE WITH MY FATHER! LET ME GO!
YOU CAN'T JUST TAKE EVERYTHING! YOU CAN'T!
LET GO! LET ME GO, YOU BASTARD!
LET ME... LET ME...

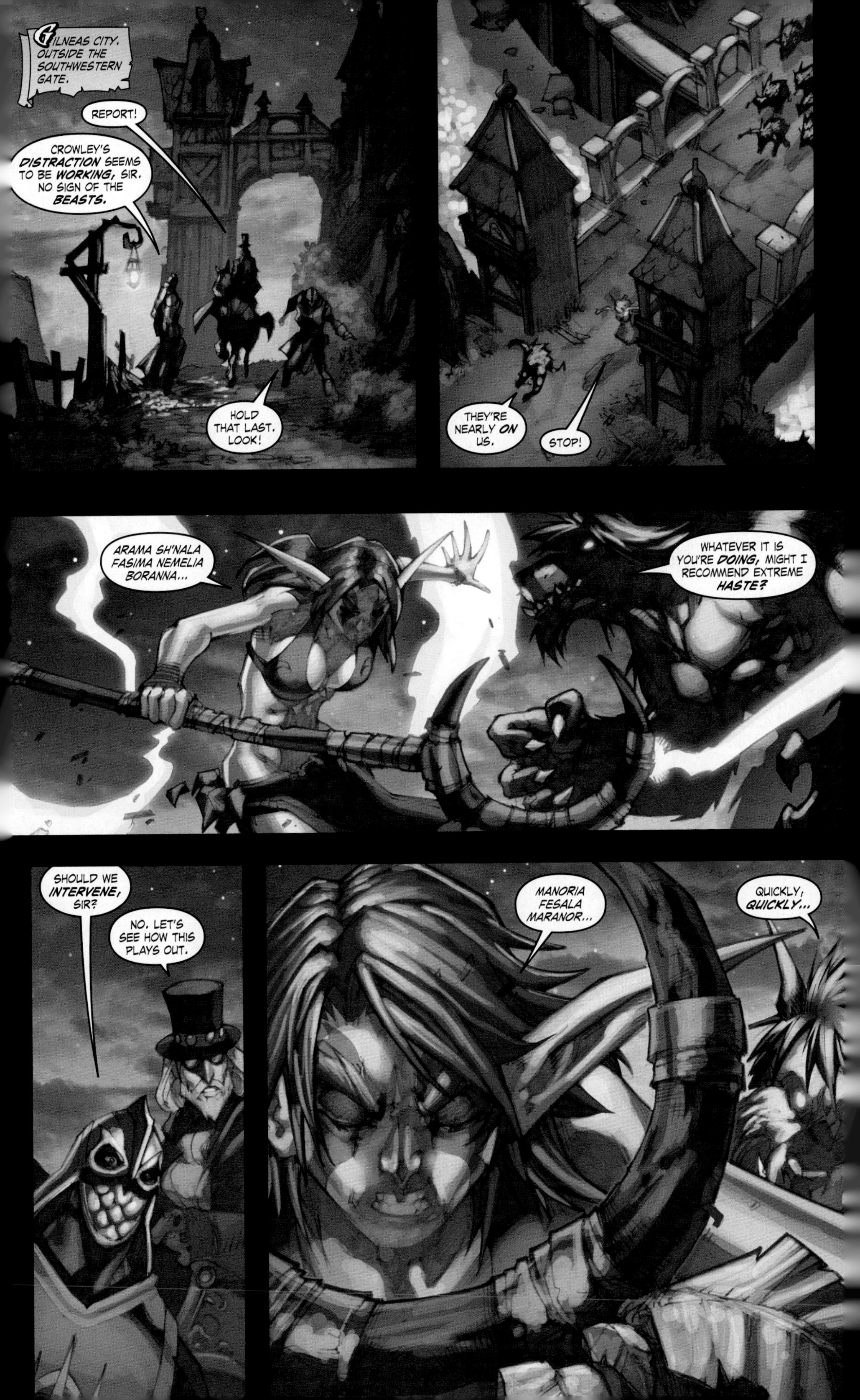
GILNEAS CITY. OUTSIDE THE SOUTHWESTERN GATE.
REPORT!
CROWLEY'S DISTRACTION SEEMS TO BE WORKING, SIR. NO SIGN OF THE BEASTS.
HOLD THAT LAST. LOOK!
THEY'RE NEARLY ON US.
STOP!
ARAMA SH'NALA FASIMA NEMELIA BORANNA...
WHATEVER IT IS YOU'RE DOING, MIGHT I RECOMMEND EXTREME HASTE?
SHOULD WE INTERVENE, SIR?
NO. LET'S SEE HOW THIS PLAYS OUT.
MANORIA FESALA MARANOR...
QUICKLY, QUICKLY...

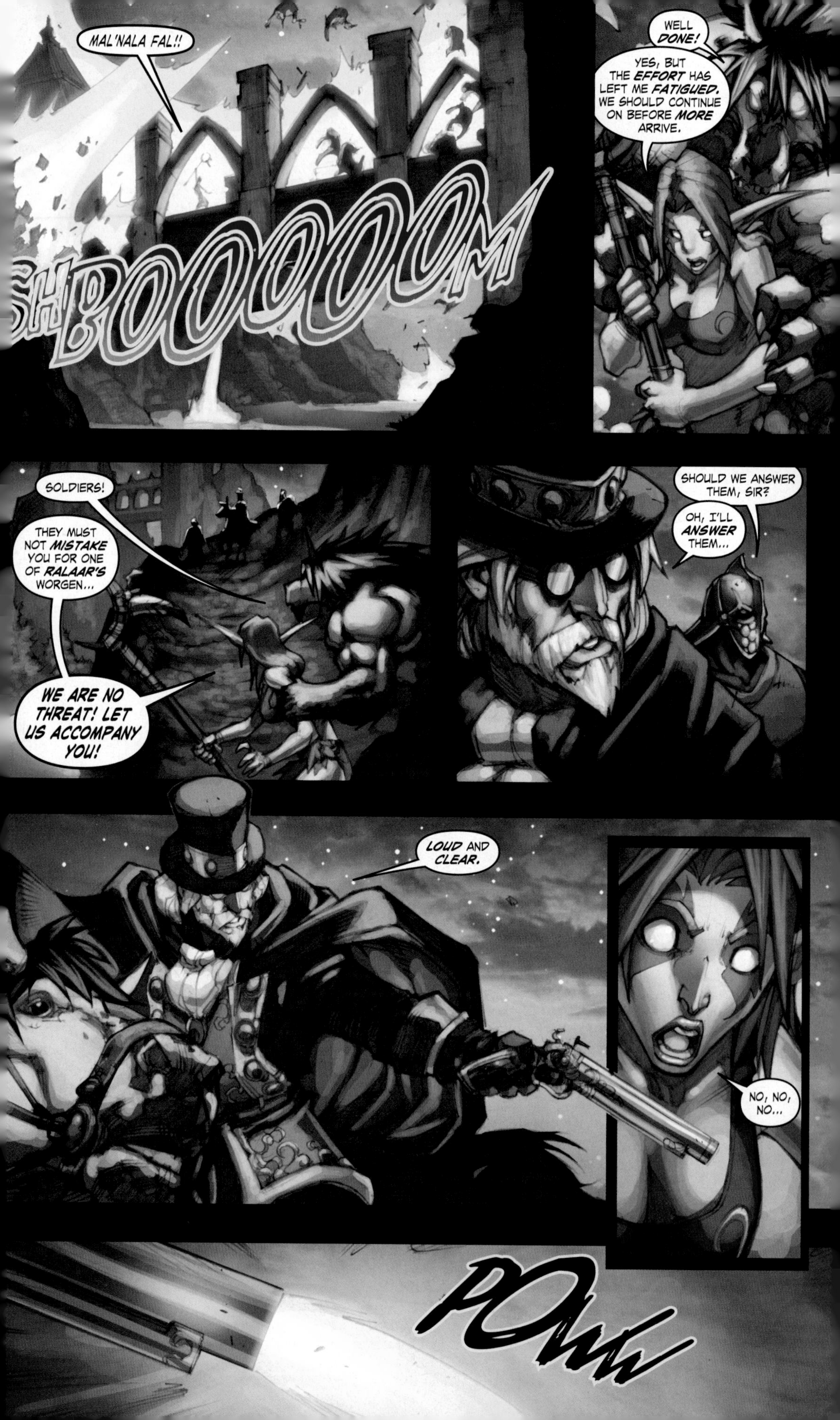
MAL'NALA FAL!!
SHBOOOOOOM
WELL DONE!
YES, BUT THE EFFORT HAS LEFT ME FATIGUED. WE SHOULD CONTINUE ON BEFORE MORE ARRIVE.
SOLDIERS!
THEY MUST NOT MISTAKE YOU FOR ONE OF RALAAR'S WORGEN...
WE ARE NO THREAT! LET US ACCOMPANY YOU!
SHOULD WE ANSWER THEM, SIR?
OH, I'LL ANSWER THEM...
LOUD AND CLEAR.
NO, NO, NO...
POW

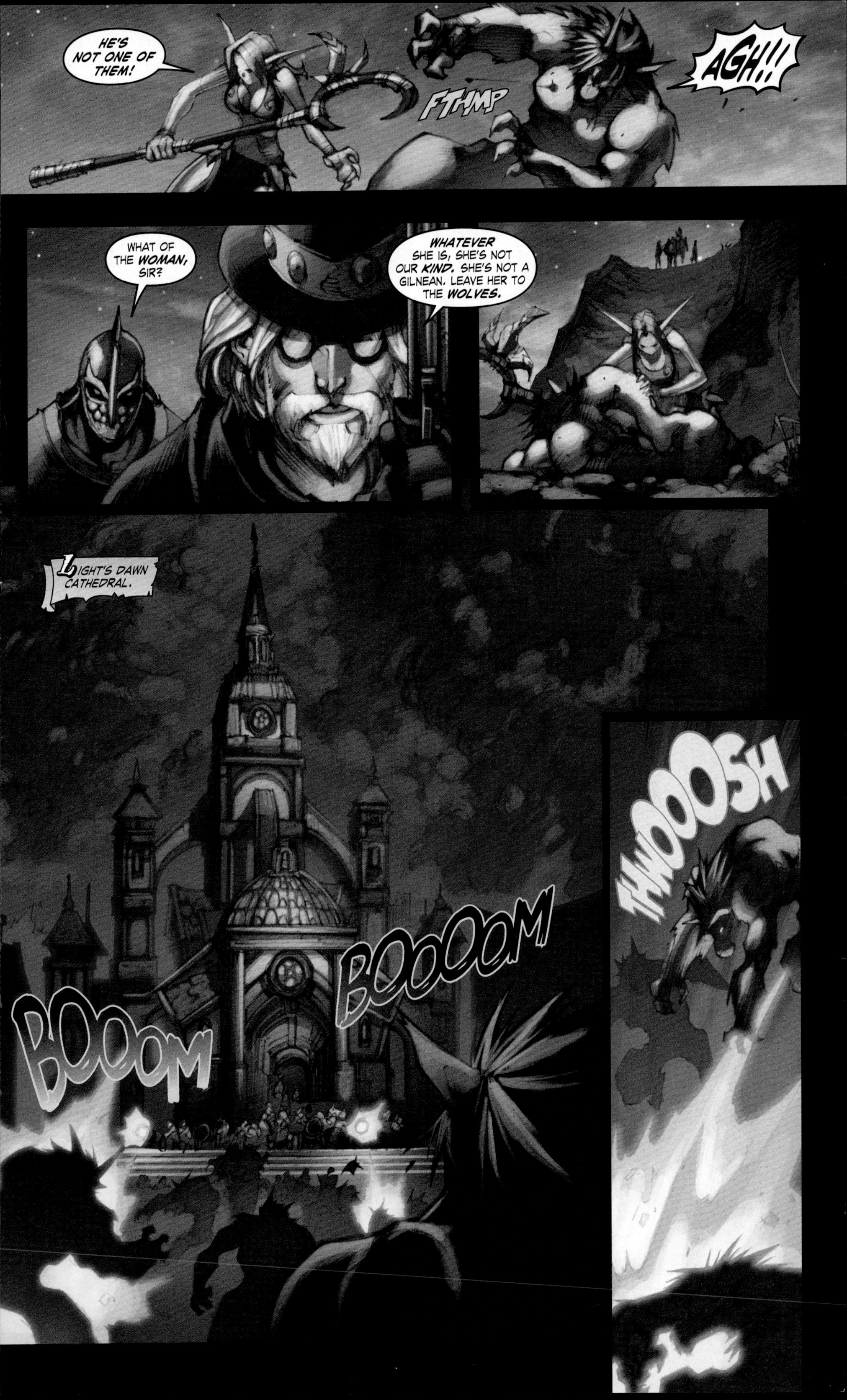
HE'S NOT ONE OF THEM!
FTHMP
AGH!!
WHAT OF THE WOMAN, SIR?
WHATEVER SHE IS, SHE'S NOT OUR KIND. SHE'S NOT A GILNEAN. LEAVE HER TO THE WOLVES.
LIGHT'S DAWN CATHEDRAL.
BOOOM
BOOOOM
THWOOOSH

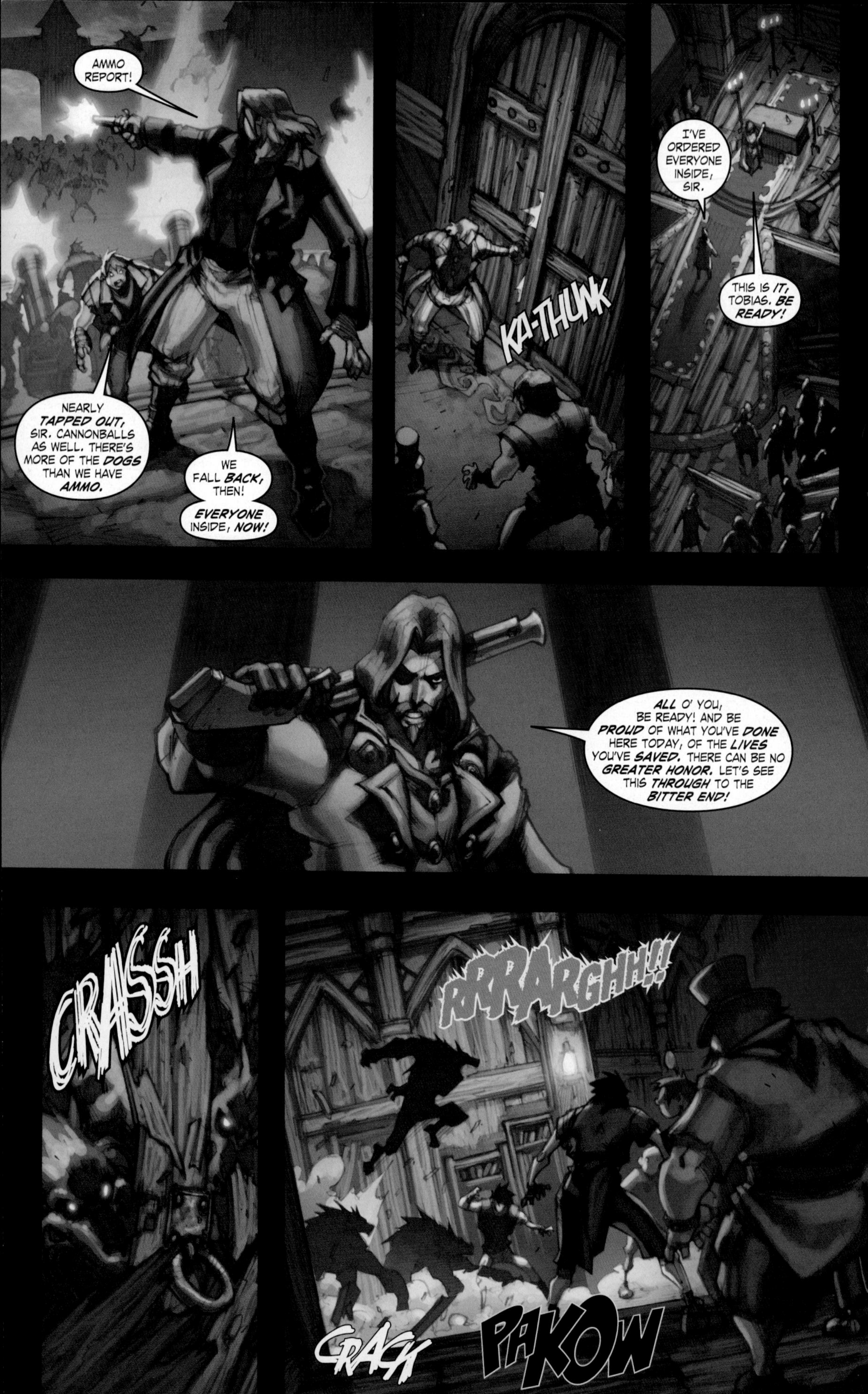
AMMO REPORT!
NEARLY TAPPED OUT, SIR. CANNONBALLS AS WELL. THERE'S MORE OF THE DOGS THAN WE HAVE AMMO.
WE FALL BACK, THEN!
EVERYONE INSIDE, NOW!
KA-THUNK
I'VE ORDERED EVERYONE INSIDE, SIR.
THIS IS IT, TOBIAS. BE READY!
ALL O' YOU, BE READY! AND BE PROUD OF WHAT YOU'VE DONE HERE TODAY, OF THE LIVES YOU'VE SAVED. THERE CAN BE NO GREATER HONOR. LET'S SEE THIS THROUGH TO THE BITTER END!
CRASSH
RRRARGHH!!
CRACK
PAKOW

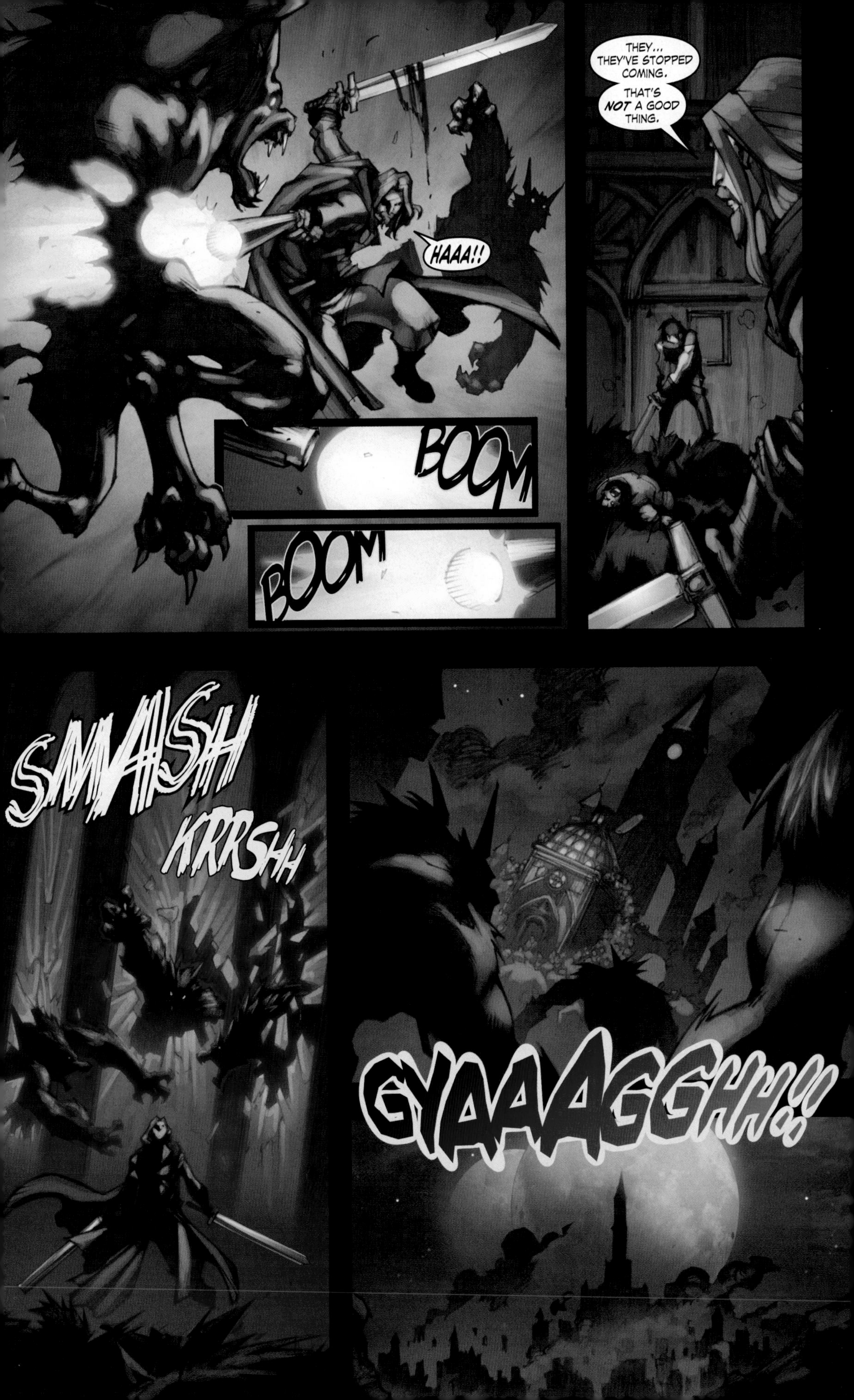
HAAA!!
BOOM
BOOM
THEY... THEY'VE STOPPED COMING.
THAT'S NOT A GOOD THING.
SMASH
KRRSHH
GYAAAGGHH!!

YOU'RE A GREAT *LEADER.* YOU'VE ALWAYS DONE WHAT YOU *BELIEVED* WAS *BEST* FOR YOUR PEOPLE. BUT IN THE RECENT PAST I FEEL AS THOUGH YOU'VE *LOST FAITH* IN YOURSELF.

IF YOU CAN JUST *FIND* A WAY TO *BELIEVE* IN YOURSELF ONCE AGAIN...YOUR *PEOPLE* WILL BELIEVE IN *YOU.* AND THEY WILL *FORGIVE* YOU. FOR *ANYTHING.*

IN MY MIND, THERE'S *NOTHING* TO *FORGIVE.*

I SHOULD GET BACK TO THE *OTHERS.*

ANYTHING...

AND WOULD *YOU* FORGIVE ME?

LIAM!

TELL GODFREY...TELL HIM THE WORGEN ARE *NOT* TO BE KILLED. I WANT HIM TO SET *TRAPS* ONLY. I WANT TO *CATCH* AS MANY OF THEM *ALIVE* AS POSSIBLE.

HE WON'T WANT TO HE IT, BUT I'L TELL HIM

SAY THAT THERE'S A *GOOD REASON.* TELL HIM THAT THEY MAY PROVE...

VALUABLE.

·END CHAPTER FOUR·

CHAPTER 5 Cover by Glenn Rane

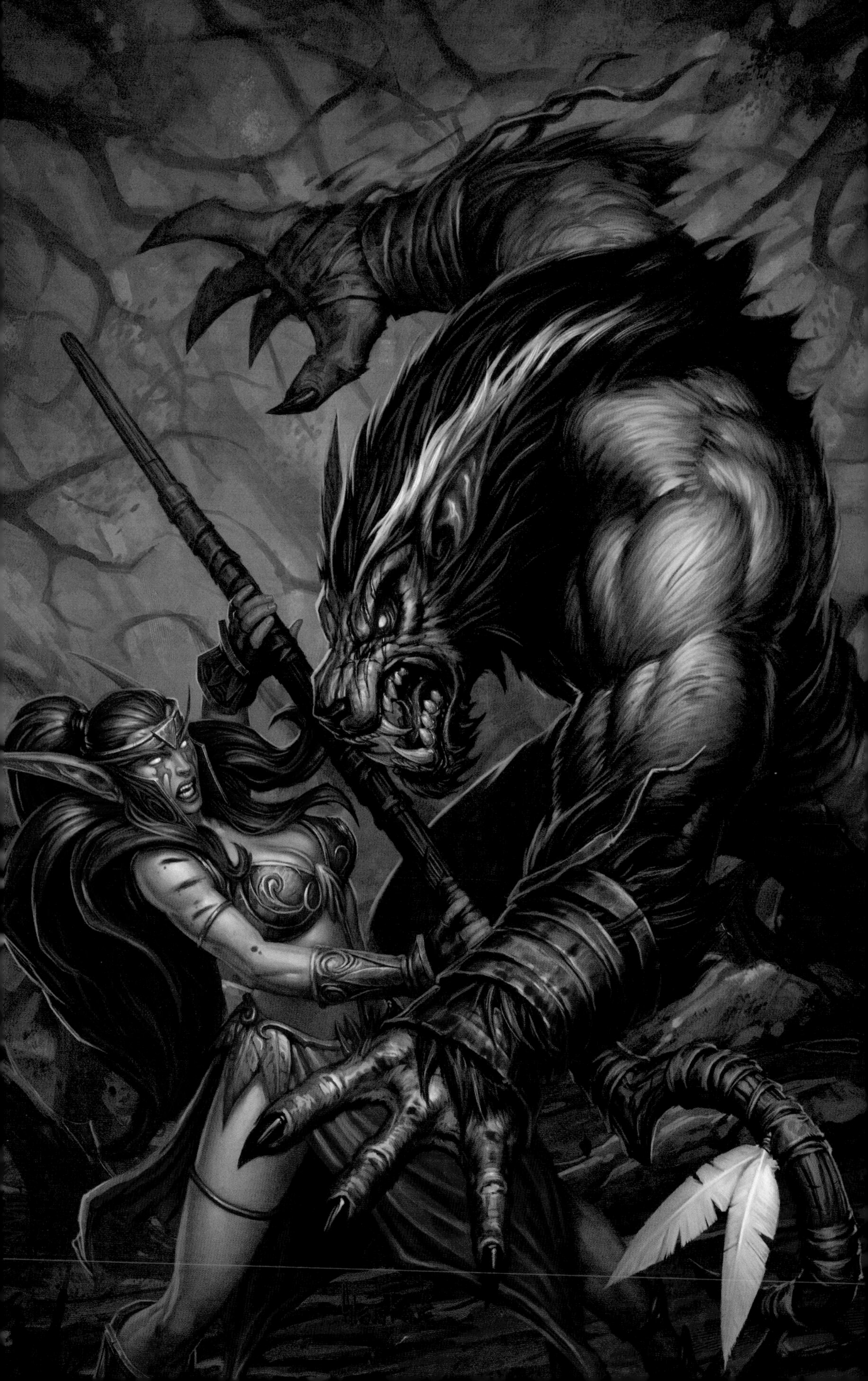

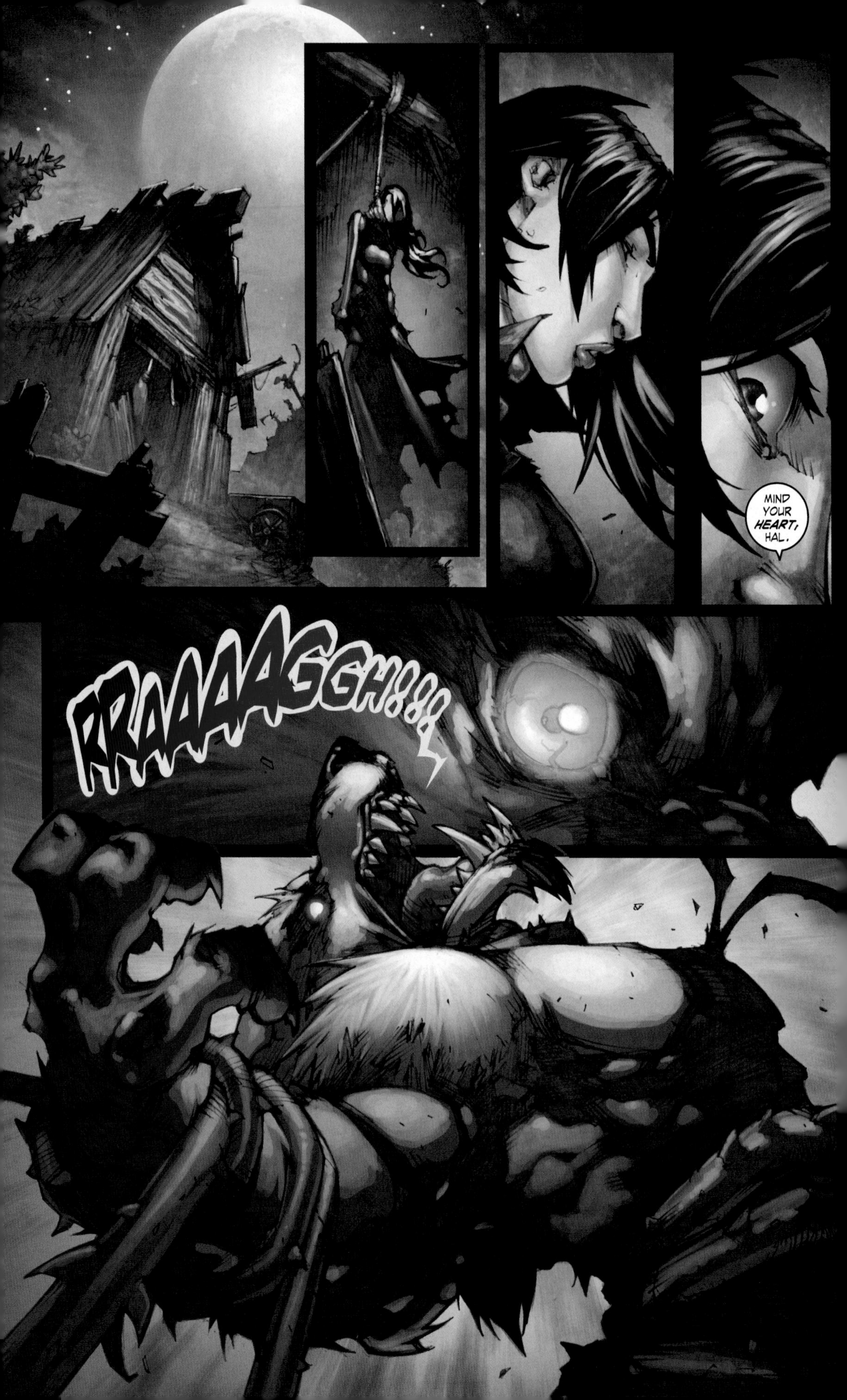
MIND YOUR HEART, HAL.
RRAAAAGGH!!!

EVEN NOW THE VINES ARE SEARCHING FOR THE *STEEL BALL,* WHICH THREATENS TO WORK ITS *WAY* TO YOUR HEART.

WHAT MANNER OF...*SADISTIC TORTURE* IS THIS? *RELEASE* ME AT *ONCE!*

BE STILL! IF THE SHOT IS NOT REMOVED *SOON...* LET US JUST SAY YOUR PAIN WILL BE *ENDED.*

SCHLLUP

IT IS DONE! *NOW* WE MAY HEAL YOU *PROPERLY.*

HM, BETTER, ADMITTEDLY. I TRUST THAT AN EXTENSION OF MY *GRATITUDE* GOES WITHOUT *SAYING.*

WELL, OF COURSE IT--

GOOD! I WON'T WASTE YOUR TIME. HOW LONG WAS I INCAPACITATED?

BE STILL. YOU MUST REST.

I HAVE TO *INSIST* THAT--

HOLD! ANOTHER *TREMOR!*

WHAT OF *GILNEAS CITY?*

OCCUPIED, BY *ALPHA PRIME* AND HIS WORGEN. NOW *REST,* BROTHER...I STILL DO NOT EVEN KNOW YOUR *NAME.*

OCCUPIED? WHAT PRECISELY IS BEING DONE TO *RETAKE* IT? *NNG!* SOMEONE, CALL OFF THESE DAMN *VINES!* WHAT IS IT YOU PEOPLE ARE *DOING* HERE?

RRRUUMBLE

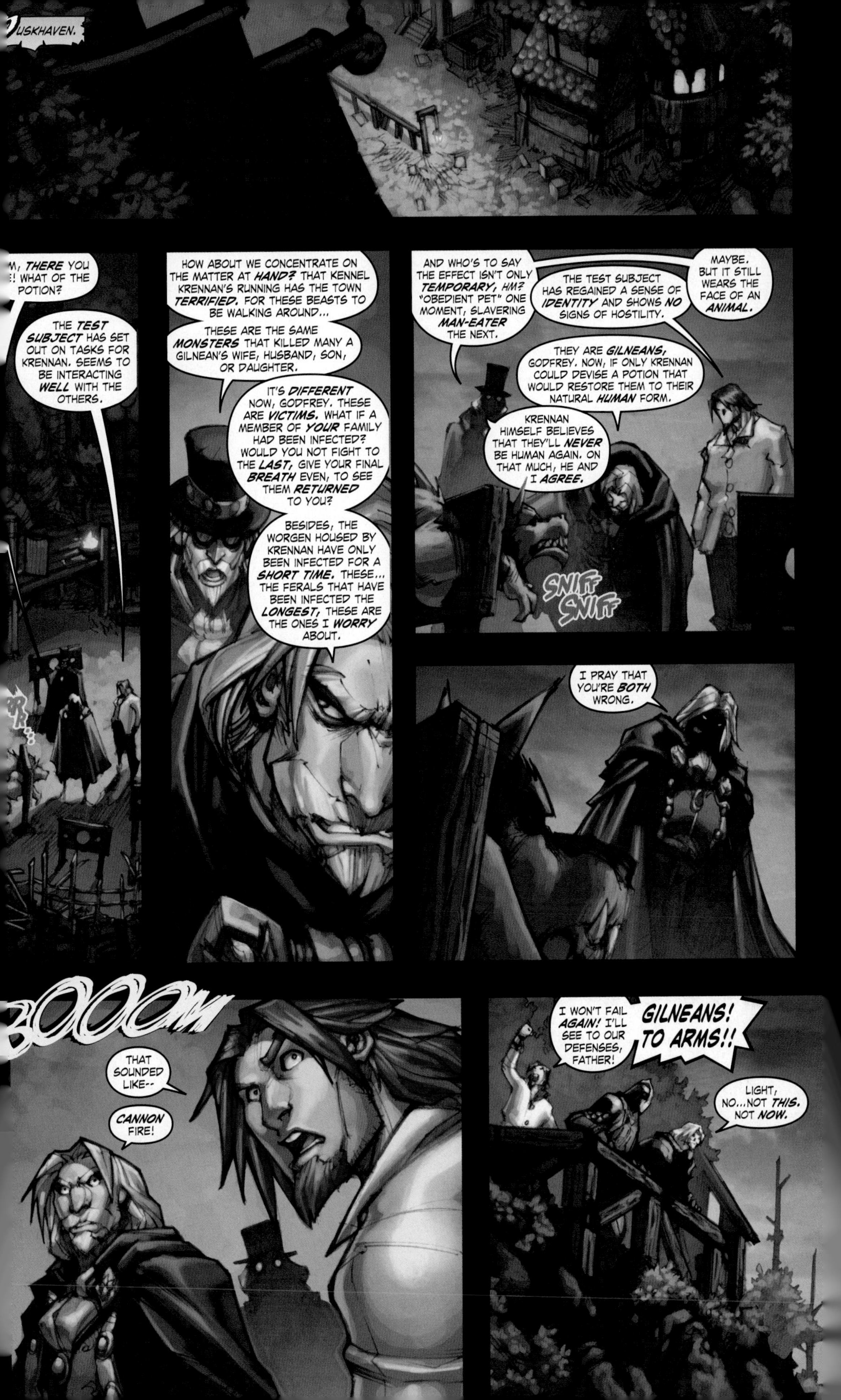

USKHAVEN.
M, THERE YOU E! WHAT OF THE POTION?
THE TEST SUBJECT HAS SET OUT ON TASKS FOR KRENNAN. SEEMS TO BE INTERACTING WELL WITH THE OTHERS.
HOW ABOUT WE CONCENTRATE ON THE MATTER AT HAND? THAT KENNEL KRENNAN'S RUNNING HAS THE TOWN TERRIFIED. FOR THESE BEASTS TO BE WALKING AROUND...
THESE ARE THE SAME MONSTERS THAT KILLED MANY A GILNEAN'S WIFE, HUSBAND, SON, OR DAUGHTER.
IT'S DIFFERENT NOW, GODFREY. THESE ARE VICTIMS. WHAT IF A MEMBER OF YOUR FAMILY HAD BEEN INFECTED? WOULD YOU NOT FIGHT TO THE LAST, GIVE YOUR FINAL BREATH EVEN, TO SEE THEM RETURNED TO YOU?
BESIDES, THE WORGEN HOUSED BY KRENNAN HAVE ONLY BEEN INFECTED FOR A SHORT TIME. THESE... THE FERALS THAT HAVE BEEN INFECTED THE LONGEST, THESE ARE THE ONES I WORRY ABOUT.
AND WHO'S TO SAY THE EFFECT ISN'T ONLY TEMPORARY, HM? "OBEDIENT PET" ONE MOMENT, SLAVERING MAN-EATER THE NEXT.
THE TEST SUBJECT HAS REGAINED A SENSE OF IDENTITY AND SHOWS NO SIGNS OF HOSTILITY.
MAYBE. BUT IT STILL WEARS THE FACE OF AN ANIMAL.
THEY ARE GILNEANS, GODFREY. NOW, IF ONLY KRENNAN COULD DEVISE A POTION THAT WOULD RESTORE THEM TO THEIR NATURAL HUMAN FORM.
KRENNAN HIMSELF BELIEVES THAT THEY'LL NEVER BE HUMAN AGAIN. ON THAT MUCH, HE AND I AGREE.
SNIFF SNIFF
I PRAY THAT YOU'RE BOTH WRONG.
BOOOOM
THAT SOUNDED LIKE--
CANNON FIRE!
I WON'T FAIL AGAIN! I'LL SEE TO OUR DEFENSES, FATHER!
GILNEANS! TO ARMS!!
LIGHT, NO...NOT THIS. NOT NOW.

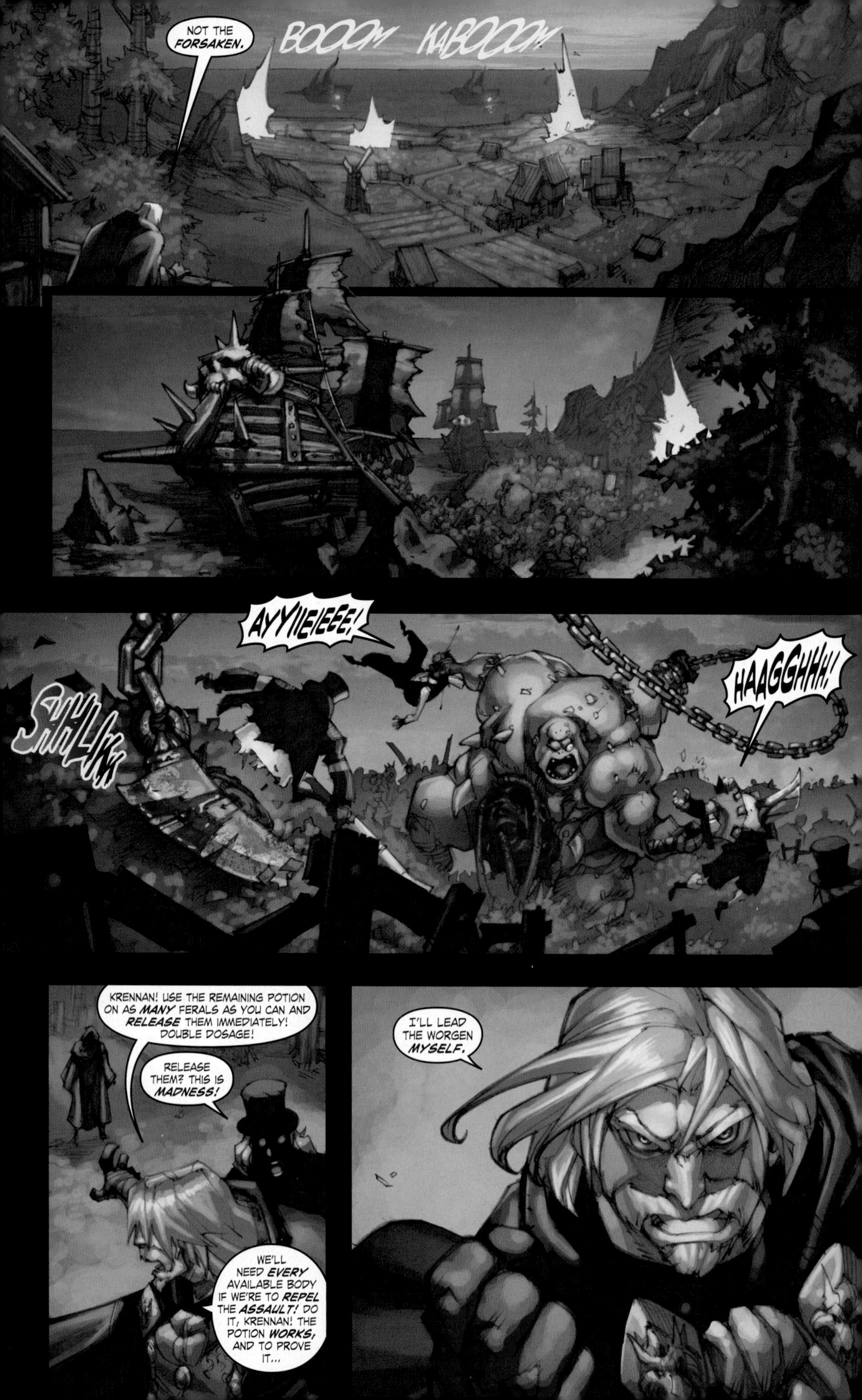
NOT THE FORSAKEN.
BOOOM KABOOOM
AYYIIEIEEE!
SHHLIKK
HAAGGHHH!
KRENNAN! USE THE REMAINING POTION ON AS MANY FERALS AS YOU CAN AND RELEASE THEM IMMEDIATELY! DOUBLE DOSAGE!
RELEASE THEM? THIS IS MADNESS!
WE'LL NEED EVERY AVAILABLE BODY IF WE'RE TO REPEL THE ASSAULT! DO IT, KRENNAN! THE POTION WORKS, AND TO PROVE IT...
I'LL LEAD THE WORGEN MYSELF.

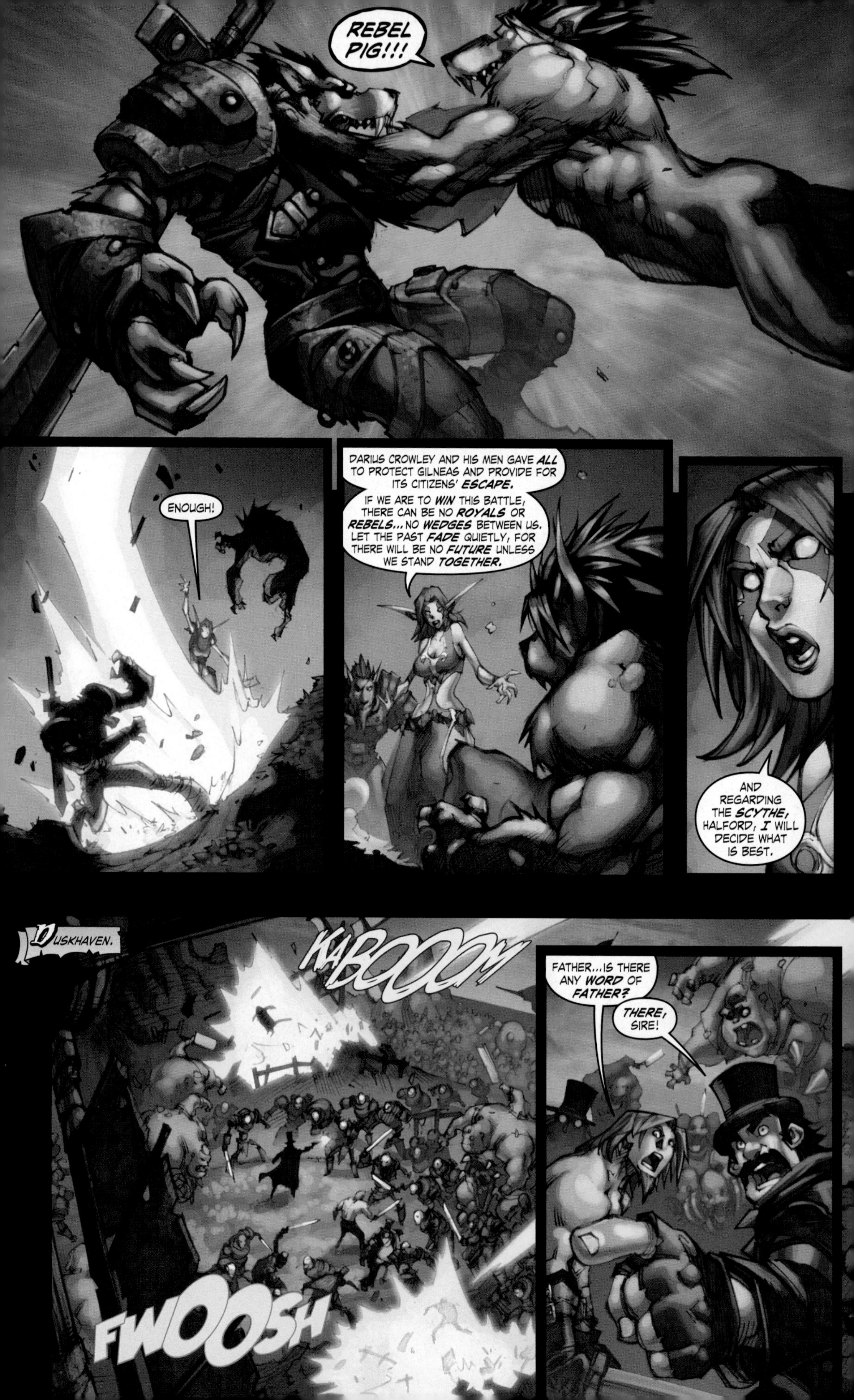

REBEL PIG!!!
ENOUGH!
DARIUS CROWLEY AND HIS MEN GAVE ALL TO PROTECT GILNEAS AND PROVIDE FOR ITS CITIZENS' ESCAPE.
IF WE ARE TO WIN THIS BATTLE, THERE CAN BE NO ROYALS OR REBELS... NO WEDGES BETWEEN US. LET THE PAST FADE QUIETLY, FOR THERE WILL BE NO FUTURE UNLESS WE STAND TOGETHER.
AND REGARDING THE SCYTHE, HALFORD, I WILL DECIDE WHAT IS BEST.
DUSKHAVEN.
KABOOOM
FATHER... IS THERE ANY WORD OF FATHER?
THERE, SIRE!
FWOOSH

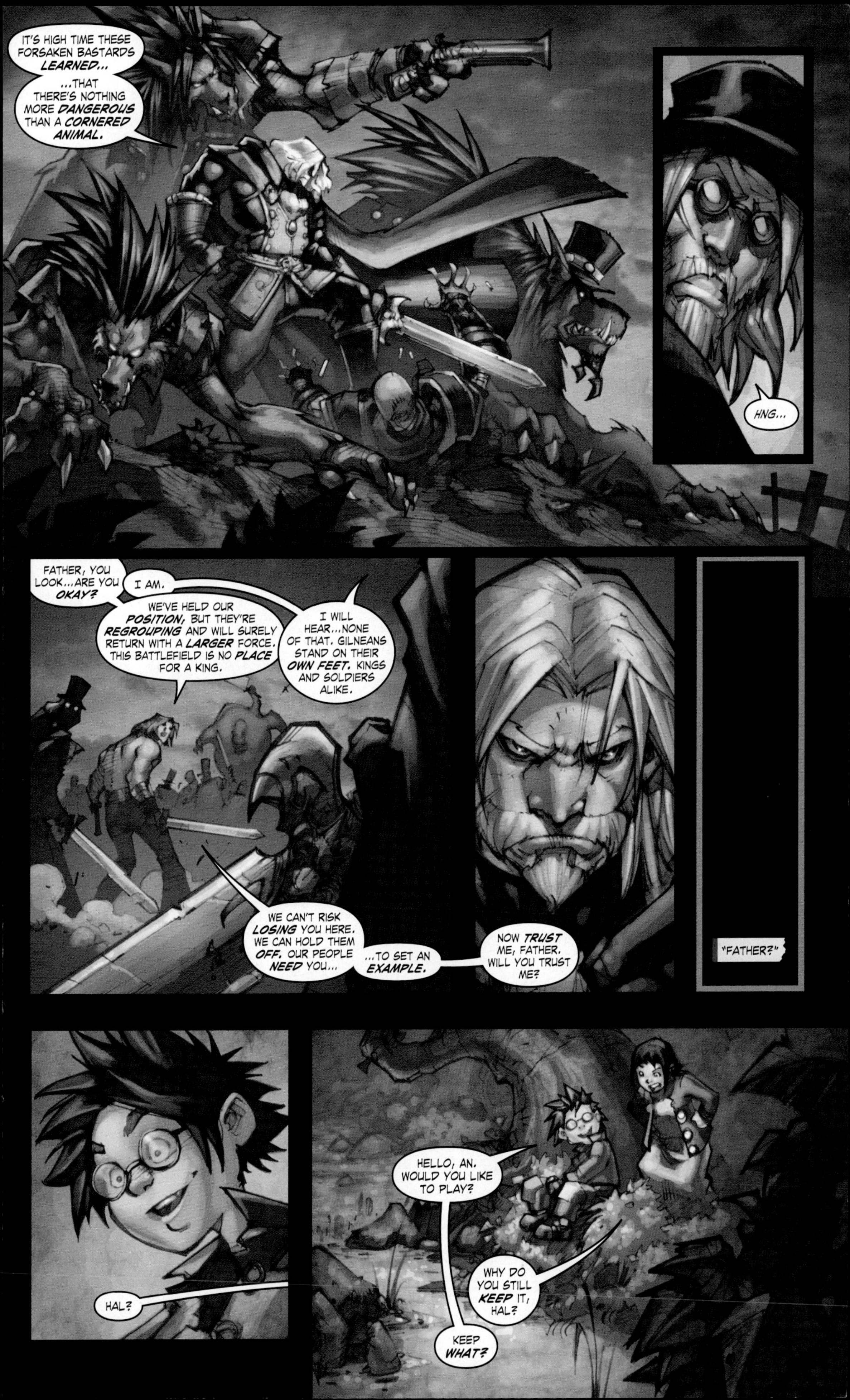
IT'S HIGH TIME THESE FORSAKEN BASTARDS LEARNED...
...THAT THERE'S NOTHING MORE DANGEROUS THAN A CORNERED ANIMAL.
HNG...
FATHER, YOU LOOK...ARE YOU OKAY?
I AM.
WE'VE HELD OUR POSITION, BUT THEY'RE REGROUPING AND WILL SURELY RETURN WITH A LARGER FORCE. THIS BATTLEFIELD IS NO PLACE FOR A KING.
I WILL HEAR...NONE OF THAT. GILNEANS STAND ON THEIR OWN FEET. KINGS AND SOLDIERS ALIKE.
WE CAN'T RISK LOSING YOU HERE. WE CAN HOLD THEM OFF. OUR PEOPLE NEED YOU...
...TO SET AN EXAMPLE.
NOW TRUST ME, FATHER. WILL YOU TRUST ME?
"FATHER?"
HAL?
HELLO, AN. WOULD YOU LIKE TO PLAY?
WHY DO YOU STILL KEEP IT, HAL?
KEEP WHAT?

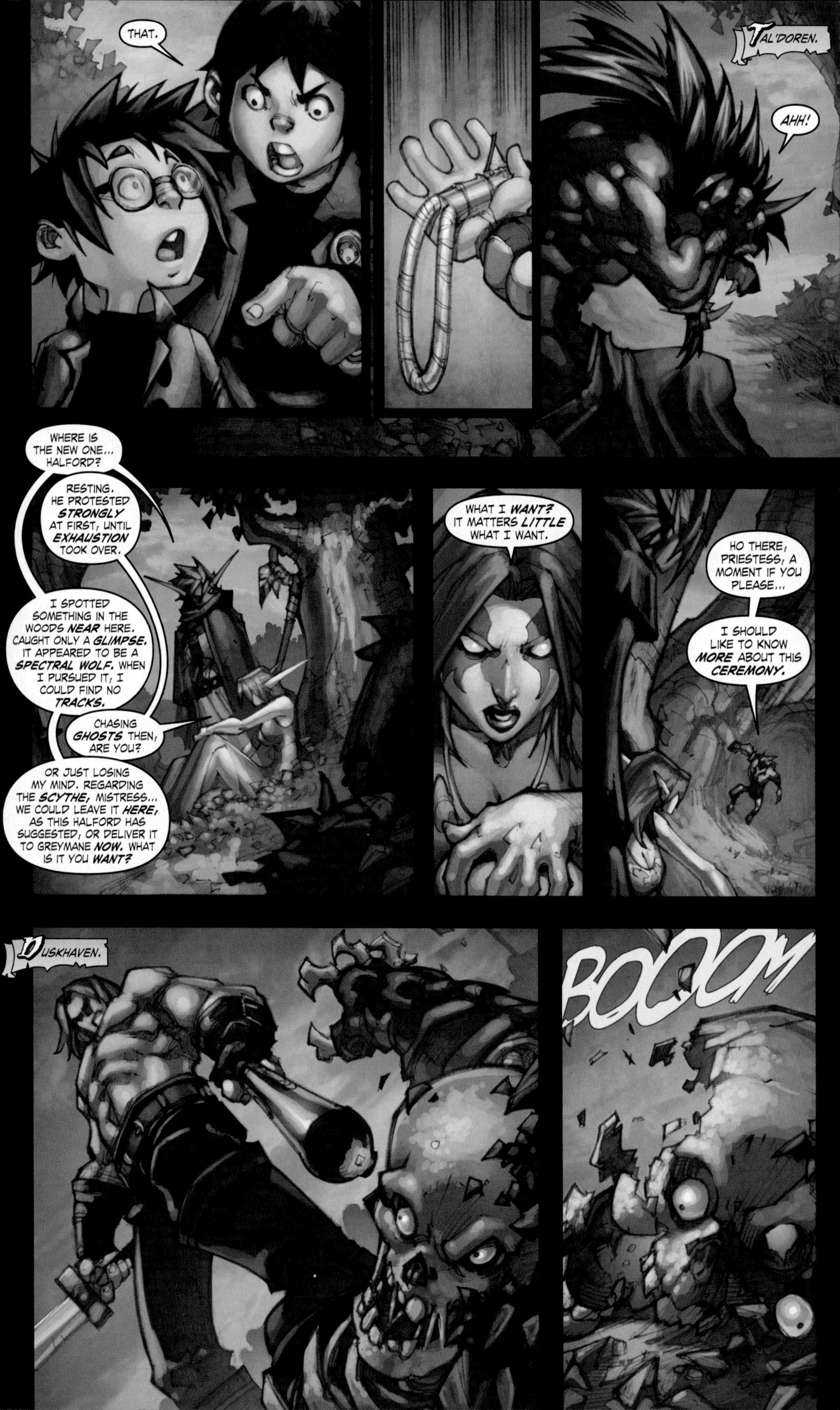
THAT.
TAL'DOREN.
AHH!
WHERE IS THE NEW ONE... HALFORD?
RESTING. HE PROTESTED STRONGLY AT FIRST, UNTIL EXHAUSTION TOOK OVER.
I SPOTTED SOMETHING IN THE WOODS NEAR HERE. CAUGHT ONLY A GLIMPSE. IT APPEARED TO BE A SPECTRAL WOLF. WHEN I PURSUED IT, I COULD FIND NO TRACKS.
CHASING GHOSTS THEN, ARE YOU?
OR JUST LOSING MY MIND. REGARDING THE SCYTHE, MISTRESS... WE COULD LEAVE IT HERE, AS THIS HALFORD HAS SUGGESTED, OR DELIVER IT TO GREYMANE NOW. WHAT IS IT YOU WANT?
WHAT I WANT? IT MATTERS LITTLE WHAT I WANT.
HO THERE, PRIESTESS, A MOMENT IF YOU PLEASE...
I SHOULD LIKE TO KNOW MORE ABOUT THIS CEREMONY.
DUSKHAVEN.
BOOOM

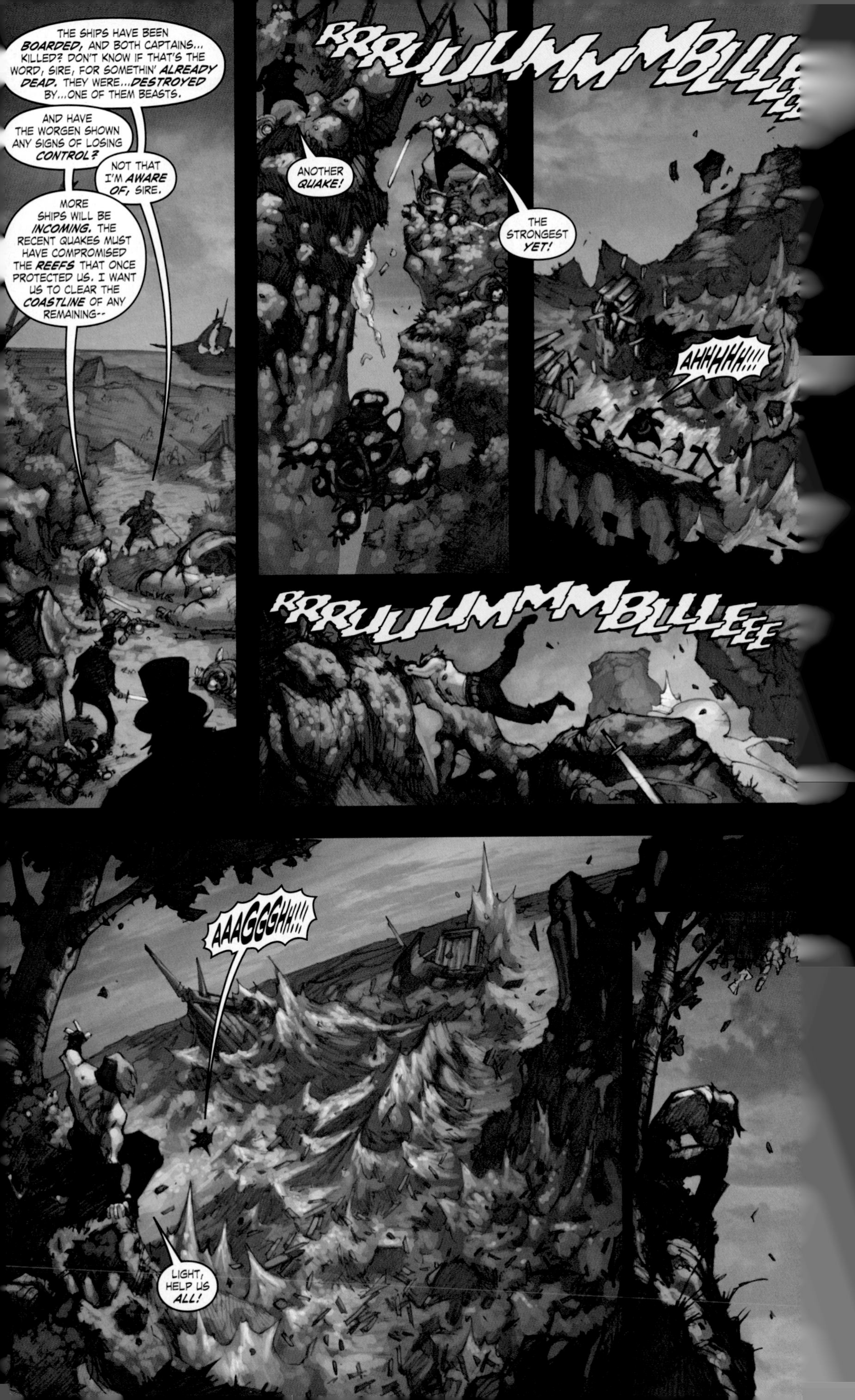

THE SHIPS HAVE BEEN BOARDED, AND BOTH CAPTAINS... KILLED? DON'T KNOW IF THAT'S THE WORD, SIRE, FOR SOMETHIN' ALREADY DEAD. THEY WERE...DESTROYED BY...ONE OF THEM BEASTS.
AND HAVE THE WORGEN SHOWN ANY SIGNS OF LOSING CONTROL?
NOT THAT I'M AWARE OF, SIRE.
MORE SHIPS WILL BE INCOMING. THE RECENT QUAKES MUST HAVE COMPROMISED THE REEFS THAT ONCE PROTECTED US. I WANT US TO CLEAR THE COASTLINE OF ANY REMAINING--
RRRUUULMMMBLLL
ANOTHER QUAKE!
THE STRONGEST YET!
AHHHHH!!!
RRRUUULMMMBLLLEEE
AAAGGGHH!!!
LIGHT, HELP US ALL!

HUMAN REFUGEES ARE TRICKLIN' INTO *STORMGLEN* NOW AS WELL. JUST A *FEW* SO FAR, BUT WORD IS, GREYMANE ORDERED FOR *ALL* THE SURVIVORS TO BE *RELOCATED* THERE.

THE *CARRIAGES* SHOULD BE COMIN' IN OVER THE NEXT SEVERAL *DAYS.*

PRIESTESS?

HM? I AM SORRY, DARIUS, IF I SEEM *DISTRACTED.* I DID NOT KNOW PEACE BLOSSOMS GREW HERE. I HAVE A SPECIAL PLACE IN MY HEART FOR THEM.

YOU BRING GOOD NEWS. THE *CLOSER* TOGETHER WE ARE, THE *STRONGER* WE WILL BE. YOU HAVE DONE *WELL,* SENDING THE LOST WORGEN TO US. OUR NUMBERS ARE *GROWING.*

...WHO HAVE *ARRIVED* THERE. I... DON'T WANT HER TO *SEE* ME JUST YET.

THERE IS NO *SHAME* IN WHAT YOU HAVE *BECOME.* YOU STILL HOLD ON TO *GUILT,* DESPITE THE *CEREMONY...* I BELIEVE IT IS WHY YOU HAVE NOT YET BEEN ABLE TO RESUME *HUMAN* FORM, EVEN BRIEFLY.

I WILL SEE HER *SOON.* BUT FOR *NOW...*

OF COURSE, I WILL GO TO STORMGLEN *MYSELF* AND MAKE CONTACT WITH ANY MORE OF *YOUR KIND* WHO *ARRIVE.*

HAD I *KNOWN* THAT THE KING WOULD BE MAKING HIS WAY THERE *NOW,* I WOULD HAVE *HELD* ON TO THE SCYTHE RATHER THAN HAVING IT *TAKEN AWAY* AND *RELOCATED* EACH NIGHT.

I'M *SURPRISED* THAT *ROYAL,* HALFORD, DIDN'T THROW A *FIT.*

NO. IN *FACT,* HE HAS BEGUN THE *CEREMONY.* AND GIVEN THE EXTENT OF HIS...*DIFFICULTIES...*

"I IMAGINE HE WILL BE *INDISPOSED* FOR A *WHILE.*"

I ALLOWED *DESPAIR* TO SPREAD WITHIN ME...A SICKNESS, A WOUND I COULD *NOT HEAL.*

IN THE END IT FELT AS IF LIFE HAD BECOME *UNBEARABLE...* AND I NO LONGER WISHED TO BE A *PART* OF IT.

YOU'RE ABLE TO SEE ME BECAUSE THE WATER GRANTED YOU *TRANQUILITY.* I'M *HERE* BECAUSE YOU *NEED* ME TO BE HERE.

YOU'RE NOT *REAL,* OF COURSE...CLEARLY THERE WAS SOME KIND OF *HALLUCINOGEN...* THOSE MOONLEAFS IN THE WELL WATER I IMBIBED.

"IMBIBED?" OH, HAL... YOU HAVEN'T *CHANGED* AT ALL.

I DON'T *BELIEVE* IN GHOSTS.

IF THAT'S *SO,* THEN YOU'RE HERE *TOO* LATE. EVEN THE *PAIN* OF WHAT YOU ENDURED... WAS NOT SO *GREAT* THAT WE COULDN'T HAVE FOUND A WAY TO *HEAL* IT TOGETHER!

YOU *GAVE UP!* DESPITE OUR DIFFERENCES DURING THE WAR, I ALWAYS *LOVED* AND *RESPECTED* YOU...AND YOU *ABANDONED* ME!

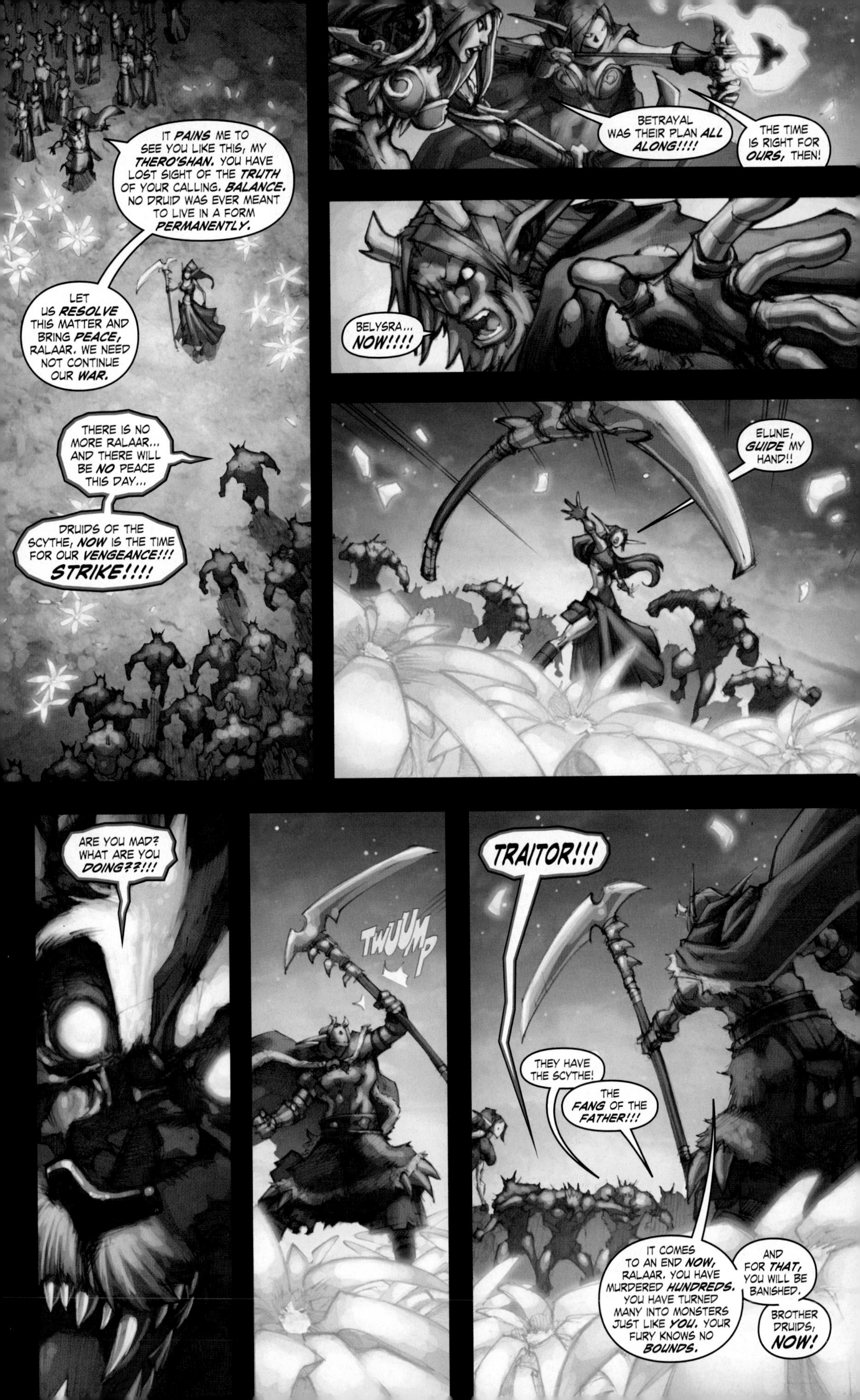
IT PAINS ME TO SEE YOU LIKE THIS, MY THERO'SHAN. YOU HAVE LOST SIGHT OF THE TRUTH OF YOUR CALLING. BALANCE. NO DRUID WAS EVER MEANT TO LIVE IN A FORM PERMANENTLY.
LET US RESOLVE THIS MATTER AND BRING PEACE, RALAAR. WE NEED NOT CONTINUE OUR WAR.
THERE IS NO MORE RALAAR... AND THERE WILL BE NO PEACE THIS DAY...
DRUIDS OF THE SCYTHE, NOW IS THE TIME FOR OUR VENGEANCE!!! STRIKE!!!!
BETRAYAL WAS THEIR PLAN ALL ALONG!!!!
THE TIME IS RIGHT FOR OURS, THEN!
BELYSRA... NOW!!!!
ELUNE, GUIDE MY HAND!!
ARE YOU MAD? WHAT ARE YOU DOING??!!!
TWUUMP
TRAITOR!!!
THEY HAVE THE SCYTHE!
THE FANG OF THE FATHER!!!
IT COMES TO AN END NOW, RALAAR. YOU HAVE MURDERED HUNDREDS. YOU HAVE TURNED MANY INTO MONSTERS JUST LIKE YOU. YOUR FURY KNOWS NO BOUNDS.
AND FOR THAT, YOU WILL BE BANISHED.
BROTHER DRUIDS, NOW!

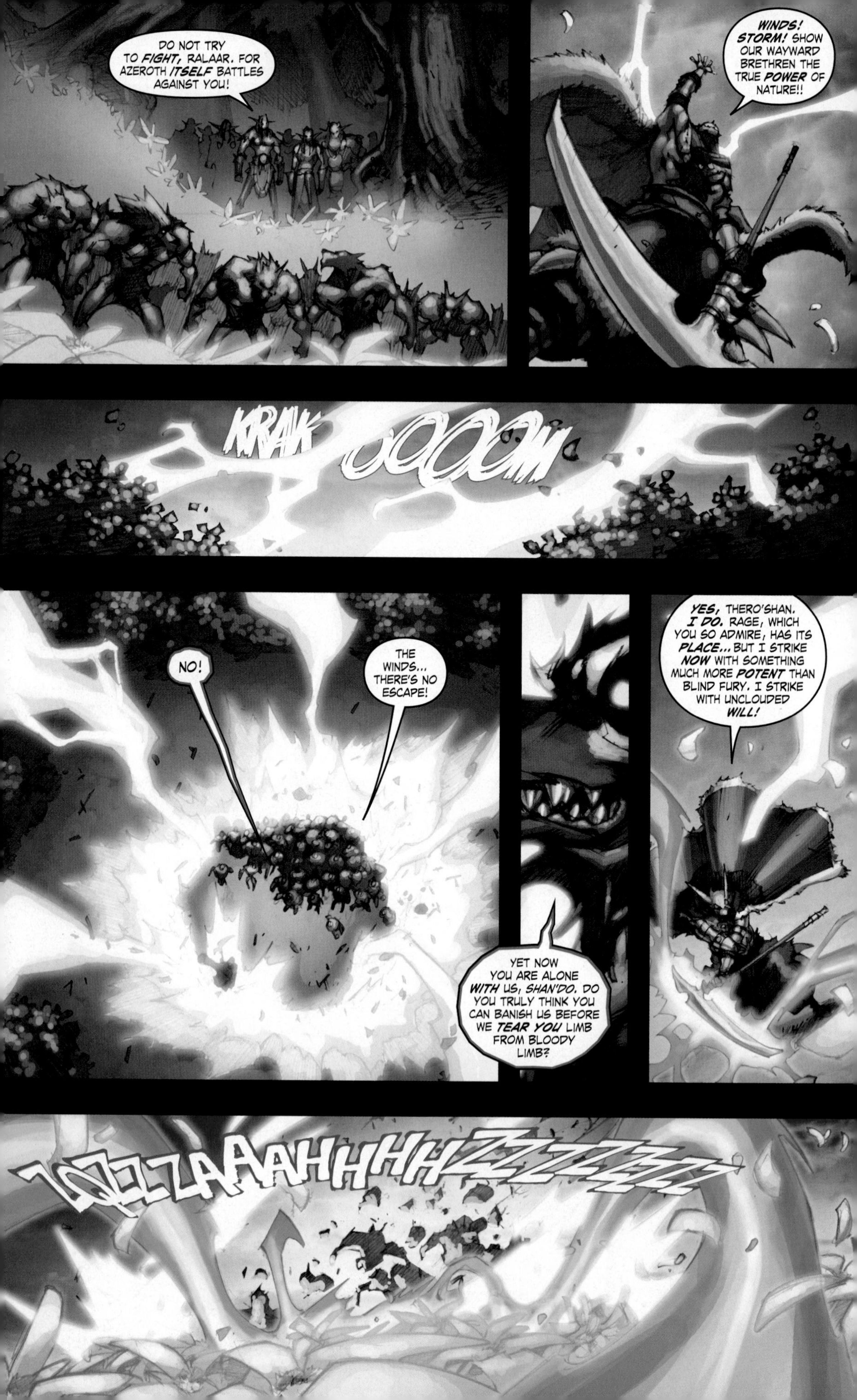
DO NOT TRY TO FIGHT, RALAAR. FOR AZEROTH ITSELF BATTLES AGAINST YOU!
WINDS! STORM! SHOW OUR WAYWARD BRETHREN THE TRUE POWER OF NATURE!!
KRAKOOOOOM
NO!
THE WINDS... THERE'S NO ESCAPE!
YET NOW YOU ARE ALONE WITH US, SHAN'DO. DO YOU TRULY THINK YOU CAN BANISH US BEFORE WE TEAR YOU LIMB FROM BLOODY LIMB?
YES, THERO'SHAN. I DO. RAGE, WHICH YOU SO ADMIRE, HAS ITS PLACE... BUT I STRIKE NOW WITH SOMETHING MUCH MORE POTENT THAN BLIND FURY. I STRIKE WITH UNCLOUDED WILL!
ZZZZAAAHHHHZZZZZZZZ

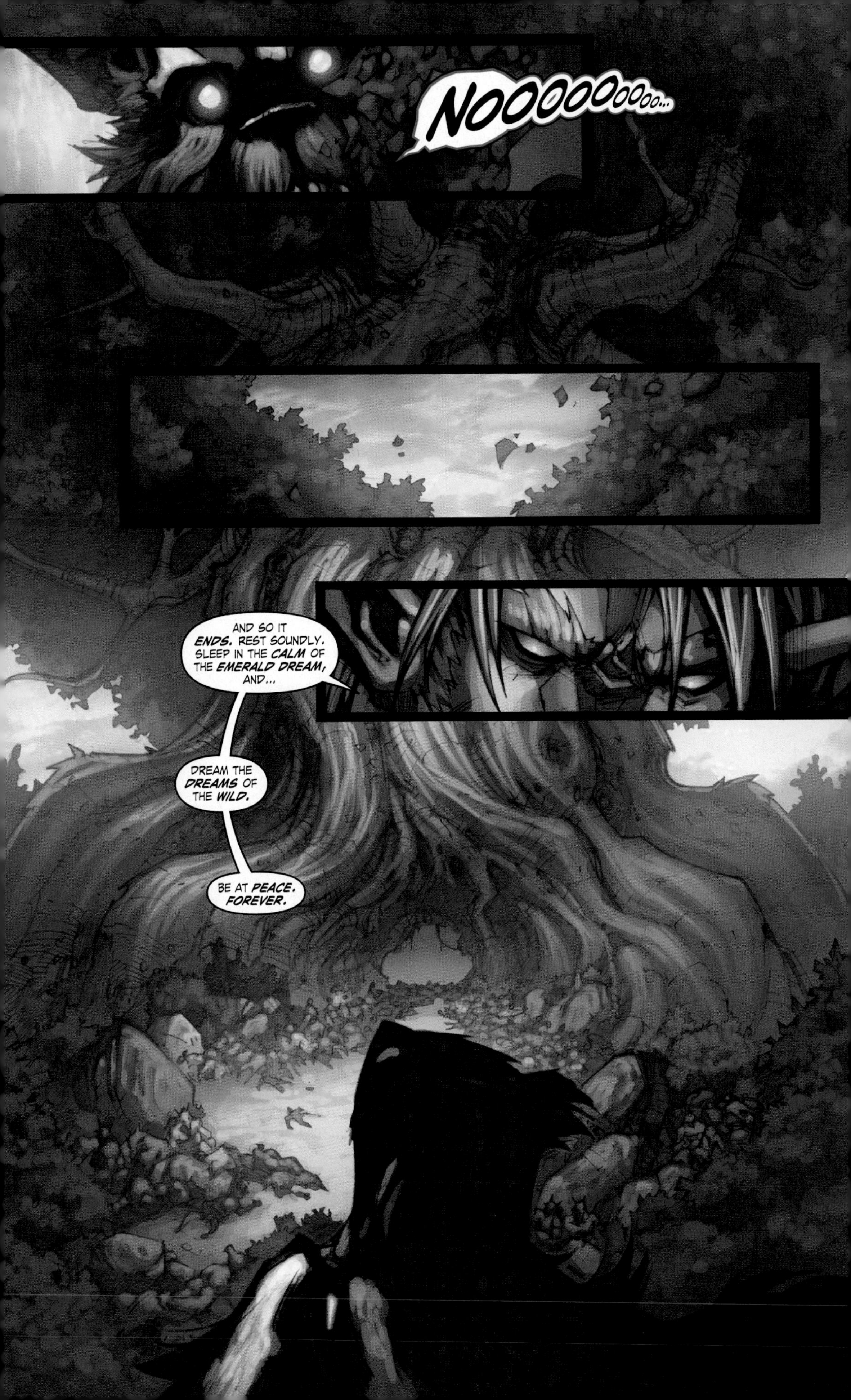
NOOOOOooo...
AND SO IT ENDS. REST SOUNDLY. SLEEP IN THE CALM OF THE EMERALD DREAM, AND...
DREAM THE DREAMS OF THE WILD.
BE AT PEACE. FOREVER.

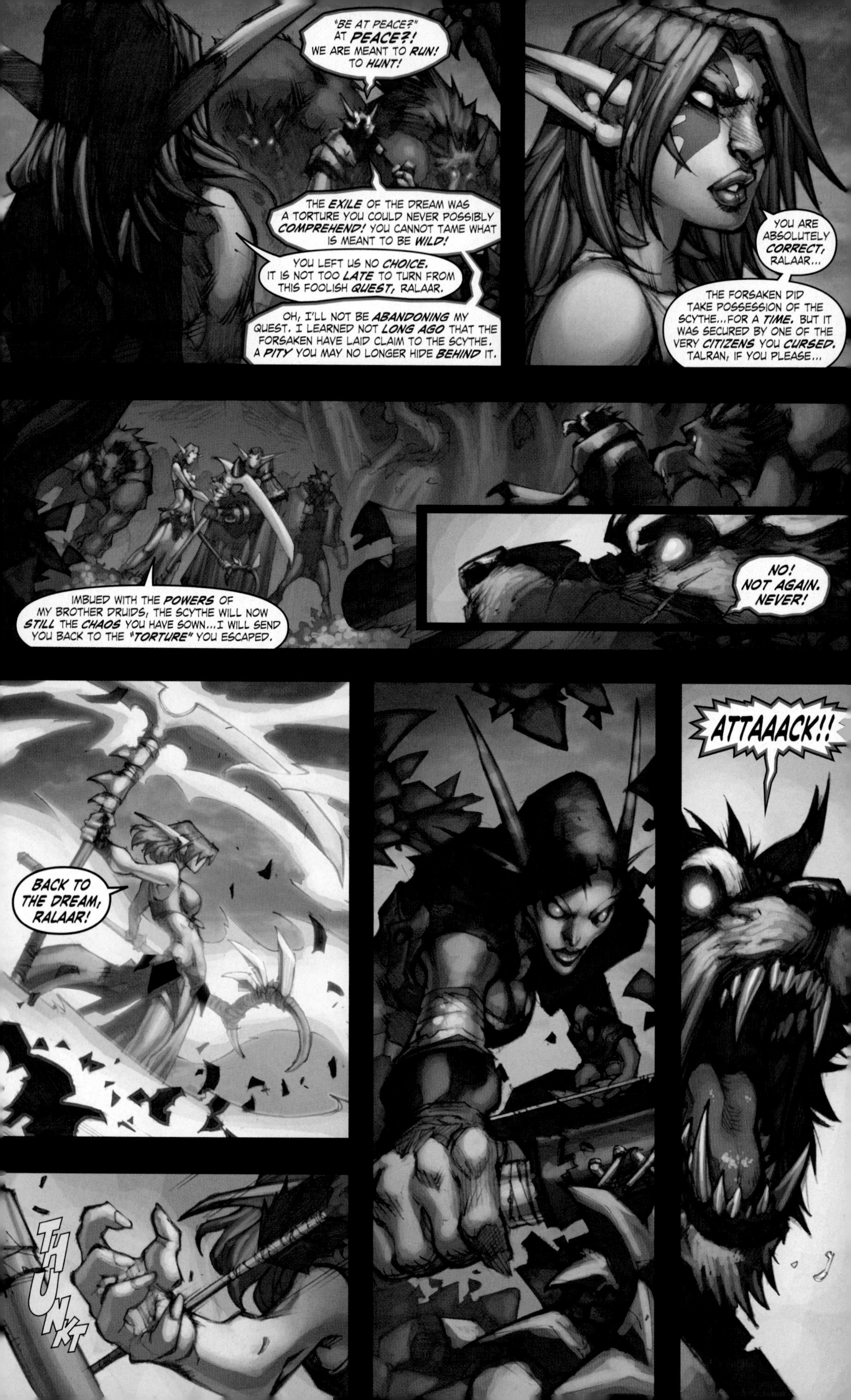
"BE AT PEACE?" AT PEACE?! WE ARE MEANT TO RUN! TO HUNT!
THE EXILE OF THE DREAM WAS A TORTURE YOU COULD NEVER POSSIBLY COMPREHEND! YOU CANNOT TAME WHAT IS MEANT TO BE WILD!
YOU LEFT US NO CHOICE. IT IS NOT TOO LATE TO TURN FROM THIS FOOLISH QUEST, RALAAR.
OH, I'LL NOT BE ABANDONING MY QUEST. I LEARNED NOT LONG AGO THAT THE FORSAKEN HAVE LAID CLAIM TO THE SCYTHE. A PITY YOU MAY NO LONGER HIDE BEHIND IT.
YOU ARE ABSOLUTELY CORRECT, RALAAR...
THE FORSAKEN DID TAKE POSSESSION OF THE SCYTHE...FOR A TIME. BUT IT WAS SECURED BY ONE OF THE VERY CITIZENS YOU CURSED. TALRAN, IF YOU PLEASE...
IMBUED WITH THE POWERS OF MY BROTHER DRUIDS, THE SCYTHE WILL NOW STILL THE CHAOS YOU HAVE SOWN...I WILL SEND YOU BACK TO THE "TORTURE" YOU ESCAPED.
NO! NOT AGAIN. NEVER!
BACK TO THE DREAM, RALAAR!
ATTAAACK!!
THUNKT

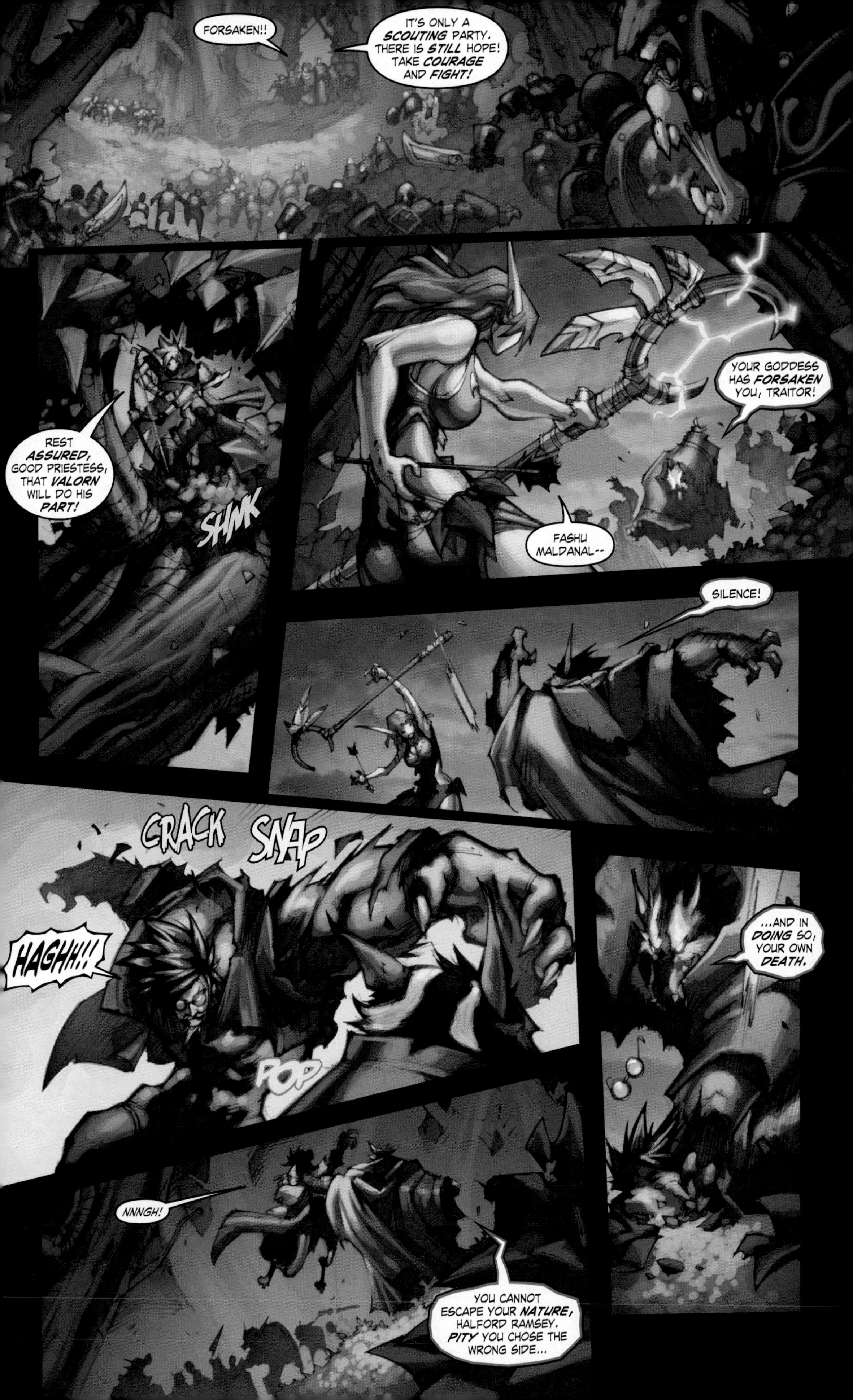
FORSAKEN!!
IT'S ONLY A SCOUTING PARTY. THERE IS STILL HOPE! TAKE COURAGE AND FIGHT!
REST ASSURED, GOOD PRIESTESS, THAT VALORN WILL DO HIS PART!
SHMK
YOUR GODDESS HAS FORSAKEN YOU, TRAITOR!
FASHU MALDANAL--
SILENCE!
CRACK
SNAP
HAGHH!!
POP
...AND IN DOING SO, YOUR OWN DEATH.
NNNGH!
YOU CANNOT ESCAPE YOUR NATURE, HALFORD RAMSEY. PITY YOU CHOSE THE WRONG SIDE...

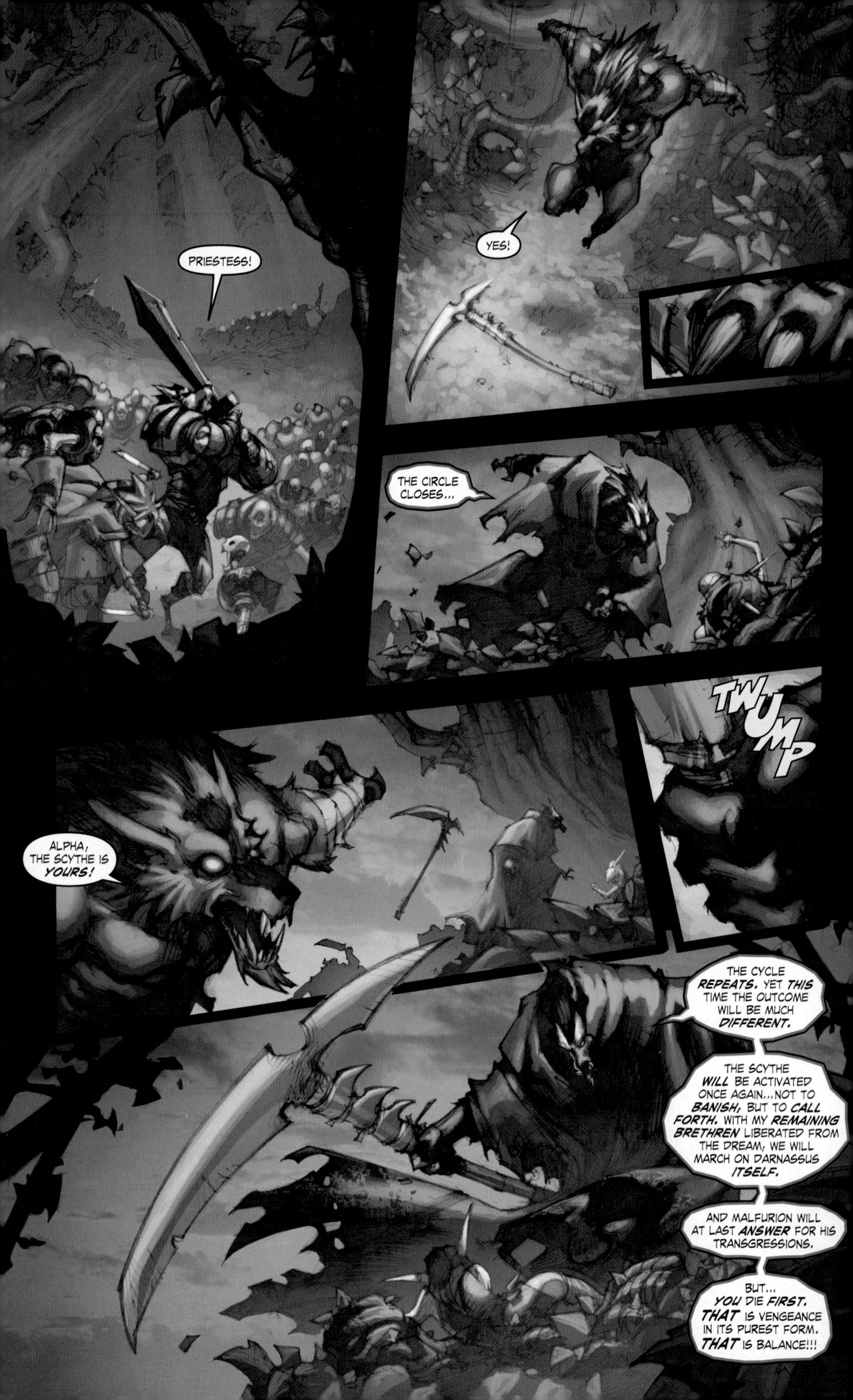
PRIESTESS!
YES!
THE CIRCLE CLOSES...
TWUMP
ALPHA, THE SCYTHE IS *YOURS!*
THE CYCLE *REPEATS.* YET *THIS* TIME THE OUTCOME WILL BE MUCH *DIFFERENT.*
THE SCYTHE *WILL* BE ACTIVATED ONCE AGAIN...NOT TO *BANISH,* BUT TO *CALL FORTH.* WITH MY *REMAINING BRETHREN* LIBERATED FROM THE DREAM, WE WILL MARCH ON DARNASSUS *ITSELF.*
AND MALFURION WILL AT LAST *ANSWER* FOR HIS TRANSGRESSIONS.
BUT... *YOU* DIE *FIRST.* *THAT* IS VENGEANCE IN ITS PUREST FORM. *THAT* IS BALANCE!!!

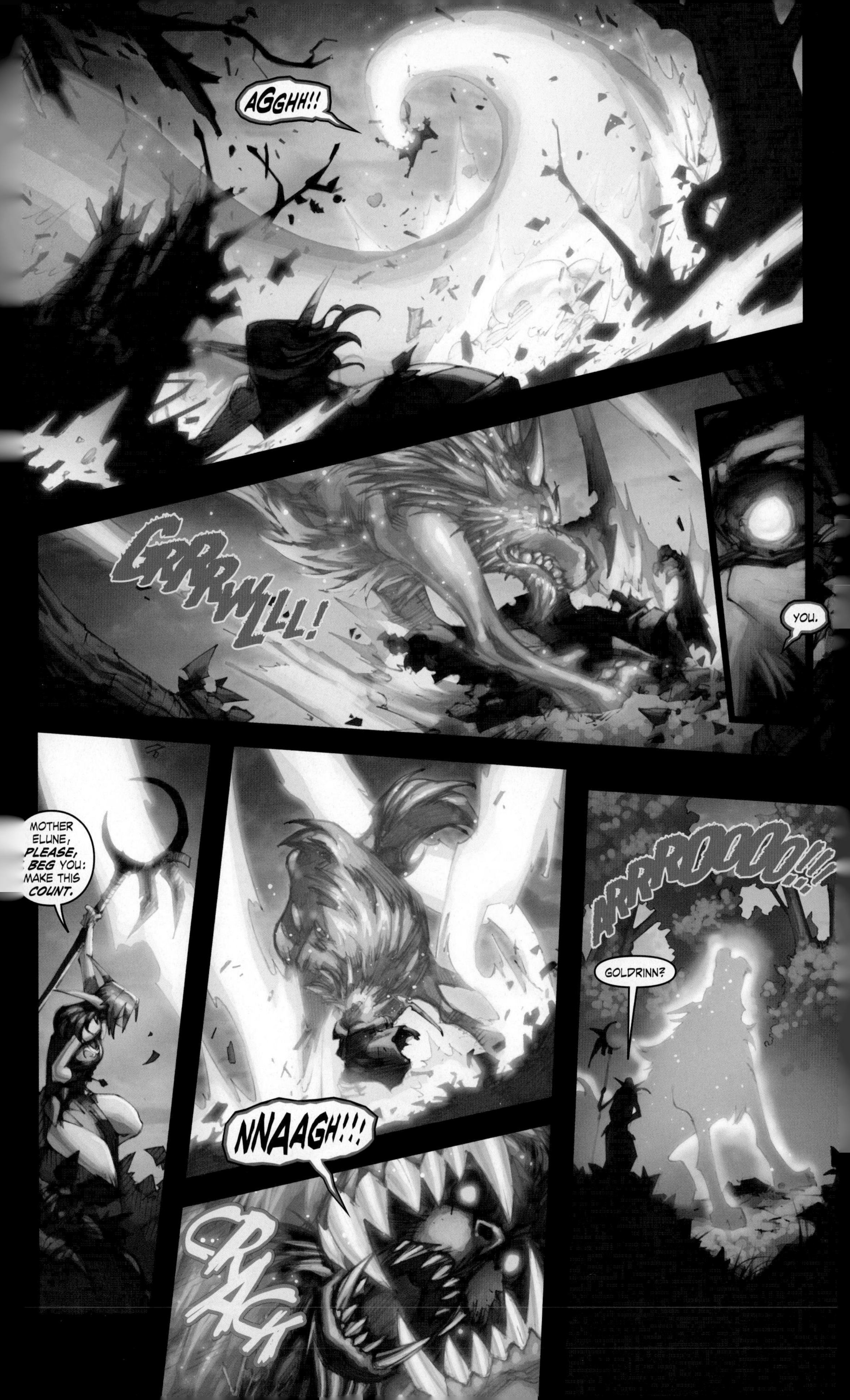
AGGHH!!
GRRRWLLL!
YOU.
MOTHER ELUNE, PLEASE, BEG YOU: MAKE THIS COUNT.
NNAAGH!!!
CRACK
ARRRROOOO!!!
GOLDRINN?

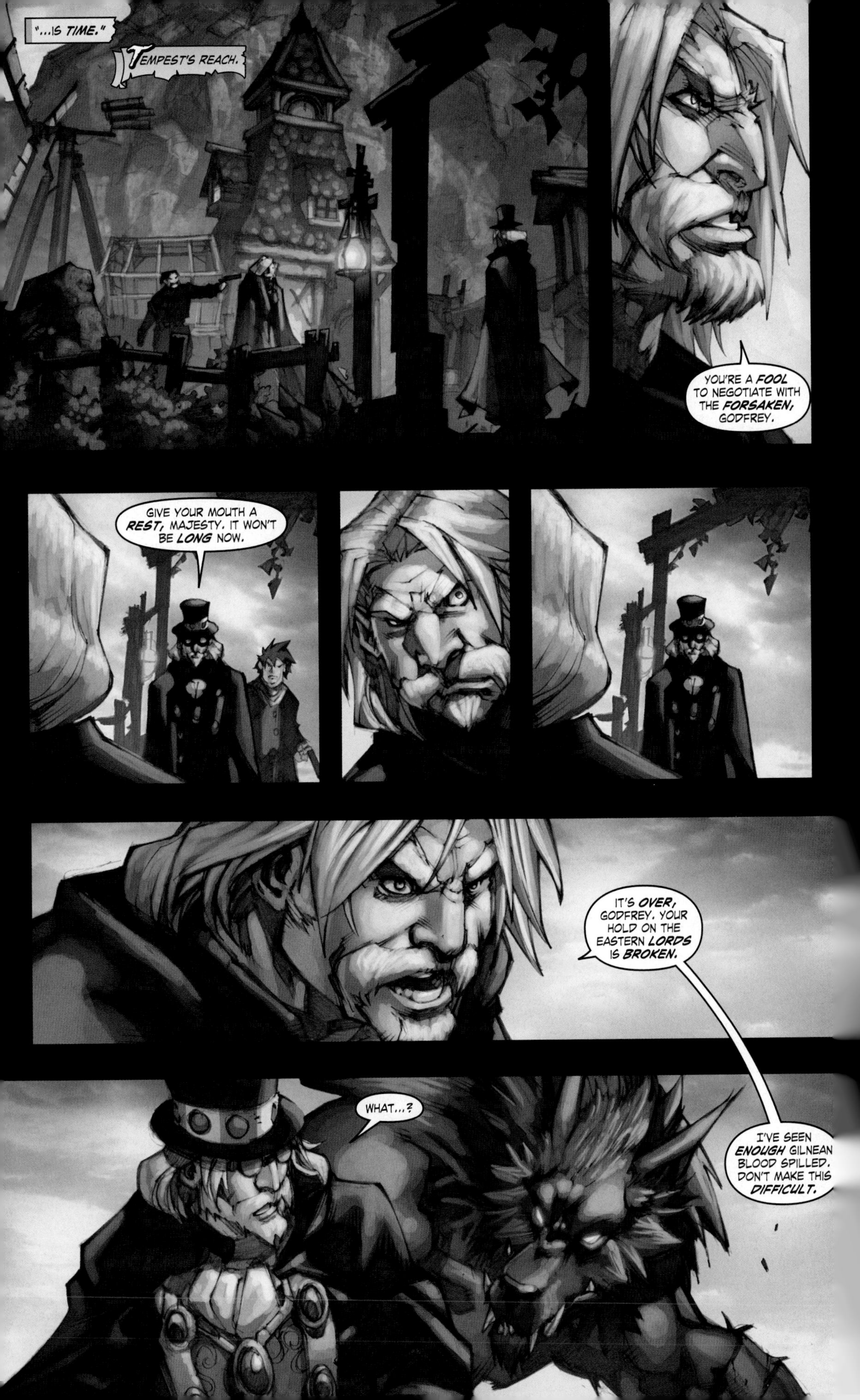
"...IS TIME."
TEMPEST'S REACH.
YOU'RE A FOOL TO NEGOTIATE WITH THE FORSAKEN, GODFREY.
GIVE YOUR MOUTH A REST, MAJESTY. IT WON'T BE LONG NOW.
IT'S OVER, GODFREY. YOUR HOLD ON THE EASTERN LORDS IS BROKEN.
WHAT...?
I'VE SEEN ENOUGH GILNEAN BLOOD SPILLED. DON'T MAKE THIS DIFFICULT.

GODFREY, *NO!!*

NO... I'D SOONER *DIE* THAN HAVE ONE OF *YOUR KIND* FOR A *KING!*

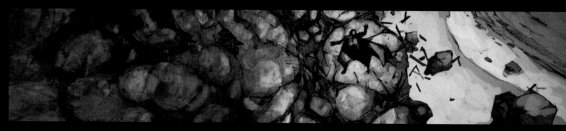

THEY'RE READY TO *HEAR* YOU, FATHER.

OUTSIDE GILNEAS CITY. DAYS LATER.

FIRST, THERE'S SOMETHING I WISH TO *SHARE* WITH YOU...SOMETHING *IMPORTANT.*

OUR NATION'S *GREAT WALL* HAS ISOLATED *MORE* THAN A KINGDOM. IT'S ISOLATED THE *LIES* OF ITS *KING* AS WELL. THE TIME HAS *COME* NOW...

...FOR THE *WALLS* TO COME *DOWN.*

YOU REMEMBER ARUGAL?

YES, OF COURSE, THAT *IMBECILE* OF AN *ARCHMAGE!* HE RECKLESSLY CAST THE *SPELL* THAT *PULLED* THE WORGEN INTO OUR *WORLD.*

WHAT YOU HAVE *NOT* KNOWN, WHAT I'VE NEVER *TOLD* YOU, IS THAT ARUGAL...

"...DID NOT ACT ON HIS *OWN.*"

LET'S *HAVE IT* THEN, MASTER MAGE...TELL ME YOU'VE DISCERNED A *SOLUTION* TO THIS *MADNESS.*

MY RESEARCH HAS LED ME TO THE WORKS OF A POWERFUL SORCERER, *UR.* WITH THIS *KNOWLEDGE,* I MAY BE ABLE TO CONJURE A MEANS OF *DEFEATING* THIS SO-CALLED *SCOURGE...*

FOR I HAVE DIVINED THE *PRESENCE* OF A *HOST* OF BEINGS...TRAPPED WITHIN WHAT I CAN ONLY DESCRIBE AS ANOTHER *DIMENSION...*

MY LIEGE, NOT EVEN THIS GREAT WALL WILL *HOLD* AGAINST SO *MANY.*

WHAT CAN BE *SAID* OF SUCH A *SIGHT?* IT IS...AN UNRELENTING *TIDE* OF *DEATH.* IF I WEREN'T SEEING IT WITH THESE *WEARY EYES,* I WOULD SCARCELY *COMPREHEND* IT.

BESTIAL CREATURES IMBUED WITH *PRETERNATURAL* STRENGTH AND PURE *FEROCITY.* AT THIS TIME THEY'RE IN SOME SORT OF *RESTING STATE,* BUT I...SENSED...THAT THEY WISH TO BE *FREED.*

I DESIRE TO *PROCEED,* MY LORD, BUT I REQUIRE YOUR *BLESSING.*

I MUST SEE THESE CREATURES *FIRST,* ARCHMAGE... SUMMON ONE. I WILL RESERVE MY DECISION UNTIL *THEN.*

I HAD LITTLE ASSURANCE THAT THE WORGEN WOULD BE OUR *SALVATION,* BUT IF SOMETHING WASN'T *DONE,* THE UNDEAD WOULD HAVE *SWARMED* THE *STREETS* OF GILNEAS CITY.

THE SCOURGE'S NUMBERS *DWARFED* THOSE OF EVEN THE CURRENT RANKS OF FORSAKEN.

"AT FIRST ARUGAL'S WEAPONS *WORKED.* THEY WERE A FORCE UNLIKE *ANY* WE HAD EVER SEEN: *VICIOUS, UNYIELDING,* AND EXACTLY THE BEASTS WE NEEDED TO FIGHT THE MONSTERS AT OUR *GATES.*

"I WAS *WARNED* BY MANY GENERALS THAT THEY WERE *RECKLESS, WILD,* BUT WE WERE FRIGHTENED AND BURNING WITH *RAGE* FROM THE *LOSS* OF SO MANY GILNEAN SOLDIERS.

"I DID NOT *HEED* THEIR WARNINGS... HOW COULD I HAVE *KNOWN* WHAT WAS TO *COME?*

"THEY WERE IMPOSSIBLE TO *CONTROL.* WITH THE SCOURGE IN *RETREAT,* THE WORGEN TURNED THEIR FURY...

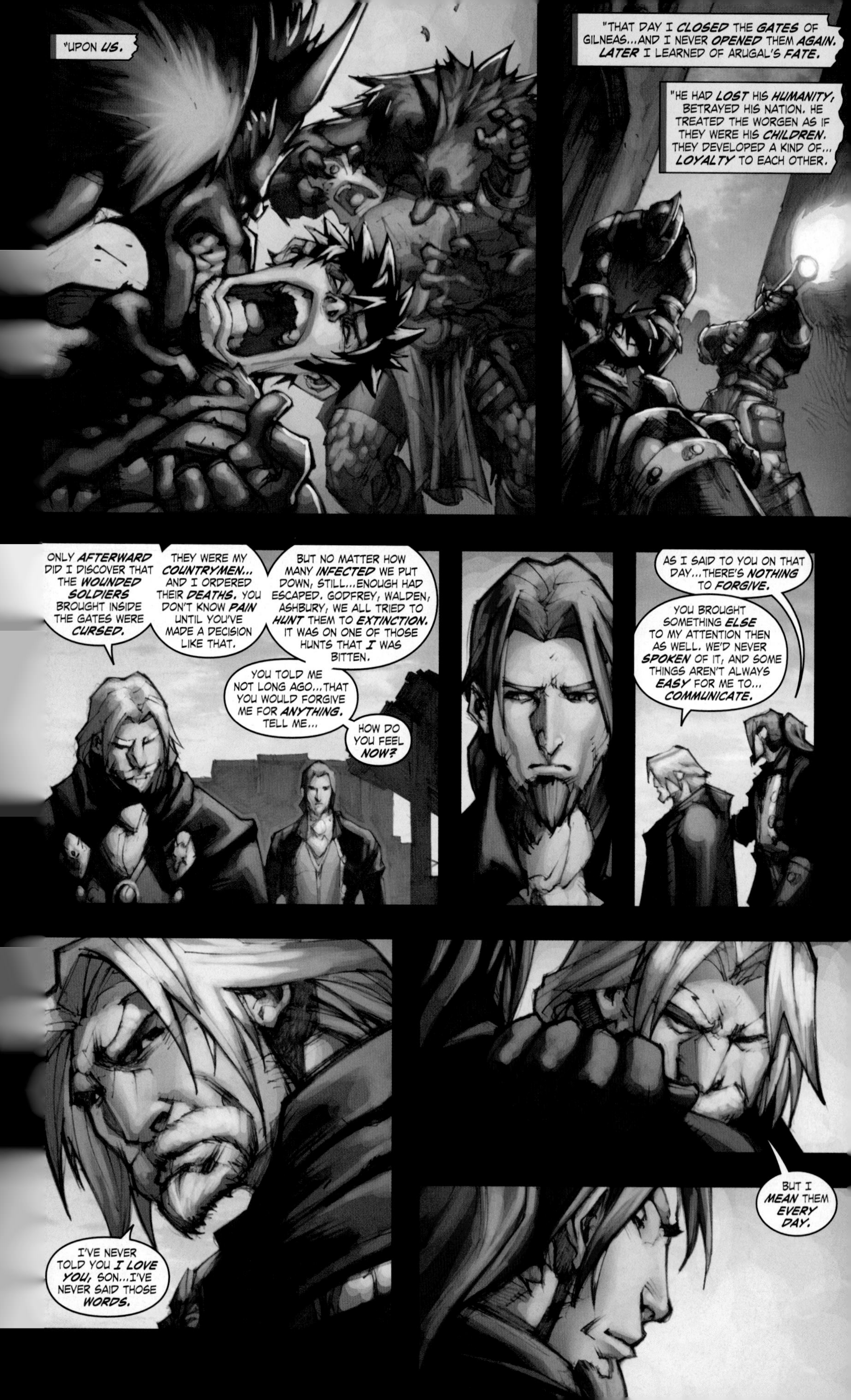
"UPON US.
"THAT DAY I CLOSED THE GATES OF GILNEAS...AND I NEVER OPENED THEM AGAIN. LATER I LEARNED OF ARUGAL'S FATE.
"HE HAD LOST HIS HUMANITY, BETRAYED HIS NATION. HE TREATED THE WORGEN AS IF THEY WERE HIS CHILDREN. THEY DEVELOPED A KIND OF... LOYALTY TO EACH OTHER.
ONLY AFTERWARD DID I DISCOVER THAT THE WOUNDED SOLDIERS BROUGHT INSIDE THE GATES WERE CURSED.
THEY WERE MY COUNTRYMEN... AND I ORDERED THEIR DEATHS. YOU DON'T KNOW PAIN UNTIL YOU'VE MADE A DECISION LIKE THAT.
BUT NO MATTER HOW MANY INFECTED WE PUT DOWN, STILL...ENOUGH HAD ESCAPED. GODFREY, WALDEN, ASHBURY, WE ALL TRIED TO HUNT THEM TO EXTINCTION. IT WAS ON ONE OF THOSE HUNTS THAT I WAS BITTEN.
YOU TOLD ME NOT LONG AGO...THAT YOU WOULD FORGIVE ME FOR ANYTHING. TELL ME...
HOW DO YOU FEEL NOW?
AS I SAID TO YOU ON THAT DAY...THERE'S NOTHING TO FORGIVE.
YOU BROUGHT SOMETHING ELSE TO MY ATTENTION THEN AS WELL. WE'D NEVER SPOKEN OF IT, AND SOME THINGS AREN'T ALWAYS EASY FOR ME TO... COMMUNICATE.
I'VE NEVER TOLD YOU I LOVE YOU, SON...I'VE NEVER SAID THOSE WORDS.
BUT I MEAN THEM EVERY DAY.

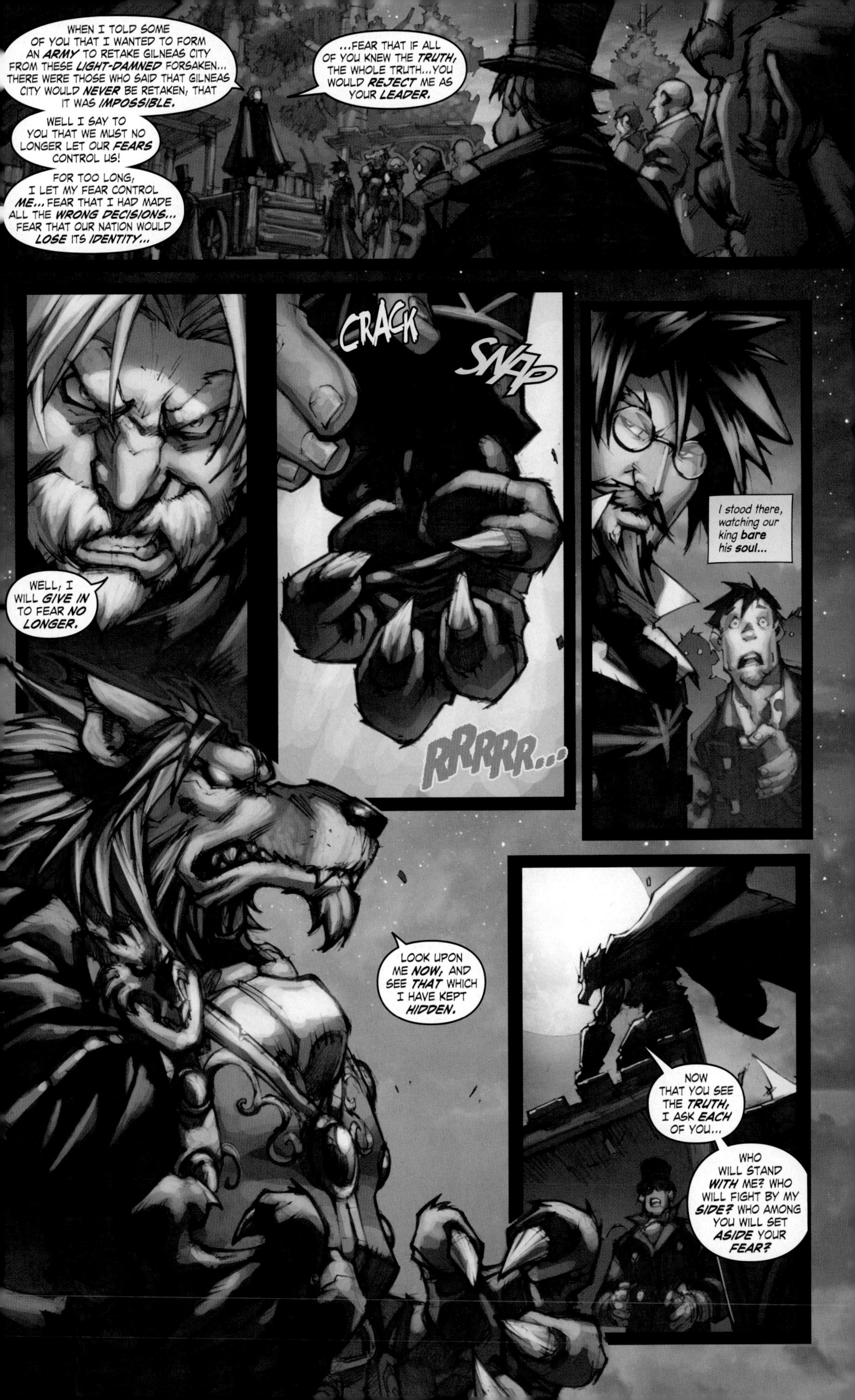
WHEN I TOLD SOME OF YOU THAT I WANTED TO FORM AN ARMY TO RETAKE GILNEAS CITY FROM THESE LIGHT-DAMNED FORSAKEN... THERE WERE THOSE WHO SAID THAT GILNEAS CITY WOULD NEVER BE RETAKEN, THAT IT WAS IMPOSSIBLE.
WELL I SAY TO YOU THAT WE MUST NO LONGER LET OUR FEARS CONTROL US!
FOR TOO LONG, I LET MY FEAR CONTROL ME... FEAR THAT I HAD MADE ALL THE WRONG DECISIONS... FEAR THAT OUR NATION WOULD LOSE ITS IDENTITY...
...FEAR THAT IF ALL OF YOU KNEW THE TRUTH, THE WHOLE TRUTH...YOU WOULD REJECT ME AS YOUR LEADER.
WELL, I WILL GIVE IN TO FEAR NO LONGER.
CRACK
SNAP
RRRRR...
I stood there, watching our king bare his soul...
LOOK UPON ME NOW, AND SEE THAT WHICH I HAVE KEPT HIDDEN.
NOW THAT YOU SEE THE TRUTH, I ASK EACH OF YOU...
WHO WILL STAND WITH ME? WHO WILL FIGHT BY MY SIDE? WHO AMONG YOU WILL SET ASIDE YOUR FEAR?

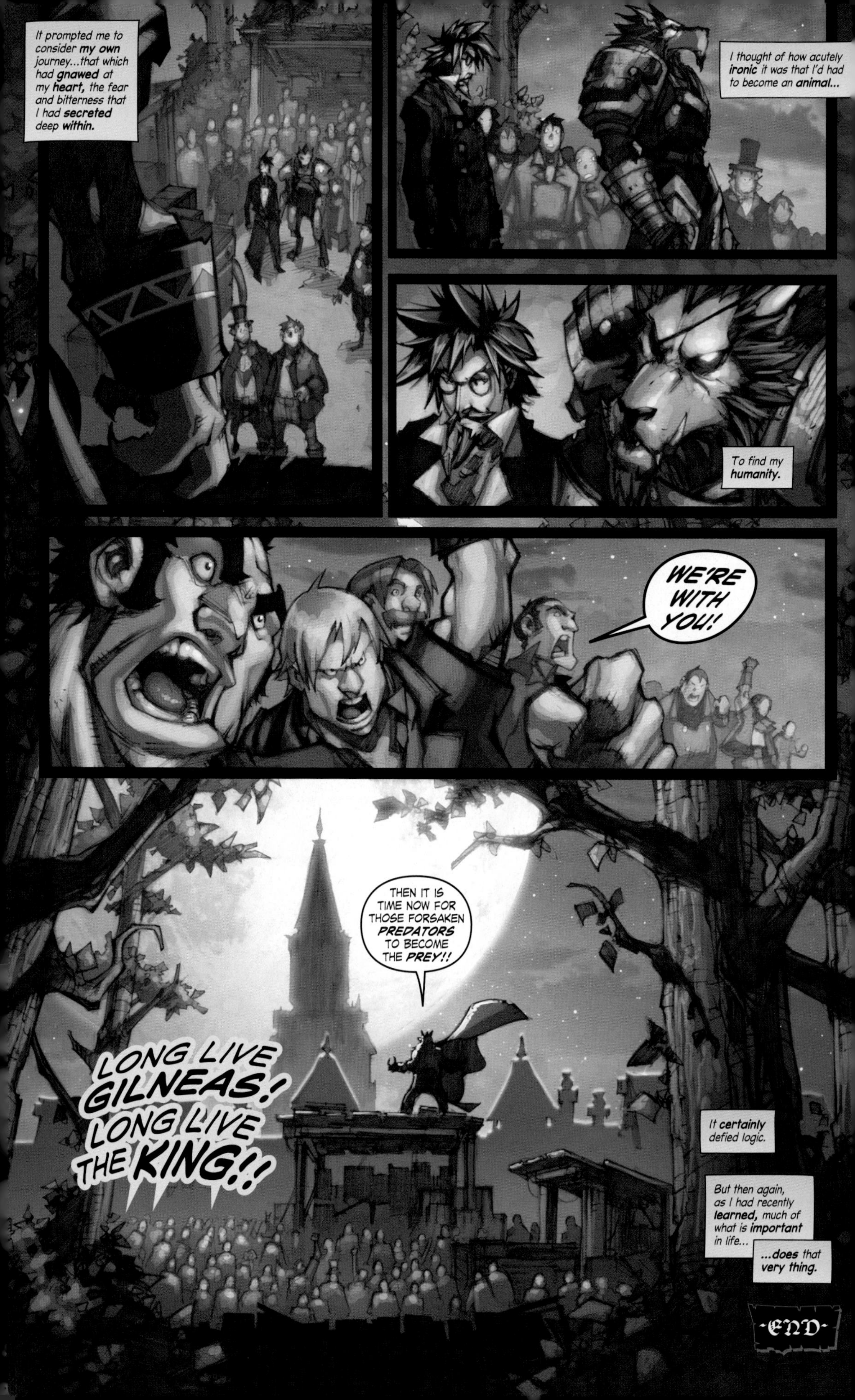

It prompted me to consider my own journey...that which had gnawed at my heart, the fear and bitterness that I had secreted deep within.
I thought of how acutely ironic it was that I'd had to become an animal...
To find my humanity.
WE'RE WITH YOU!
THEN IT IS TIME NOW FOR THOSE FORSAKEN PREDATORS TO BECOME THE PREY!!
LONG LIVE GILNEAS! LONG LIVE THE KING!!
It certainly defied logic.
But then again, as I had recently learned, much of what is important in life...
...does that very thing.
-END-

EPILOGUE

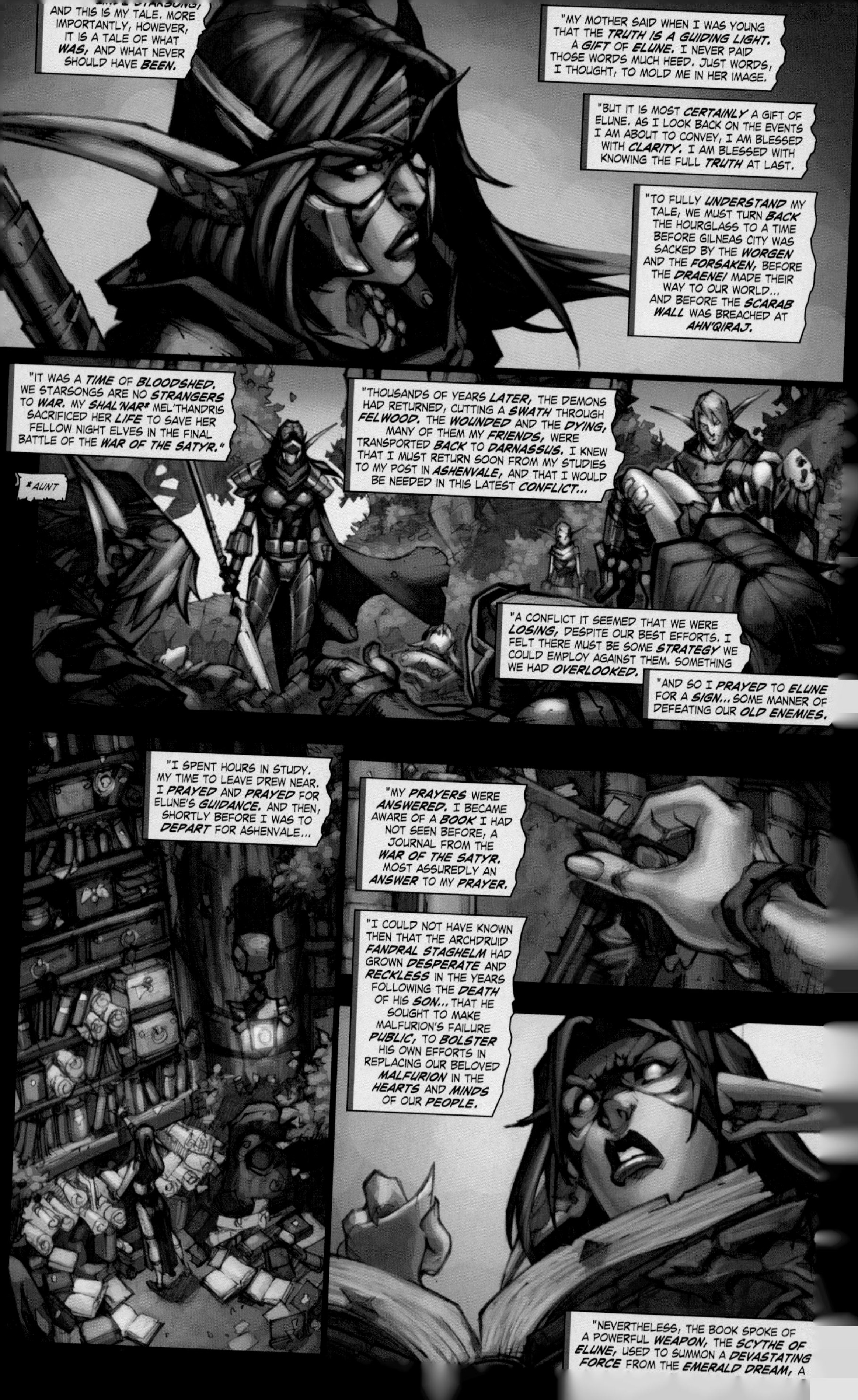
AND THIS IS MY TALE. MORE IMPORTANTLY, HOWEVER, IT IS A TALE OF WHAT WAS, AND WHAT NEVER SHOULD HAVE BEEN.
"MY MOTHER SAID WHEN I WAS YOUNG THAT THE TRUTH IS A GUIDING LIGHT. A GIFT OF ELUNE. I NEVER PAID THOSE WORDS MUCH HEED. JUST WORDS, I THOUGHT, TO MOLD ME IN HER IMAGE.
"BUT IT IS MOST CERTAINLY A GIFT OF ELUNE. AS I LOOK BACK ON THE EVENTS I AM ABOUT TO CONVEY, I AM BLESSED WITH CLARITY. I AM BLESSED WITH KNOWING THE FULL TRUTH AT LAST.
"TO FULLY UNDERSTAND MY TALE, WE MUST TURN BACK THE HOURGLASS TO A TIME BEFORE GILNEAS CITY WAS SACKED BY THE WORGEN AND THE FORSAKEN, BEFORE THE DRAENEI MADE THEIR WAY TO OUR WORLD... AND BEFORE THE SCARAB WALL WAS BREACHED AT AHN'QIRAJ.
"IT WAS A TIME OF BLOODSHED. WE STARSONGS ARE NO STRANGERS TO WAR. MY SHAL'NAR* MEL'THANDRIS SACRIFICED HER LIFE TO SAVE HER FELLOW NIGHT ELVES IN THE FINAL BATTLE OF THE WAR OF THE SATYR."
*AUNT
"THOUSANDS OF YEARS LATER, THE DEMONS HAD RETURNED, CUTTING A SWATH THROUGH FELWOOD. THE WOUNDED AND THE DYING, MANY OF THEM MY FRIENDS, WERE TRANSPORTED BACK TO DARNASSUS. I KNEW THAT I MUST RETURN SOON FROM MY STUDIES TO MY POST IN ASHENVALE, AND THAT I WOULD BE NEEDED IN THIS LATEST CONFLICT...
"A CONFLICT IT SEEMED THAT WE WERE LOSING, DESPITE OUR BEST EFFORTS. I FELT THERE MUST BE SOME STRATEGY WE COULD EMPLOY AGAINST THEM. SOMETHING WE HAD OVERLOOKED.
"AND SO I PRAYED TO ELUNE FOR A SIGN... SOME MANNER OF DEFEATING OUR OLD ENEMIES.
"I SPENT HOURS IN STUDY. MY TIME TO LEAVE DREW NEAR. I PRAYED AND PRAYED FOR ELUNE'S GUIDANCE. AND THEN, SHORTLY BEFORE I WAS TO DEPART FOR ASHENVALE...
"MY PRAYERS WERE ANSWERED. I BECAME AWARE OF A BOOK I HAD NOT SEEN BEFORE, A JOURNAL FROM THE WAR OF THE SATYR. MOST ASSUREDLY AN ANSWER TO MY PRAYER.
"I COULD NOT HAVE KNOWN THEN THAT THE ARCHDRUID FANDRAL STAGHELM HAD GROWN DESPERATE AND RECKLESS IN THE YEARS FOLLOWING THE DEATH OF HIS SON... THAT HE SOUGHT TO MAKE MALFURION'S FAILURE PUBLIC, TO BOLSTER HIS OWN EFFORTS IN REPLACING OUR BELOVED MALFURION IN THE HEARTS AND MINDS OF OUR PEOPLE.
"NEVERTHELESS, THE BOOK SPOKE OF A POWERFUL WEAPON, THE SCYTHE OF ELUNE, USED TO SUMMON A DEVASTATING FORCE FROM THE EMERALD DREAM, A

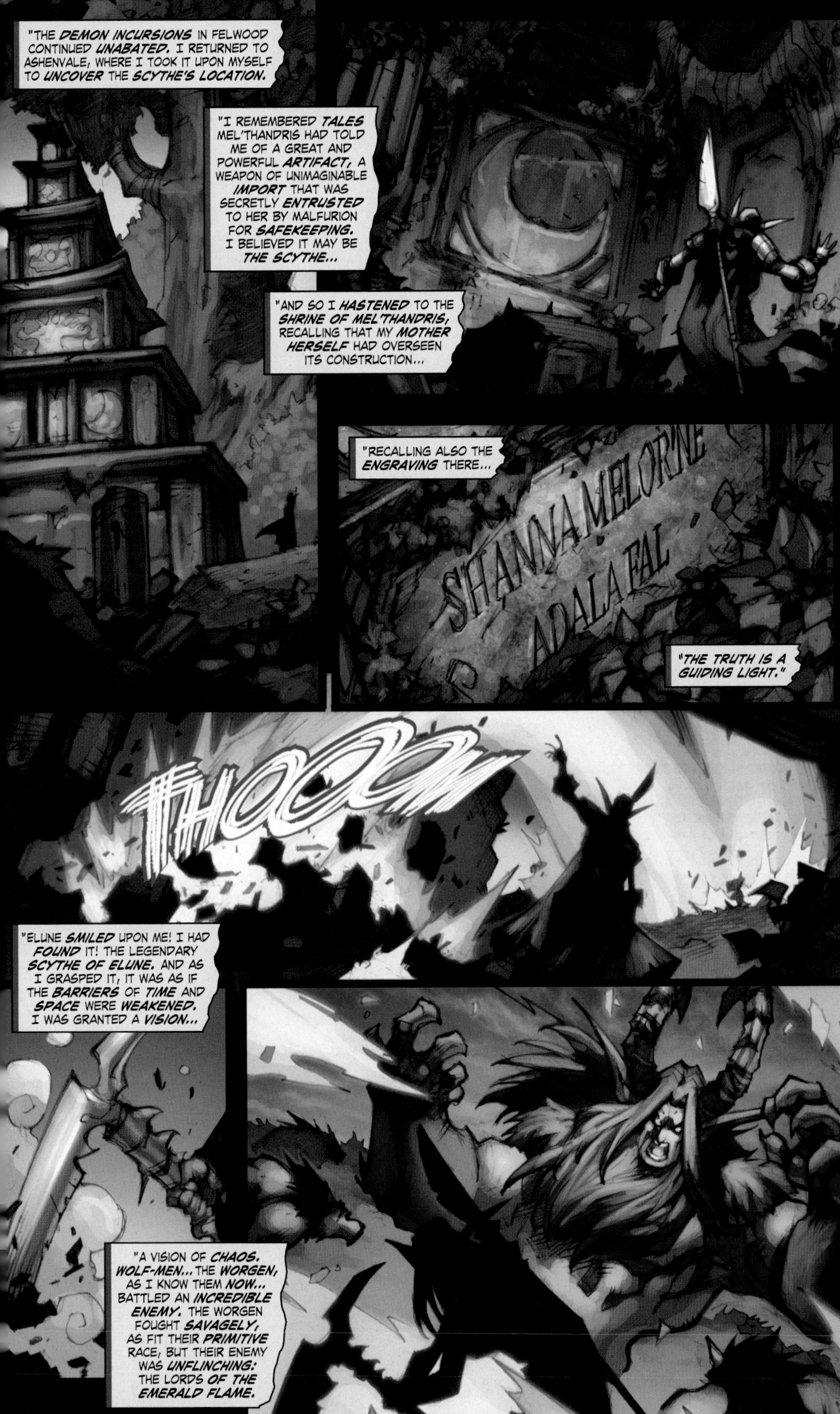
"THE DEMON INCURSIONS IN FELWOOD CONTINUED UNABATED. I RETURNED TO ASHENVALE, WHERE I TOOK IT UPON MYSELF TO UNCOVER THE SCYTHE'S LOCATION.
"I REMEMBERED TALES MEL'THANDRIS HAD TOLD ME OF A GREAT AND POWERFUL ARTIFACT, A WEAPON OF UNIMAGINABLE IMPORT THAT WAS SECRETLY ENTRUSTED TO HER BY MALFURION FOR SAFEKEEPING. I BELIEVED IT MAY BE THE SCYTHE...
"AND SO I HASTENED TO THE SHRINE OF MEL'THANDRIS, RECALLING THAT MY MOTHER HERSELF HAD OVERSEEN ITS CONSTRUCTION...
"RECALLING ALSO THE ENGRAVING THERE...
SHANNA MELORNE
ADALA FAL
"THE TRUTH IS A GUIDING LIGHT."
THOOOOM
"ELUNE SMILED UPON ME! I HAD FOUND IT! THE LEGENDARY SCYTHE OF ELUNE. AND AS I GRASPED IT, IT WAS AS IF THE BARRIERS OF TIME AND SPACE WERE WEAKENED. I WAS GRANTED A VISION...
"A VISION OF CHAOS. WOLF-MEN... THE WORGEN, AS I KNOW THEM NOW... BATTLED AN INCREDIBLE ENEMY. THE WORGEN FOUGHT SAVAGELY, AS FIT THEIR PRIMITIVE RACE, BUT THEIR ENEMY WAS UNFLINCHING: THE LORDS OF THE EMERALD FLAME.

"BY *FOCUSING* ON THE SCYTHE, I WAS ABLE TO *COMMUNICATE* WITH THE *WORGEN.* THEY *HEARD* AND *UNDERSTOOD* ME. I LEARNED THAT BY FURTHER CHANNELING THE *ENERGY* OF THE SCYTHE, I MIGHT ACTUALLY BE ABLE TO DRAW THE WORGEN *OUT.*

"MY ATTEMPTS WERE A *SUCCESS!* I CALLED FORTH A *SCORE* AND A *HALF* OF THE DEADLY BEASTS. BY THE *GRACE* OF *ELUNE*--AS I BELIEVED IT TO BE-- THE *FORESTS* WOULD BE *CLEANSED.*

"I HAD THE WEAPON I *NEEDED.* THE *TIME* HAD *COME* TO CONFRONT THE DEMON INVADERS OF FELWOOD. TO TIP THE *SCALES* IN OUR *FAVOR!*

"FOR A TIME, ALL WENT *WELL.* YET SOMETHING WAS AMISS. I NOTED THAT THE NUMBERS OF THE WORGEN CONTINUED TO *INCREASE* WITHOUT MY *INTERVENTION!*

"AS THE BATTLES *WORE ON,* MY CONCERN *GREW.* A PACK SET OUT AND WOULD NOT *ANSWER* MY CALL TO *RETURN.* I WAS LOSING *CONTROL.*

"THE BEASTS CONTINUED TO *MULTIPLY,* THEIR SHEER *FEROCITY* IN BATTLE WAS *TERRIFYING.* WHAT, IN THE NAME OF *ELUNE,* HAD I SET *LOOSE?*

"I ORDERED THE REMAINING WORGEN TO *HOLD* AT THE *SHRINE* OF *MEL'THANDRIS,* A COMMAND THAT THEY SEEMED *CONTENT* TO *OBEY.* I RETURNED TO THE LIBRARY OF DARNASSUS TO SEEK MORE *KNOWLEDGE* OF THE BEASTS. YET, NOT ONE *SCRAP* OF INFORMATION ABOUT THE WORGEN COULD I *FIND.*

"I DID, HOWEVER, HEAR *WHISPERS.* REPORTS OF A *WIZARD* OF THE *KIRIN TOR* NAMED *ARUGAL* WHO PURPORTEDLY HAD SUMMONED WORGEN *AS WELL.*

"ONLY NOW DO I KNOW THAT ARUGAL'S SUMMONING HAD IN FACT *WEAKENED* THE *BARRIER* TO THE WORGEN, *ALLOWING* ME TO COMMUNICATE WITH THEM.

"I SET OUT THE VERY *NEXT DAY* FOR THE *EASTERN KINGDOMS.*

UPON MY *ARRIVAL* AT *BOOTY BAY,* I SENT WORD OF MY SOJOURN TO THE WIZARD *ARUGAL.*

"BUT THERE WAS *ANOTHER* ALSO, A *SUBJECT* OF PRIME'S WHO *COVETED* THE SCYTHE, WHO SOUGHT TO *USURP* THE POWER OF HIS *MASTER. VARKAS* WAS HIS CURSED NAME.

"AGAIN, MY CURRENT STATE OF *ALL-KNOWING* HAS *PARTED* THE *VEIL* OF MYSTERY. I AM AWARE OF THE ONE CALLED *ALPHA PRIME,* MASTER OF THE WORGEN IN *SILVERPINE FOREST,* WHO *HELD* THE MADDENED *ARUGAL* UNDER HIS *SWAY.*

"HOW *EAGER* PRIME WAS TO RECEIVE THE SCYTHE! IF *ONLY* I HAD KNOWN *THEN.*

"*VARKAS* STRUCK OUT, WITH THREE OTHERS WHO WOULD *DEFY* PRIME, TO *INTERCEPT* THE SCYTHE. I BECAME AN OBLIVIOUS *TARGET,* SET *SQUARELY* IN THEIR *SIGHTS.*

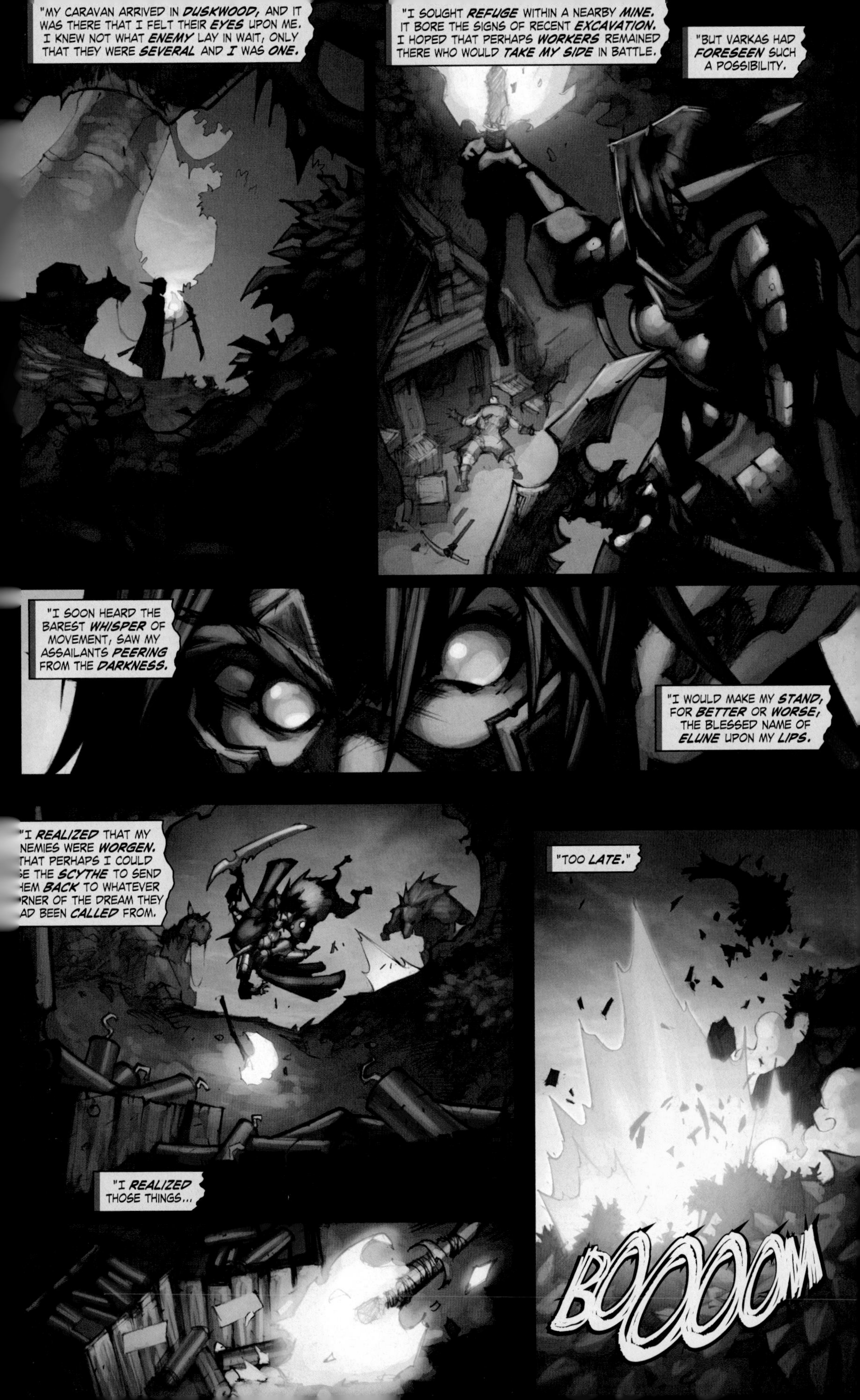
"MY CARAVAN ARRIVED IN DUSKWOOD, AND IT WAS THERE THAT I FELT THEIR EYES UPON ME. I KNEW NOT WHAT ENEMY LAY IN WAIT, ONLY THAT THEY WERE SEVERAL AND I WAS ONE.
"I SOUGHT REFUGE WITHIN A NEARBY MINE. IT BORE THE SIGNS OF RECENT EXCAVATION. I HOPED THAT PERHAPS WORKERS REMAINED THERE WHO WOULD TAKE MY SIDE IN BATTLE.
"BUT VARKAS HAD FORESEEN SUCH A POSSIBILITY.
"I SOON HEARD THE BAREST WHISPER OF MOVEMENT, SAW MY ASSAILANTS PEERING FROM THE DARKNESS.
"I WOULD MAKE MY STAND, FOR BETTER OR WORSE; THE BLESSED NAME OF ELUNE UPON MY LIPS.
"I REALIZED THAT MY NEMIES WERE WORGEN. THAT PERHAPS I COULD SE THE SCYTHE TO SEND HEM BACK TO WHATEVER ORNER OF THE DREAM THEY AD BEEN CALLED FROM.
"I REALIZED THOSE THINGS...
"TOO LATE."
BOOOOOM

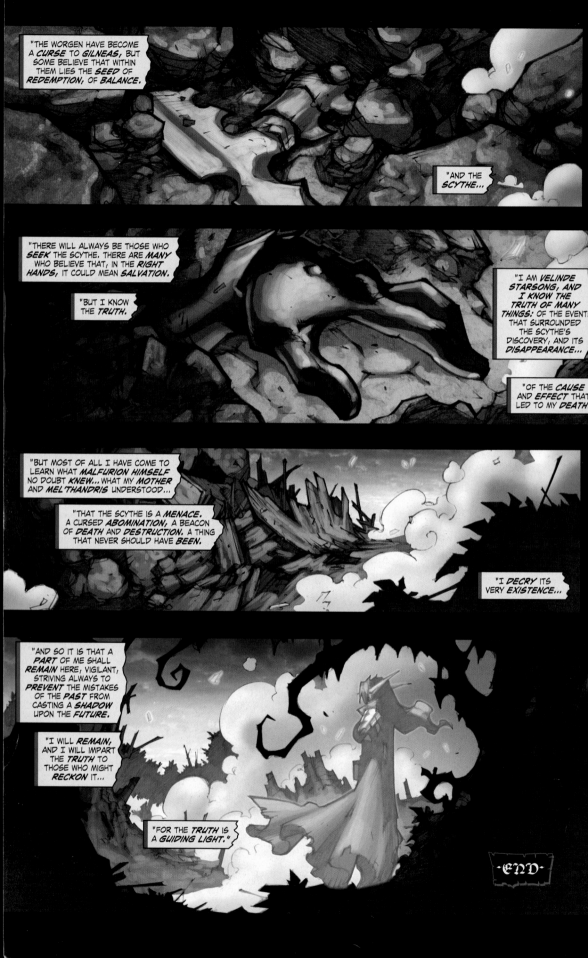

"THE WORGEN HAVE BECOME A *CURSE* TO *GILNEAS*, BUT SOME BELIEVE THAT WITHIN THEM LIES THE *SEED* OF *REDEMPTION*, OF *BALANCE*.

"AND THE *SCYTHE*...

"THERE WILL ALWAYS BE THOSE WHO *SEEK* THE SCYTHE. THERE ARE *MANY* WHO BELIEVE THAT, IN THE *RIGHT HANDS*, IT COULD MEAN *SALVATION*.

"BUT I KNOW THE *TRUTH*.

"I AM *VELINDE STARSONG*, AND I KNOW THE *TRUTH* OF MANY *THINGS*: OF THE EVENT? THAT SURROUNDED THE SCYTHE'S DISCOVERY, AND ITS *DISAPPEARANCE*...

"OF THE *CAUSE* AND *EFFECT* THAT LED TO MY *DEATH*

"BUT MOST OF ALL I HAVE COME TO LEARN WHAT *MALFURION HIMSELF* NO DOUBT *KNEW*... WHAT MY *MOTHER* AND *MEL'THANDRIS* UNDERSTOOD...

"THAT THE SCYTHE IS A *MENACE*. A CURSED *ABOMINATION*, A BEACON OF *DEATH* AND *DESTRUCTION*. A THING THAT NEVER SHOULD HAVE *BEEN*.

"I *DECRY* ITS VERY *EXISTENCE*...

"AND SO IT IS THAT A *PART* OF ME SHALL *REMAIN* HERE, VIGILANT; STRIVING ALWAYS TO *PREVENT* THE MISTAKES OF THE *PAST* FROM CASTING A *SHADOW* UPON THE *FUTURE*.

"I WILL *REMAIN*, AND I WILL IMPART THE *TRUTH* TO THOSE WHO MIGHT *RECKON* IT...

"FOR THE *TRUTH* IS A *GUIDING LIGHT*."

·END·

World of Warcraft: Curse of the Worgen

FURTHER READING

If you'd like to read more about the characters, situations, and settings featured in this comic book, the sources listed below offer additional pieces of the story of Azeroth.

More information about King Genn Greymane is revealed in *World of Warcraft: Wolfheart* and *Warcraft: Day of the Dragon* by Richard A. Knaak; *World of Warcraft: Tides of Darkness* by Aaron Rosenberg; *World of Warcraft: Beyond the Dark Portal* by Aaron Rosenberg and Christie Golden; and the short story "Lord of His Pack" by James Waugh (on http://us.battle.net/wow/en/game/lore/).

Malfurion Stormrage plays a key role in *World of Warcraft: Wolfheart* by Richard A. Knaak. Further insight regarding his past is offered in *World of Warcraft: Stormrage* and the *War of the Ancients Trilogy* (*Warcraft: The Well of Eternity*, *Warcraft: The Demon Soul*, and *Warcraft: The Sundering*) by Richard A. Knaak, as well as the short story "Seeds of Faith" by Valerie Watrous (on http://us.battle.net/wow/en/game/lore/).

In the *War of the Ancients Trilogy* by Richard A. Knaak, Tyrande Whisperwind reluctantly establishes herself as the leader of the night elves. Other exciting events in Tyrande's life are portrayed in *World of Warcraft: Wolfheart* and *World of Warcraft: Stormrage* by Richard A. Knaak; issue #6 of the monthly *World of Warcraft* comic book by Walter Simonson, Ludo Lullabi, and Sandra Hope; and the short story "Seeds of Faith" by Valerie Watrous (on http://us.battle.net/wow/en/game/lore/).

You can learn more about Shandris Feathermoon in *World of Warcraft: Wolfheart*, *World of Warcraft: Stormrage*, and *Warcraft: The Demon Soul* and *Warcraft: The Sundering* (books two and three of the *War of the Ancients Trilogy*) by Richard A. Knaak, as well as "Seeds of Faith," a short story by Valerie Watrous (on http://us.battle.net/wow/en/game/lore/).

Other details about the worgen curse and Gilneas, including characters such as Vincent Godfrey, Darius Crowley, and Baron Ashbury, are disclosed in the short story "Lord of His Pack" by James Waugh (on http://us.battle.net/wow/en/game/lore/).

Legends abound concerning the wolf Ancient, Goldrinn. You can learn more about him in *World of Warcraft: Stormrage* and *World of Warcraft: Wolfheart* by Richard A. Knaak, as well as issue #3 of the monthly *World of Warcraft* comic book by Walter Simonson, Ludo Lullabi, and Sandra Hope.

The history of the great demigod Cenarius and his ties to the night elves are further explored in the *War of the Ancients Trilogy* and *World of Warcraft: Stormrage* by Richard A. Knaak.

The fate of King Genn Greymane's family following the events of the *World of Warcraft: Curse of the Worgen* comic book is touched on in the short story "Lord of His Pack" by James Waugh (on http://us.battle.net/wow/en/game/lore/).

WORLD OF WARCRAFT

WORLD OF WARCRAFT
SIMONSON • LULLABI • HOPE

An amnesiac washes up on the shores of Kalimdor, starting the epic quest of the warrior Lo'Gosh, and his unlikely allies Broll Bearmantle and Valeera Sanguinar. Striking uneasy relationships with other races, as well as each other, they must fight both the Alliance and the Horde as they struggle to uncover the secrets of Lo'Gosh's past! Written by Walter Simonson (THE JUDAS COIN, Thor) and illustrated by Ludo Lullabi (Lanfeust Quest) and Sandra Hope (JUSTICE LEAGUE OF AMERICA), this is the latest saga set in the World of Warcraft!

WORLD OF WARCRAFT: BOOK 2

WORLD OF WARCRAFT
SIMONSON • BURAN • BOWDEN

Simonson • Buran Bowden

WORLD OF WARCRAFT: BOOK 3

WORLD OF WARCRAFT

Simonson • Buran Bowden

WORLD OF WARCRAFT: BOOK 4

WORLD OF WARCRAFT

Simonson • Buran Bowden

SEARCH THE GRAPHIC NOVELS SECTION OF
DCCOMICS.COM
FOR ART AND INFORMATION ON ALL OF OUR BOOKS!